THE
FATAL
KNOT

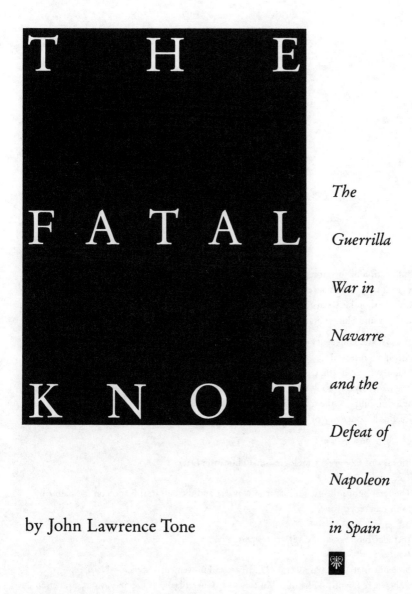

THE FATAL KNOT

The Guerrilla War in Navarre and the Defeat of Napoleon in Spain

by John Lawrence Tone

THE UNIVERSITY OF NORTH CAROLINA PRESS
Chapel Hill and London

Publication of this book was aided by
a grant from the Program for Cultural
Cooperation between Spain's Ministry of
Culture and United States Universities.

Manufactured in the United States of America
The paper in this book meets the guidelines for permanence
and durability of the Committee on Production Guidelines
for Book Longevity of the Council on Library Resources.

98 97 96 95 94   5 4 3 2 1

Library of Congress Cataloging-in-Publication Data
Tone, John Lawrence.
The fatal knot : the guerrilla war in Navarre and the defeat of Napoleon in Spain / by
John Lawrence Tone.
p. cm.
Includes bibliographical references and index.
ISBN 0-8078-2169-1
1. Peninsular War, 1807–1814—Underground movements—Spain—Navarre.
2. Navarre (Spain)—History, Military. 3. Guerrillas. 4. Espoz y Mina, Francisco,
1781–1836—Military leadership. 5. Spain—History—Napoleonic Conquest,
1808–1813. I. Title.
DC231.T63 1994
940.2'7—dc20   94-4237 CIP

❦ *Contents*

❦ Acknowledgments

I gathered the evidence used in this study during several extended research trips to Spain and France. The Institution for Latin American and Iberian Studies at Columbia University supported an initial foray into Spanish archives in 1983. The Fulbright Program awarded me a Fellowship for 1984–85, allowing me to complete a substantial portion of the work done in the archives in Madrid and Navarre. Grants from the National Endowment for the Humanities and the American Philosophical Society in 1990 made it possible for me to work in the French military archives in Vincennes. Without the generous financial assistance of these four bodies, this work would not have been possible.

I first became interested in modern Spanish history and the Spanish guerrillas while attending the lectures of Professor Edward Malefakis at Columbia University. Since that time, he has been my greatest supporter, helping to direct this work from its infancy. I also owe great debts to Professor Robert Paxton and Professor Isser Woloch for their invaluable critical reading and assistance. In Spain, Professor Miguel Artola gave me the single greatest piece of advice I received when he insisted that I focus my work in the notarial archives of Navarre, which in the end produced some of the richest materials used in this book.

I must not forget the support and friendship of my colleagues at the Georgia Institute of Technology or the help of my friends in the Atlanta Seminar on the Comparative History of Labor, Industrialization, Technology, and Society. The constant intellectual stimulation provided by this environment I could not do without. I would also like to thank

Professor Renato Barahona, Professor Owen Connelly, and Professor Michael Fellman for their helpful reading of the manuscript.

Finally, I wish to thank my wife, Professor Andrea Tone, for the gift of love, which makes everything possible.

T H E

FATAL

KNOT

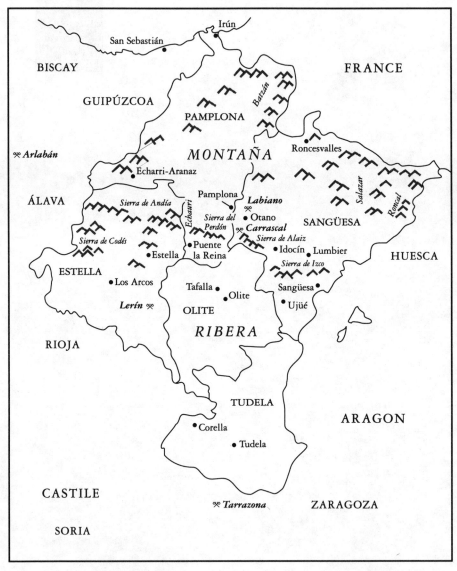

BISCAY

GUIPÚZCOA

San Sebastián

Irún

FRANCE

PAMPLONA

Batzán

✻ *Arlabán*

MONTAÑA

Roncesvalles

Echarri-Aranaz

Sierra de Andía

Pamplona

ÁLAVA

Sierra del Perdón

Echarri

Labiano

✻
Otano

✻ *Carrascal*

Salazar

Roncal

SANGÜESA

Sierra de Codés

Sierra de Alaiz

Idocín

Lumbier

HUESCA

Estella

Puente la Reina

Sierra de Izco

ESTELLA

Los Arcos

Tafalla

Olite

Sangüesa

Ujüé

Lerín ✻

OLITE

RIOJA

RIBERA

TUDELA

Corella

ARAGON

Tudela

CASTILE

SORIA

✻ *Tarrazona*

ZARAGOZA

Navarre, 1808–1815

✤ Introduction

That unfortunate war destroyed me; it divided my forces, multiplied my obliga-
tions, undermined my morale. . . . All the circumstances of my disasters are bound
up in that fatal knot.—Napoleon Bonaparte on the Spanish war, *Mémorial de*
Sainte-Hélène, 1823

I N 1808 NAPOLEON seized Spain, ending an alliance with the
Spanish Bourbons that dated back to 1796. By the summer of
1808 French troops occupied Madrid and the most important
forts in the country. The Bourbons, their armies in disarray, were forced
to abdicate, and Napoleon turned Spain over to his older brother, Joseph.
Spain seemed the easy prize Napoleon had predicted it would be.

The Spanish people, however, proved more resilient than its government and armies. With their cities occupied, their royal family deposed,
and half of their ruling elite co-opted by the Bonaparte regime, Spaniards
formed a revolutionary government, raised new armies, and initiated
a war of liberation against France. The English took advantage of the
Spanish resistance to place an expeditionary army in Portugal, and during the next six years, English, Portuguese, and Spanish forces battled
France in Iberia when most of Europe lay prostrate before Napoleon.
As the emperor himself later observed, it was the long, costly war in
Spain that led to his destruction.

Napoleon sacrificed 300,000 men in Iberia.[1] As damaging to France
as the number of casualties, however, was the burden of maintaining
large numbers of troops in the peninsula for six years. From 1810 to 1812
Napoleon had 400,000 men in Spain and Portugal, and he maintained

an army of some 250,000 in Spain through 1812.[2] In contrast, Welling-ton's English troops never numbered more than 60,000, and Spanish and Portuguese forces, though large, were poorly led and by themselves no real threat, especially after 1809. How, then, did the Allied forces avoid destruction by Napoleon's host?

The answer to this riddle is that the Allies never faced the bulk of Napoleon's armies. Most of the time, French troops were not fighting Wellington or the Spanish regulars. Rather, they were assigned to the occupation of a nominally pacified Spain, where a guerrilla insurgency threatened the French regime at its roots.[3] Spanish guerrillas forced Napoleon to expend hundreds of thousands of French troops in occupation duties, eliminating the emperor's numerical superiority over the Allies. In the summer of 1811, for example, the French used 70,000 troops to maintain the lines of communication in the zone of guerrilla activity between Madrid and the French border. Many of the men diverted to this task had been intended for Marshal Masséna at one of the war's most critical junctures. Masséna lost Portugal, while his reinforcements chased guerrillas fruitlessly around Navarre, Aragon, and other northern provinces.[4] The implications of French military dispositions in garrisons, requisition parties, convoy duty, and antiinsurgency units rather than in facing Allied concentrations cannot be mistaken. Guerrillas, in symbiosis with the regular Allied armies, destroyed Napoleon's regime in Spain.

Spain may be said to have invented guerrilla war. The word *guerrilla*, or "little war," which before 1808 described the usual skirmishes fought by detachments and screening units of regular armies, became transformed during the war with France and entered the military lexicon carrying the meaning familiar in the twentieth century: the irregular war of civilians against the occupation forces of a foreign power or an unpopular regime. By mid-1809 it had become clear that neither the Spanish nor the Anglo-Portuguese armies could drive the French from Spain. Spanish patriots learned, therefore, to accept the consequences of a militarized population and to embrace the new warfare. An editorial of the day enjoined people to enlist with the guerrillas: "From now on you must show a renewed martial vigor, aided by a novel system of war unknown to military tacticians. It is necessary to counter these 'warriors on a large scale' with war on a small scale, with guerrillas and more guerrillas."[5]

Armed peasants made chaos of French communications and performed other tasks of value to both English and Spanish regular forces. Partisans scoured the countryside of French spies and sympathizers and brought a continuous stream of information to the Allies.[6] The guerrillas also effected a kind of psychological warfare in which the French had to be constantly on the alert, while the Allied armies could rest securely in the midst of a vigilant peasantry. The guerrilla war was a long and demoralizing nightmare for France. In the regions of insurgency, where each peasant was a potential guerrilla, there could be no campaigning season, no safe havens, no truces. Everywhere and always there existed the possibility of a hostile encounter.[7] This constant terror made the Spanish war uniquely exhausting to Napoleon's armies and ruined their effectiveness in battle. Occupation troops in guerrilla war are rapidly demoralized—and morale among French soldiers in Spain was notoriously low. Fresh replacements, however, lacked the training and experience to match the hardened forces of the insurgents. As the fighting dragged on in Spain, the French faced an ever bolder guerrilla movement forged by years of struggle and infused with the confidence that comes from an almost daily train of small victories. By 1811 the best guerrilla forces were able to face equal numbers of French troops and defeat them in battle.

Success in guerrilla war, however, is not measured only by the number of battles won and the effect of espionage and terror. Guerrilla war is, above all, about controlling the fruits of the rural economy. In Spain, the guerrillas denied the enemy systematic, peaceful contact with much of the countryside, making the collection of taxes fitful, costly, and, in some areas, impossible for the French. In guerrilla country, the French governed only where they actually had troops in place. When these troops were withdrawn, the territory reverted to the guerrillas, becoming valueless to the French, if not a positive drain on their resources. War in Spain did not pay Napoleon as it had in other parts of Europe. On the contrary, guerrilla action made the occupation of Spain a constant burden and made the Spanish war unwinnable.

The guerrillas gained wide fame for their ability to defy imperial troops and taught European nationalists that, under certain circumstances, popular forces could be as effective as professional armies. In Spain, Europe witnessed a new movement that, by bringing previously disfranchised strata of society into the political and military arena, had the potential to liberate the Continent. The lesson that resistance to Napoleon might continue even after military defeat was learned as far afield as Austria and Russia.[8]

Despite the importance of the guerrillas in shaping Spain and Europe, historians have paid scant attention to them. In England and France, the historical literature has always focused on Wellington and Napoleon, and the guerrillas have been considered a sideshow, little more than bandits.[9] Even in Spain, where scholars have at least acknowledged the importance of the insurgency, there has never been a clear notion of who the guerrillas were or why they fought. Spanish patriots portrayed the resistance as a unanimous, nationwide, and irresistible movement, and said the guerrillas fought for king, country, and the Catholic faith. In turn, this interpretation became embedded in the historiography.[10] In fact, however, it is based on a set of myths.

First, guerrilla warfare was not a unanimous, national effort. Although small parties of guerrillas operated throughout Spain during at least part of the war, the heart of guerrilla country can be more closely defined than this. The greatest of the insurgent armies operated in northern Spain, from Upper Aragon through Soria, Navarre, Rioja, the Basque provinces, parts of Old Castile, Asturias, León, and Galicia. It was in this region that the famous Empecinado earned his name and the guerrilla-priest Merino gained his evil reputation. In the center of this band of insurgent territory, Navarre, under Francisco Espoz y Mina, produced the largest and most effective guerrilla army in Spain. Thus, guerrilla war was in large measure particular to northern Spain, above all to Navarre and the surrounding provinces.

This work focuses on Navarre, because it produced the most perfect guerrilla movement in Spain. Mina gained a virtual monopoly of military force in Navarre and Upper Aragon, established a court system, took over the tariff operations at the borders, and exacted contributions from the population. For a time, therefore, a guerrilla army governed the region. Even in Navarre, however, guerrilla war was not ubiquitous and unanimous. In a general sense, this proposition hardly needs defending, since only a minority of the population in any war actually engages in battle or directly aids the combatants. Yet, the myth of unanimity has prevented historians from asking the basic questions: who fought and who supported the guerrillas? I will argue that even in the guerrilla stronghold of Navarre it was a particular social class in a special rural setting in the northern half of the province that produced effective guerrilla resistance and that many Navarrese remained quiescent or collaborated with France.

Second, loyalties to king, country, and religion do not begin to describe the motivations of the Navarrese guerrillas. People in pacified areas of southern Spain no doubt loved their nation, faith, and royal family as much as the Navarrese, yet they did not produce a powerful guerrilla movement, while Navarre did. The fact is that the guerrilla genius of the Navarrese did not flow from superior patriotism or piety, but from the nature of rural society in Navarre. The dispersion of the population, the unarticulated peasant economy, and the tradition of strong village government were some of the factors that contributed to the success of the Navarrese guerrillas. To understand the insurgency, therefore, this work will examine the peasant world of Navarre, which gave birth to and nurtured the guerrilla forces.

This peasant world in 1808 was almost entirely Basque-speaking. It might seem tempting, therefore, to associate Basque ethnicity or some peculiar Basque historical experience with *guerrillerismo*, the notion that some people are more naturally suited to guerrilla warfare than others. However, there is no reason to believe that ethnicity ever determines warlike tendencies, nor did the Basque people have any special tradition of guerrilla resistance to central authority in the early modern period that could account for a cultural disposition to combativeness. The Basque region became associated with Carlism and guerrilla warfare in the nineteenth century, but that tradition was anchored in the experience of the Napoleonic occupation, not in any secular history of resistance predating 1808. Therefore, "Basqueness" can form no part of any rational explanation for the success of the Navarrese guerrillas.

Finally, Mina's army was no juggernaut, and victory was not inevitable. The record is clear: the guerrilla movement went through several phases of disintegration and reconstruction, and its success owed much to the chance of battle, politics, and personality. For this reason, a social history of Navarre is insufficient to explain the power of the insurgency there. Only by consulting the chronological record can Mina's victory and the nature of the guerrillas' contribution to Napoleon's downfall be understood. This work is, therefore, both social history and narrative.

The first two chapters are a portrait of Navarre in 1808 and an analysis of the conditions that fostered guerrilla warfare there. The remaining chapters recount the Napoleonic invasion, describe the career of Mina and his guerrillas, and explain the success of the insurgency as a function of both structural features of Navarrese society and the contingencies of politics and war.

1 ❀ Guerrilla Country

NAVARRE LIES IN the shape of a rough diamond wedged between France to the north and Castile to the south. To the east is Aragon and to the west the Basque provinces. From the northern tip of Navarre to the southern measures just under 100 miles, and at the widest point from east to west the distance spanned is about 75 miles.[1] Despite its limited size, Navarre possesses a more varied landscape and climate than many larger territories. Spain is famous for its continental variety, from the cool, moist mountains of Cantabria and the chill plateaus of Castile to the gardens of the Levant and the deserts of Murcia. Navarre mirrors these vast differences and concentrates them even further within its small territory, a fact that has earned the province the nickname "Little Spain." The modern visitor to Navarre can in an hour's drive go from green hills and leaden skies in the Northwest to brown lands under a high canopy of blue in the South.

For administrative purposes, Navarre under the old regime was divided into five *merindades*, roughly equivalent to counties, but geographers customarily divide Navarre into two regions, the North, or *Montaña*, and the South, or *Ribera*. (The merindades were Pamplona and Sangüesa in the North, Tudela and Olite in the South, and Estella, which lay partly in the Montaña and partly in the Ribera.) Topography is the foundation for this division. The Pyrenees and the eastern marches of the Basque-Cantabrian mountain range create distinct northern and southern hemispheres in Navarre. The line running from the Sierra of Leyre in the East through the Sierras of Izco, Alaiz, Perdón, Andía,

Urbasa, and Santiago de Lóquiz, and terminating in the Sierra of Codés in the West, defines the boundary between the "Two Navarres." North of the Leyre-Codés line the land is typically over 2,000 feet above sea level, in some places as high as 7,000 feet. To the south the mountains flatten out into a gentler landscape of valleys and plains.

The elevation of the Montaña does not make it particularly remarkable: even Madrid is as high. But Madrid lies in the center of a high plain, whereas the Montaña of Navarre is a land of dramatic precipices, gorges, hidden valleys, and box canyons with their secret exits. This land, so suited to the requirements of partisan warfare, was the first of many factors that made northern Navarre, together with contiguous and similar areas of northern Aragon and the Basque provinces, a nightmare for French troops. Mountains provided a last refuge to the guerrillas, who could always seek temporary asylum in heights that were impassable to French cavalry and artillery units. Geography thus partially negated the technological and organizational superiority of the French. By guarding key passes and occupying strategic heights, the guerrillas could even eliminate the numerical advantage enjoyed by their enemies. By contrast, the French could more easily hold the open landscape of southern Navarre, which gave the edge to cavalry and artillery.[2]

The French never felt secure in the Montaña, where straggling or drawing duty in a foraging detachment could bring an inglorious death.[3] Rough terrain, though, was just the beginning of their difficulties. The Montaña possessed a particular demography, economy, politics, culture, and even language (the Leyre-Codés line corresponded to the southern limit of Basque) that set it apart from the Ribera and from most of Spain and that gave the region special motives and aptitudes for guerrilla war.

The origins of the Montaña's peculiarities are partly climatic and partly historical. The climate in Navarre is, of course, intimately linked to physical relief, for the mountains do more than create a broken terrain; they also act as a barrier to the moisture-laden breezes blowing from the Cantabrian Sea. Against this wall, the wet ocean air exhausts itself, giving northwestern Navarre, parts of which receive seventy-nine inches of rainfall a year, a maritime climate. South of the mountain barrier, in the rain shadow of the Cantabrian massifs, southern Navarre is a dry plain, receiving only fifteen inches of rain a year in some places and depending on irrigation from the Ebro River and its tributaries. In few areas of the world does such a strong pluviometric contrast occur over such a small distance.

Immunity to drought and proximity to the sea had helped to preserve the population of the Montaña from the demographic setbacks of the seventeenth century, and by 1808 the merindades of Pamplona and Estella were among the most densely settled rural areas in Spain.[4] By that date, however, the population of the Montaña had ceased to expand. Partly, this was the result of the disruptions caused by the French occupation of 1795 and the economic dislocations of the war with England.[5] The essential reason for demographic stagnation in the Montaña, however, was that the region had experienced no fundamental social and technological change to raise agricultural or industrial productivity. Steady growth had, therefore, created a condition of overpopulation relative to the Montaña's fixed resources.[6]

Indeed, to maintain its vital equilibrium, the Montaña had begun to export people. Under the prevailing system of rigid primogeniture, younger children had to emigrate or accede to life under the tutelage of an older sibling. In this system, young men were especially likely to emigrate—to America, to Madrid, and to the agro-towns of the Ribera, where paid agricultural labor was seasonally available.[7] The English blockade of Spain and Spanish America after 1796 had curtailed the option of emigration to America, and the economic contraction caused by the blockade made work in Madrid and the Ribera more difficult to find as well. What the French found in the Montaña in 1808, therefore, was densely populated, rugged country full of young men with no prospects. Thus, the availability of men for Mina's army of guerrillas was the result, in part, of a particular economic and demographic conjuncture in the Montaña.

Climatic differences also helped to create a very particular type of agriculture and human geography in the Montaña favorable to guerrilla war. The wet, steep land of northern Navarre was ideally suited to small farms. On a small plot in the Montaña, intense labor combined with generous rainfall could redeem the intrinsic deficiencies of the terrain. The tendency was, therefore, toward small, subsistence holdings, which, in turn, helped to disperse the population over the countryside. Indeed, the town—with the exception of Pamplona—was a structure historically alien to the area, and people lived instead in small settlements and even in isolated farmhouses. The Montaña contained 700 individual *poblaciones*, almost as many as in all Andalusia (753). An average of 207 people lived in each of the settlements of the Montaña, and hundreds of villages had populations of 50 or less.

In contrast, small holdings could not compete well in the dry Ribera, since farmers of small plots had difficulty surviving even a single year of drought. The solution there, as in most of Spain, was extensive agriculture, the construction of irrigation projects, and the application of paid gang labor, all of which encouraged a concentration of landownership.[8] This agricultural regime, by requiring concentrations of labor and by generating commercial surpluses, encouraged the growth of towns. The Ribera merindades of Navarre were even "urban" by contemporary standards. In Tudela, for example, 28,112 people lived in only 27 towns, an average of 1,041 in each. The city of Tudela had a population of 7,295, Corella 3,935, and Tafalla 3,347, and 25 other towns had populations between 1,000 and 3,000.

The suitability of the Ribera to large estates had been reinforced by historical circumstances. As they had done in all the territories of the Western Empire, the Romans brought a system of production based on slave labor and *latifundia* to the Ebro basin, which was the northern borderland of effective Roman power in the region. Urban life followed the latifundia, as estate owners and their laborers lived in cities. This system was maintained by successive Visigothic and Moslem conquerors, whose political power always closely followed the old parameters of urban settlement established by Rome. The Reconquest of the Ribera in the Middle Ages by the Kingdom of Navarre increased the concentration of landownership and the growth of towns in the region. In the lands taken from the Moslems, the Navarrese monarchs, unhindered by a concern for the inhabitants, parceled out vast estates to the nobles and church. Thus, the urban pattern of settlement created by Rome and favored by the climate survived into the Napoleonic era. Great lords, residing in the towns, owned all of the land. Also in the towns, though in less comfortable surroundings, were the propertyless agricultural laborers.

These historical pressures had, to a large degree, passed over the Montaña. In the foothills of the Pyrenees and the Cantabrian mountains, Rome had encountered the decisive boundary to the expansion of the slave economy. (Pamplona was an outpost in the unsubdued Basque

Montaña.) Neither had the Visigoths and Moors been able to absorb the Basque people. Even the medieval monarchs of Navarre had failed completely to transform the tribal Montaña into a feudal society. Thus, while a system of large estates based successively on slave, serf, and paid labor had existed in the Ribera since ancient times, the Basques in the Montaña had been left to achieve a system of landownership centered on the small, family-sized exploitation.

In the Montaña people lived in *caseríos*, the typical dwelling of the Basques.[9] The caserío was a large house, usually built of stone. It was designed to contain the family, the animals, the tools, the harvest—in fact, everything belonging to the household. In the Pamplona and Lumbier basins, the heart of the Navarrese Montaña and of the guerrilla war, caseríos tended to be grouped in hamlets and small villages. Caseríos are impressive structures, even today. They can seem more like fortifications than homes, and, to French soldiers, the caseríos lent the Montaña the appearance of a country covered with innumerable small citadels.[10] In fact, they could be and were converted to this use by both the guerrillas and the French.

The dispersion of the population in small villages and hamlets gave the Montaña an important fighting edge.[11] To tax this population, the French had to send small detachments into each village, but this made them vulnerable to guerrilla attack. The solution was to send in a larger force, but this was not cost effective, given the limited money and goods that could be raised in a small municipality. Thus, the French never succeeded in maintaining their presence in the land of the caserío, which was so well suited to the guerrilla strategy. On the other hand, dominating the Ribera, where the population was concentrated in a handful of towns, was an easier task. Even areas of the Ribera that did contribute volunteers to Mina's army, could not themselves, by the very nature of their human geography, be the site of armed guerrilla struggle.

Another of the Montaña's assets for war was the relative lack of social differentiation that existed there. One indication of this was, paradoxically, the large number of nobles in the region. The census of 1796–97 counted 19,010 nobles in Navarre, equal to 7–8 percent of the population, a high figure by almost any standard. The vast majority of these nobles lived in the Montaña. West of Pamplona, in the valley of Larráun, for example, 80 percent of the population was noble; to the north of the capital, in the valley of Baztán, the figure was 60 percent, and in the Pyrenees of Sangüesa around 30 percent. In the Ribera, on the other hand, only about 1 percent of the population was born noble.[12]

The value of a thing, however, falls when it is superabundant, and in northern Navarre, thousands of *hidalgos*, the lowest degree of noble, were barely distinguishable from the peasant commoners among whom they lived. In the Ribera, a hidalgo normally possessed enough property to avoid engaging in trade or manual labor. In contrast, the hidalgos of the Montaña (and of the northern Spanish littoral generally) worked as tavernkeepers, cobblers, blacksmiths, and carpenters.[13] Foreigners readily noticed the lack of social stratification associated with nobility in the region. The muddling of the line between nobles and commoners inspired one French observer to ask whether the institution had any purpose in a region "where a crowd of muledrivers is noble; where domestic servants, when they come of age, display the pedigrees of their ancestors."[14]

It would have been more fruitful to ask what purpose nobility in the Montaña did not serve. It did not, for example, serve as an important source of discontent as it did in the Ribera and in most of Spain south of the Ebro-Duero demarcation. In these regions nobles were a special interest attracted to the French government by promises to quell popular revolution and to redistribute upward the spoils of war.[15] In the Montaña this tactic was not possible. The hidalgo of northern Navarre was farther from the rich noble of Madrid or Seville than he was from a common peasant.

In these conditions the concept of derogation—the loss of nobility through the exercise of ignoble trades—had little meaning. Nobility was not always defined by an officially executed title, nor was it so easily lost. The Montaña, like much of the Basque-Cantabrian region, had remained free from "contamination" by the Moors, and nobility was considered to pass through the blood and to belong inalienably to all native inhabitants, regardless of their economic role or station in life. In the Montaña entire villages, even whole valleys were populated almost exclusively by the noble born. As a result, the people developed a sense of racial and moral superiority to other Spaniards, and this sense of distinction helped to engender a strong feeling of community. Put another way, the Navarrese hidalgo's primary allegiances were likely to run vertically into the local community rather than horizontally across the noble estate. This fact is extremely important. At decisive moments, fear and loathing of the populace brought Castilian and Aragonese nobles together in solidarity against the resistance movement and in favor of the regime imposed from above by the French. The nature of nobility in the Navarrese Montaña prevented this from happening.

There were additional reasons why noble status distinguished its owner less in the Navarrese Montaña than elsewhere. It is true that even the poorest hidalgo in Navarre enjoyed certain privileges that set him apart from commoners, including the right to be addressed as *Don* or *Doña* and to display coats of arms, the privilege of carrying weapons in public, exemption from arrest for nonpayment of debts, and access to certain offices. These rights were not inconsiderable. However, the main institutions from which nobles drew their wealth and power—the seigneurial jurisdiction, or *señorío*, and the entail, or *mayorazgo*—barely existed in northern Navarre. The number of señoríos was high in Spain, amounting to some 50 percent of all municipalities.[16] Around Madrid and Valencia señoríos accounted for between 60 percent and 70 percent of all towns and villages and for 86 percent in the province of Guadalajara. In Navarre, however, property burdened with señorial dues and rents was extremely rare. Only thirty-eight towns and forty-three villages, amounting to 10 percent of all settlements, fell under señorial jurisdiction in Navarre. In addition, most of these señoríos were extremely small, often amounting to no more than one or two dwellings. Thus, señoríos accounted for 10 percent of all villages, but less than 1 percent of the population lived under señorial jurisdiction.[17]

The mayorazgo allowed nobles (as well as wealthy commoners) to protect properties from seizure, sale, and division. These entails varied in size from great latifundia in Andalusia to small plots in the Basque country.[18] As with the señoríos, the greatest number of mayorazgos in Navarre as well as the largest and most valuable existed in the Ribera, whereas in the Montaña they were of little consequence. For example, a survey conducted in 1802 revealed no mayorazgos in the valley of Ergoyena just northwest of Pamplona. In the village of Echarri-Aranaz, also in the Northwest, there was one "very old and poor" entailed estate, whose exact location, size, and value nobody seemed to recall.[19]

Finally, señores in the Montaña tended to lease their land to peasants at very low prices. The reasons for this are simple. Since there was little commercial development in the Montaña due to an absence of urban markets, and since excess population tended to migrate from the region, land values remained steady, and there was no pressure to raise rents. Indeed, tenants sometimes paid entirely symbolic sums to their over-lords, as if in mere memory of ancient señorial ownership, and typical rents in the region ran between 2 percent and 6 percent of the value of an average harvest.[20] This was one of the reasons why the Bonapartes' abolition of señoríos in 1809 received less than an enthusiastic response in the Montaña.[21]

The situation in the Ribera was entirely different. In the city of Tudela, 77 individuals, mostly nobles, in a population of 7,572 controlled all of the land. They directly exploited 67 percent of the arable land, some 7,400 acres, and leased out the remaining 3,000 acres to 250 individuals. About 11 percent of this total (1,180 acres) was locked up in 23 entails owned by 19 nobles.[22] In Corella, 16 nobles held 445 acres in entails, amounting to 12.5 percent of all the arable land. The remaining 3,112 acres was shared between these and 49 other proprietors, and most was exploited directly.[23]

Urban property in the Ribera was also concentrated in few, usually noble, hands. In Corella the noble family of Virto de Vera owned 11 percent and the Marqués de Santa Cara 5 percent of all urban dwellings. Most remaining houses were owned by just a handful of people, many of them interrelated, and this forced the vast majority of the population to rent.[24] In the Montaña, on the other hand, many more dwellings were occupied by their owners. For example, only ten individuals in the vil-lage of Echauri owned more than one house, and over 42 percent of the dwellings were occupied by their owners.[25]

The weakness of the señorial regime and the lack of correspondence between nobility and wealth in the Montaña narrowed the fundamen-tal social division between commoners and nobles so characteristic of the old regime in the Ribera and in most of Europe. Few peasants paid any form of feudal rent; those who did paid low rents; and in some areas, most peasants were themselves nobles. Noble privilege had been exploited by Napoleon to divide conquered peoples in Europe and to help consolidate a ring of satellite kingdoms around France.[26] This same strategy was also effective in much of Spain, including the Ribera of Navarre, where elites feared the mob more than the French and were easily induced to collaborate.[27] Mina recalled in his memoirs that he had received no help from any titled noble, owner of a mayorazgo, or wealthy individual.[28] In the Montaña, however, where mayorazgos were rare and where most nobles did not even have officially executed titles much less vast property or wealth, Mina found many supporters. Thus, the nature of nobility in the Montaña allowed the area to meet the challenge of the French occupation from a position of unity and strength.

The church in Navarre occupied a position similar to the nobility. It had less wealth and property but a heavier presence, especially in the Montaña, than the church in the rest of Spain. For this reason, the church in Navarre, like the noble estate, produced less social division than it did in the rest of Spain. Navarrese clerics enjoyed the same valuable privileges, including exemption from some taxes, as clergy elsewhere. However, the two greatest sources of revenue for the church—the tithe and rents from property—were much less lucrative in Navarre than in Castile and Aragon.

It has been estimated that in nineteenth-century Spain the church skimmed off half of the net agricultural product in the form of the tithe.[29] In addition, the Spanish church not only preserved its medieval jurisdictions or *señoríos ecclesiásticos*, it had, like the nobility, taken advantage of the penury of the Hapsburg monarchy in the seventeenth century to acquire new ones. A total of 9 cities, 375 towns, and 2,299 villages and hamlets were señoríos of the church, the equivalent of 14 percent of all Spanish municipalities, a large figure by European standards at the time and a source of chagrin to reformers in Madrid.[30] The church possessed 16,000 square miles of land, or fully 8 percent of the entire surface area of Spain and 18 percent of the arable. These properties generated 565 million reales a year in rent, the second largest item of income in the church's budget after tithes.[31]

The considerable resources of the church corresponded to the important role it played. Hospitals, charity, and education absorbed a large part of the total income. What remained provided a livelihood for 16,675 priests (.16 percent of the population), 39,489 other secular clergymen (.38 percent), and 71,487 members of the regular clergy (nearly .69 percent), for a combined total of 1.23 percent of the population.

The church in Navarre supported a larger proportion of clerics, especially parish priests, than the church in Spain as a whole. In 1786 there were 762 priests, accounting for more than .34 percent of the population, over twice the proportion of priests in the rest of Spain. An additional 1,748 other secular clergymen, many of whom performed little or no function within the church, made up another .77 percent of the population, also more than twice the national average. And 1,875 members of the regular clergy, most of them men and 70 percent of them mendicants, accounted for another .82 percent, a figure close to the Spanish average. Thus, ecclesiastics were almost 2 percent of the population in Navarre, a proportion half again as high as that for Spain.[32]

Despite the number of people it supported, the church in Navarre absorbed a considerably smaller percentage of the agricultural product and owned much less property, proportionally, than it did in the rest of Spain. Tithes brought 17.2 million reales in an average year between 1803 and 1807, equivalent to 11 percent of Navarre's agricultural product.[33] The church possessed señorial rights over only three towns and one village in Navarre. The regular clergy owned 22 square miles of land, and the secular clergy owned 9 square miles, less than 1 percent of the surface area of Navarre, compared with 8 percent in all Spain.[34]

As in the matter of noble status, religious differences between the Two Navarres, Montaña and Ribera, mirrored the differences between Navarre, as a whole, and the rest of Spain. In the Montaña, priests formed a relatively large proportion of the population (.5 percent), but the presence of the regular clergy was light (.3 percent). In the Ribera, the reverse held true: priests were rare (.1 percent of the population), while the presence of monks and nuns (1.3 percent) was everywhere evident. So common were regular clerics in the merindad of Tudela that they almost equaled the number of regular clerics in all the rest of Navarre, excluding the city of Pamplona.

The Ribera also supported a large proportion of "other" secular clerics (.8 percent of the population), which doubtless included some genuinely pious men and women, but which in large part consisted of hundreds of people who performed little discernible function in exchange for their tax-free status and other benefits.[35] This class of clergy appeared as parasites and served to cast doubt and discredit on the truly devoted servants of the church. In the Montaña only .4 percent of the population fell into this category.[36]

These figures on the distribution of the clergy within Navarre are not without implications for patterns of piety in the province. In the Montaña an unusually large priesthood administered the sacraments. In the Ribera there were simply too few pastors to say mass, a circumstance that must have resulted in a lack of even the rudiments of Christian instruction for many people, a situation not uncommon in other European

nations, where churches failed to keep pace with growing urban populations. At the same time, regular and "other" secular clerics, who in
the popular imagination were often depicted as burdens or parasites on
society, led to anticlerical sentiment in the region.[37] The call to arms in
defense of the church was, therefore, less likely to receive a response in
the Ribera than it was in the Montaña.

In addition, the church, like the nobility in Navarre, possessed more
land in the Ribera than in the Montaña. In Tudela, for example, 4 percent
of the arable was owned by six convents for men and four for women,
and almost 20 percent of the urban dwellings were in the hands of the
clergy. In Corella 10 percent of the arable was owned by two convents
for men and two for women.[38] Between the convents and the cathedral
chapter, 10 percent of the urban property in Corella was also in the
hands of the church.[39] It is no shock, then, that the city of Tudela favored
the seizure of convent property in order to release land on the market.
French reforms that promised to do just that could hardly inspire resistance. On the contrary, some Ribereños, at least, had long fought for a
repartition of church lands.[40]

In contrast, the church owned proportionally less property in the
Montaña.[41] In the village of Echarri-Aranaz, for example, there was only
half an acre belonging to the church, and in the valley of Ergoyena the
clergy had not a single acre.[42] Sometimes villages in the Montaña even
maintained control over part of the clergy's income. In Echauri, the
priest accepted what he was given from the rental of four acres of municipal land specifically set aside for the support of the parish.[43] The point
is, most people in the Montaña did not have contact with clerics who
were also their landlords, and this made it easier to imagine defending
the spiritual church.

As was the case with properties belonging to secular lords, ecclesiastical señores leased land to peasants for very small sums, usually under
censo enfiteutico. The censo was a type of feudal copyhold that allowed
peasants to acquire the usufruct of a piece of land, for which they paid a
"purchase" price as well as a yearly sum, almost always payable in kind,
to the seller. The censo lands were inheritable, passing through families
for generations without experiencing rent increases. Indeed, peasants
with church lands paid such low rents that they had become virtual
coproprietors, in almost as enviable a position as those who owned property outright.[44] Promises to redistribute such lands on the open market,

which would have led inexorably to rising land values and rents, held very little attraction for peasants in the Montaña. However, censo lands rented for more in the Ribera than they did in the Montaña. The presence of urban markets and the high quality of the irrigable land along the Ebro had caused the price of land and rents to inch upward in the Ribera.[45] And because the church collected higher rents in the Ribera, especially on irrigated land, people there were more likely than people in the Montaña to perceive the church, or elements of the church, as economically exploitative. This, in turn, would affect the willingness of peasants to answer the church's call for an anti-French "crusade" in defense of Catholicism.

The Ribera suffered in another way from the swarm of "other" secular clergymen. Many of these people were not really clerics at all, but wealthy laymen who held land under the umbrella of *obras pías* and *capellanías*, categories of church property that could be manipulated by laymen to entail estates under church protection and to exempt the crops produced on the estates from taxes.[46] The amount of arable possessed by capellanías was not enormous, from about 1 percent in Tudela to 3 percent in Corella, but this often included some of the best land.[47] As a result, Bourbon programs to seize and sell these kinds of properties met with enthusiasm among some Ribereños and were extremely successful there.[48] When the French extended nationalization programs to other forms of church property, it took little convincing to get buyers of former obras pías and capellanías to put their money down on additional lands seized from the church.[49] There is no adequate study of the process of ecclesiastical disentailment in Navarre during these years. What is evident, however, is that this kind of land reform in Navarre, whether it was carried out by Godoy, Bonaparte, or Mendizábal in the 1830s, never provoked popular resistance.[50]

The evidence produced so far with respect to the church in Navarre suggests a number of reasons why people in the Montaña would have been willing to fight for their religion, while people in the Ribera would not have been. The Montaña was well ministered, and peasants maintained an intimacy with their priests remarkable to contemporary observers.[51] French soldiers passing through Navarre were amazed to find priests "playing billiards, smoking, and drinking liquor in public houses."[52] The rough piety of the Montaña, in which priests mixed naturally with their parishioners, may have shocked some French observers, but it was an indication of the survival of a religious sensibility still capable of producing a crusade.

At the same time, the absence of regular orders and greedy "other" secular clergy, as well as the scarcity of church lands in the Montaña, had not generated the kind of anticlerical sentiment that was already evident in the Ribera and in many other areas of Spain. The French program to dissolve monasteries, abolish whole categories of clergy, and seize church property would not have been understood in the Montaña, where most people knew the church through their priest, who was no more than the "first among the parish poor."[53] In this situation, French reforms could only have appeared as vandalism and an offense to piety.

The nature of the nobility and clergy in the Montaña was conducive to social cohesion, and this helped the region produce a guerrilla insurgency. More important, however, was the character of the rest of the population. In Navarre, 91 percent of the population belonged to the so-called third estate, a term that expressed a legal distinction rather than a social reality, since within the third estate there existed the greatest variety of conditions.

Most people in both the Montaña and the Ribera depended on agriculture. Excluding nobles and clerics, whose numbers and resources—also mainly agricultural—have been considered apart, 68 percent of the remaining population that had an occupation in Navarre either exploited a plot of land directly, worked for wages on land belonging to someone else, or raised livestock. About 17 percent of the active population comprised artisans, and just over 9 percent worked in domestic service. Those constituting the remaining 6 percent were divided among military and government personnel (1 percent each), doctors, lawyers, and other professionals (2 percent), commerce and industry (1 percent), and students (1 percent).

These figures show that Navarre did not deviate much from the Spanish norm. The percentage of people in agriculture was identical; the proportion of artisans, students, merchants, and manufacturers was slightly smaller; and the proportion of domestic servants was a bit greater. However, the distinguishing mark of Navarrese society was, once again, the absolute difference between the Montaña and the Ribera in terms of the social and occupational structure of the population.

The proportion of students, merchants, professionals, royal servants, and military personnel was 2 percent lower in Navarre than in Spain as a whole. It was lowest of all in the merindad of Pamplona, somewhat higher in Sangüesa, Olite, and Estella, and approached the national average in Tudela. The weakness of these professions in the Montaña meant that clerics, as sources of information and leadership, had few rivals in their communities. On the other hand, the relative strength of these groups in the Ribera supplied a natural constituency to the collaboration, for the professional classes, including officers in the Spanish army, were everywhere in Spain among the first to pledge allegiance to the French government. As will be seen, in Tudela, men like the erudite and flexible José Yangüas y Miranda would quickly make peace with the occupation, in the hopes of reaping political and economic rewards from the Bonaparte regime.[54]

Artisans were overrepresented in the Ribera. The Ebro valley produced textiles, soap, *aguardiente*, and licorice, on a scale that employed significant numbers of people. Of course, the Montaña was not devoid of industrial activity. Textile production was important in Estella and Sangüesa, and the mining of iron and copper had been carried out on a small scale for centuries in the region. But fewer people in the Montaña, especially in the merindad of Pamplona, made their primary living from mining or manufacturing.[55] Indeed, there were even some rather large villages in which almost nobody seemed to work outside of agriculture. For example, in Echarri-Aranaz there were only 14 people working full time in industry in a population of 774.[56]

Industry was not really booming anywhere in Navarre. The crafts used old techniques, shops were small, productivity was low, and Navarre exported almost nothing.[57] An indication of the primitive nature of Navarrese industry was the preponderance of master artisans over apprentices and other employees by a ratio of two to one. Especially in the Montaña, manufacturers were normally craftsmen employing one or no apprentice and producing for small local markets.[58] The guild organization was as yet unchallenged in the Montaña. Neither the horizontal integration of the putting-out system nor the development of factories had any place in the region. There was, in other words, nothing like an industrial proletariat or even a proto-industrial work force in the Montaña.

Instead, most people in the Montaña were peasant farmers who owned their own land. In Navarre as a whole, *labradores*, or peasants who worked their own or rented land, outnumbered *jornaleros*, or day laborers, by three to one. This already made Navarre unusual. In Spain as a whole there were more jornaleros (53 percent) than labradores (48 percent). Looking more closely at the figures for labradores in Navarre, one finds that 70 percent owned the land they worked, while only 30 percent were leaseholders. This situation was reversed on the national level, where some 60 percent of the labradores rented land and only 40 percent were proprietors.[59]

These figures become even more suggestive when they are broken down within Navarre. For example, while the ratio of landed peasants to day laborers (3:1) was remarkable enough at the provincial level, in the Montaña the proportion rose to 9:1. In the merindades of Pamplona and Sangüesa only 7 percent of the active population was identified as landless laborers.[60] In many areas there were no landless peasants. Aspiroz, a village of 298 inhabitants in 1786, showed 298 peasant proprietors, 205 of whom were nobles. (It is notable that women and children were listed as nobles and proprietors.) In the village of Echauri 98 percent of the arable land was worked by its owners. There were a few leased properties, but these were small plots at prices averaging between 2 percent and 6 percent of the value of the harvest. With land so easy to come by, landlords could not charge more to their tenants. There were no day laborers in Echauri.[61] When one considers that most of the over 14,000 nobles in the region were socially in the same class as peasant proprietors, it becomes clear that the Montaña of Navarre was the land par excellence of the small farmer.

One of the mechanisms that kept land prices down in the Montaña and helped to underpin the wide property distribution was an arrangement known as the *carta de gracia*. Through the carta de gracia peasants were able to supplement their own ancestral possessions by acquiring the usufruct of others in exchange for the payment of onetime "purchase" prices.[62] The true owner of a plot sold in carta de gracia was allowed to recover his property by refunding the usufruct owner the cost of the land plus improvements. This, however, occurred much less frequently than might be expected.[63] There was little incentive for landowners to spend money reconstituting their estates from lands previously sold in carta de gracia. Stagnant or declining population and the absence of markets for agricultural products made commercial exploitation of land unattractive in the Montaña. And because so many people owned land outright, it was difficult to find tenants for leaseholds: people were unwilling to pay rent for any but the very best plots of land.[64] Proprietors with more land than they could work directly or with widely dispersed lands that could not be leased were therefore satisfied to obtain what they could from sales in carta de gracia, which at least allowed them theoretically to recover ownership at a later date.

The contrast with the Ribera could not be starker. Day laborers there far outnumbered peasants who owned or leased land, by as much as 4:1 in the merindad of Tudela, where 50 percent of the active population was listed as jornaleros. There were tenant farmers, but land was hard to come by and prices were relatively high, so that even tenants were forced to work as day laborers to supplement their income. In Corella, where a few families controlled almost all of the land, there was not a single case of a leasehold peasant who did not also have to work at least part of the time as a day laborer on one of the big estates.[65]

The nature of the Ribera made it easy for the French to dominate. A handful of families owned all of the land. The French squeezed these families for taxes and requisitions and rewarded them with church property and a measure of public power. In contrast, the average person in the Ribera had nothing. Men worked for a wage, either in industry or agriculture. To such a person, it was irrelevant whether wages were supplied by a pro-Bourbon or pro-Bonaparte boss or landlord. Most men were jornaleros, unemployed for months at a time, begging or tramping great distances to find work in agricultural slow seasons.[66] Such men were extremely vulnerable. What could make them risk everything to defend the order of things against the French? The church was not likely to inspire Ribereños to die for it, and even if someone wanted to resist the French, with what resources could he do so? Most Ribereños faced the French occupation naked, and only extraordinary circumstances could have led such people into the guerrilla movement.

Things were quite different in the Montaña. Here most people owned enough land outright to avoid working for a wage or renting. Industry was primitive, almost nonexistent in places, so few people depended on wages. Thus, there had been no developments in industry or agriculture to occasion any significant social differentiation. Almost everyone was a farmer or dependent of a farmer. The nobility was not a class apart that could be used by the French to control the population, nor were most people conscious of vassalage as a burden to be removed. The church was represented for most people by the parish priest, who lived and worked among the peasants as an equal. Thus, there was nothing in the French program to attract peasants in the Montaña or induce them to collaborate.

On the contrary, as the following chapter will argue, peasant proprietors in the Montaña had special means and motives for resisting the French. Each of thousands of small farmers was forced to make a political decision every time he faced the tax collectors and the foraging parties of the enemy. Taking up arms against the French, he was protecting his or his family's ancestral home, lands, and way of life. And he could afford to resist because there were always relatives to manage the family farm during his absence. As a result of these factors, the region was ungovernable for the French. The economic independence of the peasantry in the Montaña, its dispersal over the countryside, and its close relations with the village clergy and local hidalgos were some of the major factors placing the peasant proprietors of the Montaña in a position thoroughly to frustrate the occupation. In addition, however, there were other features of life in the Montaña, including a long tradition of self-government, that prepared the people for guerrilla war.

A

T THE TIME OF the French invasion Navarre possessed a rich
agricultural economy. Relative to its size, Navarre ranked second out of thirty-three Spanish provinces in the volume of its
wheat harvest. It ranked first in the production of wine and spirits, with
one-fourth of all the liqueur, or aguardiente, produced in Spain coming
out of Navarre. It was the thirteenth largest producer of vegetable oils
and ranked ninth in the value of its livestock.[1] Industrially, Navarre was
less developed than most Spanish provinces, ranking twentieth among
thirty-three provinces in manufacturing. Moreover, most of Navarre's
manufactures served strictly local markets. In general, Navarre exported
raw materials and imported finished goods, especially from France, a
sign of the province's quasi-colonial subordination to the French economy.[2]

Industry was more important in the economy of the Ribera towns
than it was in the Montaña. As already seen in the previous chapter, the
Montaña supported few full-time workers in industry. As a result there
was little craft specialization, and manufactures in the Montaña were too
shoddy to compete even in very local markets. The Ribera, on the other
hand, produced textiles, liqueurs, and other products for local markets,
and a small but significant portion of the population made its living from
industry, broadly defined. Thus, manufactures generated 1,190 reales of
income per person in Corella, but only 95 reales in Echauri.[3]

A comparison of agriculture in the Montaña and the Ribera also re-
veals interesting differences. Ribereños had more contact with regional
markets and tended to specialize in fewer, more commercially viable

products, whereas people in the Montaña grew a wider variety of crops as a way to ensure local food supplies. Wheat was the main product in both regions. In the merindad of Tudela the wheat harvest accounted for 63 percent of all crop production, and barley made up another 28 percent. In the merindad of Pamplona, on the other hand, wheat made up only 48 percent of all crops. The Montaña also produced less rye, barley, and oats, but grew a number of lesser grains, fodder crops, and legumes whose cultivation was almost unknown in the Ribera. Maize, which was not used in the merindad of Tudela at all, was almost as important as wheat in the Pamplona region.

Then, as now, most of the wine produced in Navarre came from the Ribera, but areas of Pamplona from which the vine has retreated in modern times also produced important quantities of wine and aguardiente. The Ribera was the source of most of the olive oil in Navarre, but even here small quantities were produced in the Montaña for local use. The importance of chestnuts in the Montaña—in the merindad of Pamplona the volume of chestnuts harvested was larger than any crop but wheat, maize, and beans—indicated the survival of sylvan modes of production long since lost in the Ribera.[4]

The Montaña, just as it produced a greater variety of crops than the Ribera, also had more kinds of livestock and in greater numbers. Most families kept pigs, the commonest source of meat, and goats, which could convert leavings and the grasses of the mountains and commons into milk, cheese, and meat. There were also a large number of cattle and oxen, used for milk, meat, and labor. By contrast, pigs and goats were rare in the Ribera, and oxen were practically unknown. In the valley of Echauri there was an ox, cow, horse, goat, or pig for every 1.5 people, compared with one of these animals for every 13 people in Corella.[5]

Sheep were important in both the Ribera and the Montaña.[6] In the Ribera, however, sheep were kept by relatively few individuals in vast flocks, whereas in the Montaña many peasants had small flocks. For example, in Corella four nobles owned almost half of the total number of sheep in the city, and sixteen individuals owned 95 percent of the sheep.[7] In contrast, the top four ranchers in Echauri controlled only one-fourth of the stock of sheep, while there were dozens of individuals with small herds.[8]

Despite the subsistence orientation of farming in the Montaña, social and technical factors peculiar to the region had created an efficient agri-

culture there. As seen in the previous chapter, most families in the Montaña had access to land. Peasants owned, or more rarely rented, land in
small strips located in different, open fields. This ensured each family
the opportunity to plant a variety of crops in different soils and locations and prevented any one person from monopolizing the best land or
losing everything in an extremely localized disaster—the unpenning of
sheep, for example. The division of the land in this way was a reasonable
and time-honored system. While agricultural reformers were trying to
increase productivity by enclosing land and by introducing new techniques, peasants in the Montaña, maintaining their primitive land distribution and employing ancient methods, farmed more efficiently than
most in Europe. Seed yields on the best land were 1:8 or higher, and
average yields of 1:6 were reported in Echarri-Aranaz.[9] By comparison,
average yields in France were on the order of 1:5, in Germany 1:4, and
in White Russia 1:3.[10]

Climate was partly responsible for this high productivity. Steady rainfall and mild weather meant that two crops could be grown each year.
By alternating crops of wheat and maize with crops of legumes, it was
less necessary to rest the land. And the large numbers of livestock provided the fertilizer necessary to replenish the soil.[11] These advantages
were reinforced by the social organization of labor. Widespread private
ownership in small communities had produced a hardworking peasantry
notable for its devotion to the land and its use of cooperative labor arrangements.[12] It was this social advantage, above all else, that helped
produce such high yields in northern Navarre, not the application of
capital or any technical advance.

Indeed, peasants in the Montaña employed the most ancient agricultural implement in Europe, the neolithic *laya*, a kind of spade, rather
than (or in addition to) the plow. The laya was used exclusively by the
Basques. The small size of the plots and the steep terrain made this ancient technology more practical than the plow. The Romans in their day
had already viewed the laya as an atavism, yet the advantages it offered
ensured its use right into the twentieth century. For one thing, the laya
was cheap. Anyone could own a set of them. Access to costly plows and
draft animals was one factor that had worked to stratify European peasants, but in the Montaña the laya allowed poorer peasants to compete
with their richer neighbors, and this reinforced the egalitarian tendency
of society in the region.

One of the most important facts about the laya was that it required communal labor. Two or more families including several generations of men, women, and children worked together, first on one family's land, then on another's. This communal arrangement placed a premium on interfamilial cooperation and helped to knit communities together in ways nothing else could.[13]

A further important attribute of the laya was the way it helped to empower women. Since Roman times, visitors to the Basque region had remarked, with either pleasure or horror, that women there seemed to have a great deal of power. Some scholars have even called Basque society "matriarchal," though this doubtless overstates the evidence. However, it is reasonable to say that the laya removed some of the obstacles for women in agriculture. Although using the laya was extremely arduous, it did not require the same kind of strength or the domination of animals that plowing did. The control of draft animals and tillage is an important factor in man's dominance of woman in agrarian societies. Women in the Montaña faced no such labor disadvantage, and this may have helped to confirm their equality in other spheres as well—for example, in inheritance customs.

Peasants in the Montaña practiced strict primogeniture. This meant that the eldest child, whether male or female, inherited. Thus, women had equal access to the land.[14] Moreover, even after marriage, a woman retained control over her property. When she died, her landed possessions, minus the funeral expenses and any dowry she had brought to her husband's family, reverted to her parents, sisters, brothers, or other relations.[15] The most important aspect of the laya and of women's place in Basque society from the perspective of the guerrilla war was that women in the Montaña were accustomed to inheriting land and taking an active part in all of the processes of production, including tillage. Therefore, the absence of a large number of men—whether they were working in the Ribera or fighting the French—did not entail the disruption of agricultural production. The situation in the Ribera was very different. There was almost no wage work for women and children in the agro-towns of the Ribera. If the young men from such communities had suddenly taken to the hills, it would have spelled economic collapse and brought disaster to those left behind.[16] In other words, the labor system in the Montaña favored guerrilla war, whereas that in the Ribera discouraged it.

Primogeniture had other favorable effects on the Montaña. Regions that did not practice primogeniture often suffered from extreme *minifundism*, as had occurred in Galicia, where land was divided, leased, and subleased to so many heirs that most peasants there had barely an Irish level of subsistence. In Navarre primogeniture preserved a relatively prosperous peasantry with good-sized estates. The Mina family, for example, possessed a house and outbuildings with eighty-eight acres of land.[17] Of course, younger children, unless they could marry an heir or heiress, were disinherited by this system and had to emigrate, join the clergy, or turn to other pursuits outside agriculture, including war.

All of these factors created in the Montaña a prosperous peasantry that produced rich harvests of grains and livestock, and sufficient oils and wine to meet its own needs. The region could have exported some crops, but actually exported very little. The wide distribution of property ensured this. Neither feudal nor market mechanisms for extracting surplus production, in the form of rents or underpaid labor, respectively, had ever really penetrated the Montaña. With the products of agriculture distributed among 100,000 independent producers and among myriad sites of production, most of Navarre's agricultural wealth was consumed at or near the production site.[18] There was, then, little means for extracting wealth from the peasants in the Montaña.[19]

This feature of the Montaña was one of the greatest obstacles for the French regime and a great source of strength for the guerrilla movement. The peasants' control of production placed them in direct conflict with the taxing and requisitioning apparatus of the French government. In the Ribera, the French could force taxes and requisitions from a few big landowners. These collections cut into profits, but they did not threaten the lives of the landed elite. Moreover, the French compensated landowners in the Ribera with access to power and nationalized properties. In the Montaña, the French were forced to send agents with armed escorts into hundreds of villages to raise contributions. What they exacted from such villages directly affected the subsistence of individual property holders. As will be seen, the initial point of attack for the guerrillas was against French requisition parties in villages in the Montaña, and it was by protecting such villages from French exploitation that the guerrillas gained the allegiance of the peasantry.

Peasants in the Montaña not only had motives for resisting the French, they also had the means. Because the Montaña lay outside feudal and market systems of extraction, the cost of living was lower there than anywhere else in Spain. Wine, for example, cost 4 reales a *cántaro*, the lowest in the whole country, where the average price was 13 reales. The price of wheat in Navarre from the 1780s to 1807 ranged from 7 to 25 reales per robo, again the lowest in Spain, where the average (in 1799) was 48 reales.[20] The limited profits that could be obtained from agriculture also depressed the price of real property. Grain land around Pamplona could be paid for with the income from two harvests.[21] And the price for an acre of *tierra blanca* (unirrigated, unplanted, open-field land) could be as low as 20 to 30 reales, a few weeks wages for a day laborer.[22] The price of housing, the greatest cost for most peasants, was much lower in the Montaña than in the Ribera. Many Montañeros owned their homes, and those who rented did not pay much. In the valley of Echauri the average rent for a house was 88 reales, compared with 170 reales in Corella and 253 reales in Tudela.

In this situation, peasants were able to preserve their real property and to accumulate movable property at a remarkable rate. On 30 January 1800 officials in Echauri, on a writ from the Royal Council in Pamplona, entered the house of a local proprietor, Francisco Azanza, in order to seize his remaining property in payment of a debt he owed to another proprietor. Azanza owned a large array of furniture: fourteen chairs and two small benches, two large tables, four chests, and one mirror, among the items remaining in the house. He even possessed five paintings, items of impossible luxury for peasants in most of Spain (and the highest priced goods in the house). In the kitchen were a large number of pots and pans, ceramic casseroles, pitchers, plates, cups, utensils, and a tablecloth.[23]

In the house of more prosperous peasants, aside from the valuable tools (layas, spades, plows, yokes, etc.) and the livestock, the range of household goods was wider and the quality higher. For example, the proprietor of Ansorena, a caserío in Echauri, had a large assortment of linens, woolen blankets, pillows of wool and cotton, and rugs; in the kitchen were damask tablecloths and napkins, curtains, and surprisingly rich utensils, including a set of silverware, salt and pepper shakers of silver, and a large number of plates, bowls, and other dishes of tin; the furniture included eight tables, a bookcase with books, whose titles were not, unfortunately, inventoried, seven chests, seven regular chairs and seven Muscovy chairs, and a desk.[24] These possessions were far beyond the means of any day laborer, indeed, beyond the means of most peasants in Europe. They provided the peasant proprietor of the Montaña with a stake in society worth protecting and with the means to survive the disruptions to production resulting from the absence of men in the guerrilla campaigns.

Thus, the economy of the Montaña was both essentially subsistence-oriented and, oddly, rich. Industrially, the Montaña was unquestionably backward, with part-time artisans producing inferior goods for local sale and barter. On the other hand, the Montaña produced agricultural surpluses, which, though not spectacular, at least remained in the hands of the peasants, who could, therefore, accumulate property and movable goods.

Observers lionized the peasants of the Montaña for their work ethic, independence, and relative material wealth.[25] Theirs was not a miserly autarky, but rather a splendid isolation. However difficult life might have been in the land of the caserío, farming was more productive, housing better, and the people better fed. Some foreign observers even thought they detected in the Montaña that mythical rural middle class so desired by agrarian reformers of the Enlightenment.[26]

It is not the purpose here to portray the life of the peasants of the Montaña as one of ease. On the contrary, only through unusual industry and application were they able to maintain themselves under the natural and technological conditions then prevailing. Yet, if their lives were as difficult and short as peasants in most of Europe, they were also less brutish. Montañeros possessed a margin of subsistence far superior to that of peasants in most of Europe. It was in this margin that the guerrillas survived and flourished. The peasant world of the Montaña was, to borrow Mao's phrase, the "congenial sea" in which the guerrillas found nourishment. The nature of the economy and society in the Ribera, on the other hand, left it vulnerable to French control.

The peculiar political constitution of Navarre also contributed to the strength of the guerrilla movement in the province. Navarre was one of the few regions in Spain that had maintained its ancient constitution, or *fuero*, including the preservation of its regional congress, or *Cortes*, the most representative governing body in Spain before the revolution of 1808. Along with the other "foral provinces"—Álava, Guipúzcoa, and Vizcaya—Navarre used its autonomous institutions to gain a measure of control over taxation, tariffs, public spending, and military levies, and to preserve customary laws that were less rigid and paternalistic and more communally oriented than the Roman and Gothic law that had been adopted in Castile and Aragon.[27]

The fueros of Navarre originated in the Middle Ages as a pact between the king and the "people" for military service and contributions in the effort to oust the Moslems from the Ebro valley. In return for this service, the monarchs pledged to maintain Navarre's extensive privileges, including important customary laws and the right to protest the least infraction of any of these laws. In practice this meant that Navarre possessed institutions empowered to negotiate a social compact with each successive monarch, who had to pledge fidelity to the fueros in return for continued contributions from Navarre.

Navarre was governed by a viceroy, Royal Council, Cortes, and Diputación. The viceroy was named by the king and exercised the king's executive functions in Navarre.[28] The Royal Council was Navarre's judiciary. The seven members maintained, in consultation with the Cortes or Diputación, the right of *sobrecarta*, a kind of veto power over royal measures deemed to be *contrafueros*, that is, violations of the fundamental law of Navarre. Since by law four of the seven councillors had to be Navarrese, the Royal Council, though an appointive body, could defend Navarre's interests against Madrid.

The Cortes was divided into three estates: ecclesiastics, nobles, and commoners. The three met together for debate but voted in separate chambers. Resolutions required majority passage in each chamber, thus practically ensuring the veto of any resolutions that threatened to disturb established power relationships. The popular branch was formed of the thirty-eight municipalities (nominally representing 36 percent of the population of Navarre) that, through their size, wealth, and importance, merited a seat in the Cortes. They were far outnumbered by the members of the clergy and nobility with seats in the Cortes, so that the balance of power lay not in the cities but in the first two estates. This ensured that representation from the Montaña dominated proceedings.

Most of the time, the powers of the Cortes, including the right to collect taxes and to recruit for the army, were invested in the Diputación, a permanently standing committee elected by each Cortes upon its dissolution. The Diputación was presided by the bishop of Pamplona, and included six other representatives: two from the noble estate, two from the city of Pamplona with one vote between them, and two from other municipalities, again with one vote. This structure ensured that urban interests got a hearing while at the same time reserving final power for the nobles and the bishop of Pamplona, whenever they should wish to operate in concert. In the Diputación, too, representatives from the Montaña had the final word.

One of the most valuable foral rights was control over taxation. The Diputación levied taxes and disbursed most of the revenue locally, helping to create the appearance of prosperity and order for which Navarre was famous.[29] Madrid received its revenues from Navarre in the form of an annual gift. Before granting the gift, however, the Navarrese could raise grievances over contrafueros. Once these were rectified, it would put the machinery of tax collection into motion. Spanish monarchs, so as not to threaten the already thin flow of money from Navarre, were careful to avoid contravening the Navarrese fueros. The exception proves the resilience of the foral constitution. In 1796 the Spanish government initiated an offensive against the taxing powers of Navarre, but this was so ineffective that during the first decade of the nineteenth century the crown actually spent more in Navarre than it extracted. In effect, Navarre was exempt from its fiscal duties toward the central government at the time of the French invasion.

The fueros exempted the Navarrese from war except in defense of Navarre. In 1803 and again in 1806, after heated battles with Madrid, Navarre was finally forced to relinquish this privilege and accede to military levies. Nevertheless, the full levy, by which the government was supposed to be able to recruit one out of every five men of military age, was not obtained from Navarre. In 1803, the province contributed 800 men, and in 1806–7 another 1,498 men, the only "blood contribution" made by Navarre to the Spanish military in the prewar era. Again, any threat to this fuero, whether from Madrid or Paris, was likely to meet staunch resistance.

One of Navarre's most valuable privileges was its separate customs border. In the rest of Spain, the Bourbons had created a single, national market, and they had restricted the importation of finished manufactured goods and the exportation of raw materials in an attempt to encourage industrial development. Navarre, however, controlled its own borders and was exempt from these restrictions. Thousands of Navarrese depended on the sale of raw materials, especially wool, to France. Thousands more made money by importing finished goods from France and reexporting them (illegally) to Castile and Aragon. The export of wool was particularly important to the monasteries of the Montaña, which enjoyed enormous power within the Cortes and the Diputación, and could veto any proposed change in the constitution. Drovers depended on the carrying trade, and consumers in general benefited from cheaper French manufactures. The city of Pamplona, well represented in the Cortes and Diputación, was one of the great entrepôts for French goods in Spain and stood opposed to any reform of the customs border. Finally, the foral government as a whole grew fat on its tariff revenues and was unwilling to give them up.[30] In short, there were powerful interests in Navarre prepared to defend any threat to its foral right to a separate tariff border. As a result, the Bourbons avoided threatening this aspect of the foral constitution.

Again, the exception proves how important the separate customs system was to the Navarrese. In 1717 the Bourbons had tried to extend Spanish customs to the Pyrenees. However, within a few years, as harassment of royal customs officials reached warfare proportions and smuggling absorbed previously legitimate trade, the customhouses along the Pyrenees border of Navarre cost more money to defend than they were able to collect. In 1722 Madrid admitted defeat and returned the operation to the Navarrese, withdrawing Spain's customs border back to the Ebro River.[31] This was a sign of the power of foral issues in Navarre.

Those who profited most from the separate customs were the Navarrese engaged in the illegal transit of French products into Spain. The number of people who made their living from smuggling, while impossible to count accurately due to a lack of documentation, was probably higher than in any other Spanish province judging from police records and from the observations of contemporaries.[32] One result of smuggling was the widespread availability of weapons, though this was no doubt also related to the continued economic importance of hunting in much of Navarre.[33] In the early nineteenth century Navarre had more guns per capita than any other province. The availability of weapons also had its effect on the rate of crime, which was higher in Navarre than in any province except Madrid and Logroño.[34] Indeed, in border regions of Navarre, like Roncal and Salazar, there existed a frontier atmosphere in which a large part of the population handled firearms and lived outside the law, either smuggling or having economic relations with smugglers. The possession of small arms and the habituation to lawlessness was an important resource for the guerrilla resistance after 1808, when being an outlaw and a patriot became one in the same thing. In the guerrilla army of Navarre, smugglers acted as soldiers, guides, and, ironically, as Mina's own customs officers.[35]

Thus, the foral constitution both empowered the Navarrese and gave them something worth defending. In addition, the foral government ensured its own popularity through specific legislation to control prices and commerce. Among other things, Pamplona limited the extraction of grains and other staples from Navarre. When harvests fell short in Spain, Navarrese producers felt great pressure to export cereals to Castile and Aragon, where dearths generally hit harder, causing prices to rise more than in Navarre. The Diputación, however, prohibited grain exports in bad years, consistently favoring consumers over the big producers in the Ribera.[36] In this way, the government acted to close the door on the acquisitive spirit of landowners and merchants who could have gouged consumers in both Navarre and in the rest of Spain during times of shortage.

Local governments too were able to control the price of staples. During shortages, they fixed prices locally. They used public funds to purchase cereals from abroad and prohibited local farmers who had good harvests from selling outside of the community.[37] These controls on industry and commerce were a constant source of irritation to big landowners and merchants in the Ribera who saw the future of Navarre as a supplier of cash crops for export.[38] But such measures also buttressed the position of small farmers and landless laborers, ensuring the popularity of the foral government among most people.

Aside from the material advantages they afforded, the fueros also had a strong emotional appeal in Navarre. In the abstract, they had few detractors. Even those Ribereños who would have liked to see a free market in grains and the opening of trade with Castile and Aragon agreed with the small farmer of the Montaña on the value of exemptions from royal taxes. Equally important, Navarrese believed that the constitution of Navarre, in which the king governed by compact with the Navarrese people, was a model for all Spain. The Navarrese were proud of this fact. In 1811, a Navarrese representative in Cádiz extolled the constitution of Navarre as the embodiment of the popular sovereignty missing in the rest of Spain since the time of the Hapsburgs. All Castile and Aragon had to do was to reclaim that which the Navarrese had never lost, their natural and legitimate right of self-government.[39] In reality, the vaunted sovereignty of the Navarrese people did not go very far. Yet, what mattered was that people believed in the idea of a sovereign Navarre. In the struggle with France, the Navarrese had more to defend than other Spaniards, for among other things they were fighting for an ancient and tested constitutional government.

The strength of the foral issue in Navarre was not fully understood inside France, where opinion was from the first in favor of the abolition of regional privileges. When it leaked as early as the spring of 1808 that the French had designs on Navarre and that they would certainly abolish the foral system, there was immediate reaction from Navarrese leaders. Miguel Izquierdo wrote to Madrid in the spring of 1808 describing the horror Navarrese would feel should they lose their traditional liberties.[40] Joseph Bonaparte's advisers warned him that Navarre would fight if its fueros were threatened. In 1810 Miguel Azanza, a Navarro and the most important member of Joseph's entourage, even made a special trip to Paris in part to warn Napoleon against consummating his plan to make Navarre another French department. In the War of Independence, where the combatants fought for a complex of personal, religious, dynastic, national, and regional issues, it is difficult to sort out and assign values to the various motivating factors. The trepidation of Spanish collaborators over the French plan to abolish the fueros, however, argues strongly for the influence that the foral and regional question had among the Navarrese.[41]

Under the foral constitution, municipalities in the Montaña were surprisingly democratic and powerful. This too was a source of great strength to the guerrillas. In the Montaña, municipal government was exercised by a community council open to all heads of households. Municipal offices were rotated among council members, so that every head of household eventually participated directly in government. In Echauri, which selected a treasurer and three *regidores* (town councillors) each year, twenty-eight men filled thirty-two possible vacancies from 1793 to 1800.[42] These individuals included relatively wealthy men, like Francisco Jauregui, the owner of one of the greatest flocks of sheep in the valley, and the rich labrador, Bavil Armendariz, who owned twelve houses in the village of Echauri, but also peasants of more humble means, like Gabriel Irujo, who owned a small house and whose stock of animals amounted to two goats.[43]

Madrid, to cement its control over Navarre, had tried to overthrow this system, pushing for the abolition of open elections in favor of the procedure of *insaculación*, in which officials were randomly selected from among a pool of men qualified by their property to hold office.[44] With this reform, Madrid sought to create municipal oligarchies, which could be more easily managed. The system had already been adopted in much of Castile and Aragon, but in Navarre tenacious resistance by the foral government limited insaculación to large towns and cities. Thus, most of the Ribera followed the new procedure, making government by the *veintena*, or council of twenty oligarchs, the norm in places like Tudela and Corella. Local elites, therefore, dominated the political process in the Ribera. The Montaña, on the other hand, preserved its democratic local government in all but the largest cities.[45]

Municipal governments had great powers under the passive viceregal regime that existed before 1808. Municipalities fixed wages and prices. They were responsible for most essential services, including the milling of flour and the supply of basic commodities, as well as roads, schools, and local law enforcement. The way in which municipal governments managed local services illustrates the survival of a "moral economy" in the Montaña. The contracts given to the baker, miller, innkeeper, or any one of the other local artisans were long and detailed legal documents that demonstrate how towns and villages constrained the acquisitive urge of their denizens.

The wine seller, for example, was allowed by contract to take only a customary level of profit. He paid the community for the right to do business, and he could not cease in his duties during the period of the contract without paying stiff fines. Privilege and duty were integral parts of any enterprise. On feast days and holidays the wine had to be supplied at no profit to the community. The quality of the product was closely monitored and the use of grapes or wine from outside of the community was forbidden, so long as any of the local product remained. At the same time, the wine seller was assured that no competitor could market wine in the community. Thus, the wine seller was conceived as a service provider to the community rather than as a merchant. His sphere for individual initiative was extremely limited, but at least he was secure in his niche. In effect, the closed society of the Montaña provided individuals with security in place of opportunity.

The array of powers possessed by municipalities was truly astounding. Local governments selected their priests and arranged for their payment. They controlled settlement and residence within the municipal boundaries, denying communal privileges to anyone they felt might upset the community. They allocated the tax burden communicated by the Diputación and handled conscription locally. They regulated planting and the harvest, dealt with local disturbances, and jealously controlled the ability of travelers to enter the village freely, especially vagabonds, gypsies, or other outsiders.[46]

These extensive powers were possible because of the large financial resources available to the municipalities. The first set of resources comprised the town rents. Local governments auctioned off some community services and properties in a procedure that had changed little over many generations. In Echauri, these included the mill, the bakery, the fish market, the butcher shop, the inn, the wineshop, and a fishing concession in the river Arga. When it came time to renew a license, the municipality placed notices in all the villages of the valley of Echauri. The auction lasted as long as it took to burn three candles. At each new bid, the price of the service rose one ducado (eleven reales). As a result, the rental income of the village could vary widely from year to year. In the first decade of the nineteenth century Echauri took in a minimum of 1,000 to 1,200 reales a year from these rents.[47] Larger towns and cities supplied many more services. Corella rented concessions for the sale of olive oil, salt, beans, licorice, and sausage. The city got about 24,000 reales a year from these sources during the decade before the French invasion, and another 1,500 to 2,000 reales worth of wheat from the in-kind rental of three flour mills.[48]

The second set of resources comprised the town lands. Echauri rented land to raise the priest's salary, kept pasture aside for the butcher to use for fattening livestock, and rented other properties to meet ordinary expenses. A final resource was the huge common lands. In the Montaña these lands were still normally exploited communally, usually for pasture and firewood, although governments sometimes rented pieces to individuals on a temporary basis as a way of raising extra funds.[49] Large commons in the Montaña helped to preserve the poorest members of the community from destitution, since they could keep a few animals without actually owning their own pastures. In the Ribera, on the other hand, municipalities routinely rented out commons, and communal usage had fallen into disfavor. The poor in the Ribera were, therefore, entirely dependent on wages.[50]

The democratic structure of municipal government in the Montaña naturally affected decisions on the raising and allocating of funds and on such crucial issues as conscription and the use of the commons. In 1807 the Diputación finally acceded to a military levy in Navarre after a long struggle with Madrid over the issue. Communities reserved the right to pay for exemption from this requirement, and they usually raised the money through a head tax. The valley of Echauri's contribution was set at thirteen individuals.[51] All the villages in Echauri agreed that such a levy was out of the question, since there were no vagrants to impress into service.[52] Instead, Echauri raised the 15,600 reales needed to buy exemption from military service. The government raised the money by taxing the adult male population, by taking an advance from the parish, and by utilizing surpluses in the treasury.[53] In the end, the valley fell short of the sum required, and two young men were supposed to be selected at random for the army (though no evidence exists that this actually took place).[54]

In contrast, the city of Corella, run by a closed group of noble families, found it inconvenient to pay for exemption from military conscription. The most common complaint of the city was over the surplus of laborers and the presence of a large number of destitute beggars within the city limits. Corella even encouraged its young men to enlist: over 10 percent of the armed forces drawn from Navarre came from Corella, which contributed well over one-fifth of its military-age male population to Spain's defense.[55]

In times of subsistence crisis, the democratic structure of local government in the Montaña provided a brake on the acquisitive urge and a check on the severity of crises. In 1789 there was a shortage of grain in the valley of Echauri, as elsewhere in Spain. A junta of all the regidores from the valley met to resolve the problem by purchasing wheat and corn from local sources and even from abroad, through the port of San Sebastián. The purchase and transportation of the grain from the port were handled by a resident of Pamplona, who was told to offer seventeen reales per robo of wheat, well above the price in a normal year. The price of the grain was elevated even more by the cost of transportation and the wages that had to be paid the purchasing agent. As a result, the cost per robo came to over twenty-two reales, of which the municipality paid 47 percent out of the town rents. The final price to people in Echauri was only twelve reales, scarcely more than the price in a normal year.[56]

In the Ribera, on the other hand, merchants often managed, against the wishes of the foral government, to export grain to Castile, even when harvests were short in Navarre.[57] A certain amount of grain might be set aside for relief.[58] Most of the time, however, the seasonal migration of workers from the Ribera to the cities of Aragon and Castile alleviated the responsibilities of the municipal government during the critical months of unemployment.[59]

The French gained access to the wealth of the Ribera simply by dominating the commercial and political elites, who were often glad to cooperate. Poor and landless Ribereños, on the other hand, had no reason to defend a constitution that did nothing for them. Ribereños had been demobilized and disenfranchised at the municipal and provincial level under the foral regime, and they were not likely to rise in support of such a system. Although, as will be seen, there were some young men from the Ribera who joined the resistance movement, especially in the summer of 1808 and after May 1812, it was the Montaña that contributed the vast majority of the men and supplies to the guerrilla army.

In the Montaña, foralism had brought great benefits and motivated people to defend Navarre against France. At the same time, democratic foral and municipal institutions empowered and mobilized Montañeros and proved to be another obstacle for the French occupation. The pressure of French imposts tended to unite rather than divide people in the Montaña, who were able to raise taxes through consensus rather than force, and who were able to delay the extraction of grains and animals through their control of local administration. Thus the fueros both motivated and mobilized people in the Montaña. Moreover, under foral law, the Montaña had developed some special resources with which to fight the French. Montañeros were heavily armed, both because hunting remained a common right, not a noble privilege, and because smugglers used weapons against the fiscal agents of the state. They knew secret paths to escape royal soldiers and police, and they knew how to construct makeshift boats and rafts to cross the Ebro River. All of these resources of the Montaña would be marshaled against the French after Napoleon occupied Spain in the spring of 1808.

O N THE MORNING of 9 February 1808 General D'Armagnac, at the head of 2,000 French infantrymen, entered Pamplona through the northern city gate known, ironically, as the Portal de Francia.[1] Two days earlier the French had crossed the Spanish border at Roncesvalles. Twenty feet of snow in the mountain pass had forced D'Armagnac to proceed without his artillery, and he feared for the survival of his small army should Pamplona resist.

D'Armagnac had cause for alarm. Officially, France was still Spain's ally, and Madrid accepted the presence of French troops in Spain as a security measure against their common enemy, England. However, many Spaniards had come to mistrust the intentions of Napoleon, and in Pamplona crowds filled the streets, fired by orators who spoke of driving the French from Navarre.[2] The garrison was called to arms inside the city's fortress, or Ciudadela, which was surrounded by a mob of people blocking the entrances. On 10 February an assassin knifed a French soldier to death in the street. D'Armagnac wrote to Paris that Pamplona was against him and that "the merest spark would set all Navarre ablaze."[3] The hostility of the Navarrese was justified, of course, for D'Armagnac carried secret orders from Napoleon to seize the Ciudadela.

Since the incorporation of Navarre into the Spanish monarchy in 1512, Pamplona had been one of the key points of Spanish defense against attack from the north. In 1571 Phillip II had ordered the construction of a fortress in the city to be built on a scale commensurate with his vast empire. The Ciudadela took over a century to complete and incorporated the finest elements of what would come to be called the Vauban system.

Almost as large as Pamplona itself, the Ciudadela presented an impregnable face of moats, walls, towers, parapets, and glacis to the attacker. The fortress was supposed to enable even a small garrison to hold out for months against a siege. As events turned out, however, the people of Pamplona labored to build and maintain this impressive fort for nothing. The Ciudadela, which had never had its ability to withstand a siege really tested, fell in 1808 to a simple ruse without a shot being fired.

The day after his arrival, D'Armagnac asked the viceroy of Navarre, the Marqués of Vallesantoro, for permission to enter the Ciudadela with 400 men in order to reinforce the Spanish garrison. Once inside, the French could have easily overcome the 300 troops of the garrison, many of them invalids and inexperienced militiamen. Vallesantoro knew this and wisely refused to allow entry to his French "allies" until he received specific orders from Madrid. While Vallesantoro waited for guidance from the court, D'Armagnac settled into a house that stood just outside the main gate to the Ciudadela, a location that would eventually prove useful to him.[4] There he began to consider what might be done to pacify the city. The French position in Navarre was perilous. D'Armagnac, in the midst of an unfriendly population, had no artillery, few men, and little ammunition. Without access to the citadel, his men were dangerously exposed. In this situation, D'Armagnac could not wait for permission to enter the Ciudadela, and he engineered such a subterfuge to take the fortress as might have made Odysseus blush.

The French had arranged to send an unarmed requisition party every four days to the gate of the Ciudadela, which possessed a flour mill and bakery large enough to meet the French troops' requirements. This circumstance provided the opening D'Armagnac required. On the morning of 16 February, sixty men, weapons hidden inside their cloaks, approached the fortress to collect bread. That night a heavy snowfall had blanketed the city. Some of the requisition party, while waiting outside the fort, feigned joy at the sight of the fresh snow and engaged in a vigorous snowball fight. The Spanish guards were enthralled with the sport and failed to notice that some of the French now stood upon the lowered drawbridge. Quickly, they entered the gate and disarmed the Spanish guards. During the night, D'Armagnac had secreted an additional 100 grenadiers inside his house. These men now rushed to the Ciudadela, took the armory with 10,000 muskets, and brought to a conclusion the first hostile action of the Spanish war. The most important fortress in north-central Spain had fallen to a handful of French troops armed with snowballs.

A few hours later, D'Armagnac had the following announcement posted in the streets: "Inhabitants of Pamplona: Do not interpret the recent alterations as a sign of treason or perfidy, but an act dictated by necessity for the security of my troops. Napoleon, my lord, who has signed a treaty of alliance with Spain, will back up my words." At the same time, in the cynical manner of imperial communiqués, he assured the municipal government and the Diputación of his good intentions, writing: "This act must be considered a new tie of friendship."[5]

The initial reaction in Pamplona and elsewhere to this treachery was hostile, and in some provinces there was talk of a general rising. In Valladolid a French soldier was cut down in the streets by armed citizens when the bad news from Pamplona arrived, and in an ensuing fight, two more Frenchmen were wounded.[6] In Pamplona an angry mob led by students occupied the city streets. At first, D'Armagnac cleared them with troops, but soon the crowds were augmented by armed peasants from the countryside. D'Armagnac had to withdraw to the Ciudadela, leaving the streets in the hands of his enemies. On 18 February the court finally sent Vallesantoro instructions to keep the French out of the citadel, and secretly Madrid went even further, sending a special agent whose task was to prepare Pamplona for an uprising. Of course, these efforts were too late.[7] The Ciudadela was in French hands, and D'Armagnac could congratulate himself for having acted in the nick of time.

The general's celebration was premature. Soon he found himself playing Remirro de Orco to Napoleon's Caesar Borgia. The deceitful means used to occupy the citadel had made D'Armagnac an object of loathing in Navarre and had, moreover, left a bad taste in the general's mouth. Expressing a sentiment that would become a common refrain among French officers in occupied Spain, D'Armagnac wrote that he would prefer "a state of open war" to the hypocritical situation in which he found himself. Having made the mistake of expressing disgust for his "vile mission," as he called it, D'Armagnac became disposable. When the general persisted in filing discouraging reports on the situation in Pamplona and requested additional troops, the emperor replaced him with General D'Agoult.[8] Napoleon branded D'Armagnac an inexperienced commander who had acted contrary to orders, and rumors were spread in Navarre that the emperor would rectify the situation.[9]

Soon, however, it became apparent that D'Armagnac was just one of several commanders given orders to seize Spanish forts. On 28 February General Duhesme occupied the citadel of Barcelona and the fort at Montjuich. On 5 March General Thouvenot installed himself in San Sebastián. By 18 March, when the French took control of Figueras, the most important Spanish fortresses in the North had fallen at no cost to the French. Still, the government in Madrid was too docile to object even to this pattern of treachery. King Charles IV proclaimed that the armies of his "close ally" Napoleon occupied Spanish strong points in order to protect the country from England, and he asked local authorities to maintain tranquillity at all costs.[10] In Pamplona, the initial displeasure of the people was allowed to dissipate, and the sullen crowds that had at first milled about the central plaza dispersed, leaderless.

The ease with which the French occupied the key strongholds of northern Spain must be understood in the context of almost a century of Franco-Spanish relations. After the Peace of Utrecht in 1715, Spain fell within the French orbit, as the Spanish Bourbons maintained a "Family Pact" with their cousins in Paris. The French Revolution, paradoxically, served to increase Spain's dependence on France. Initially, of course, the Spanish king, Charles IV, along with half of Europe, sought to destroy the regicides in Paris, and he brought Spain into the First Coalition in 1793. Spanish forces penetrated French territory at either end of the Pyrenees, but the success was temporary. In 1794 the Convention's armies rolled back the Spanish, especially on the western front, where Basque nationalists in Guipúzcoa and Navarre greeted the revolutionary troops as liberators.[11] With French troops as far west as Bilbao and as far south as the Ebro River, and with separatist and republican conspiracies surfacing in the Basque region and even in Madrid, the Spanish government had little choice but to sue for peace on any terms. Negotiating for Spain was the prime minister, Manuel Godoy, an army officer who held power by virtue of his influence over the weak king, Charles, and his queen, María Luisa. By the Treaty of Basel, signed on 22 July 1795, Spain returned to the French camp, and in the following year, the two countries concluded a formal alliance at San Ildefonso. The treaties earned Godoy the title "Prince of the Peace" and confirmed his position as the court favorite and virtual ruler of Spain for most of the next twelve years. After 1795 Godoy's political future and the future of the country were tied more firmly than ever to the destiny of France.

Friendship with France, in the polarized international climate of the time, meant certain war with England, but such a prospect was far from unpopular in Spain. England was the traditional enemy, the modern Carthage, threatening Spanish interests around the globe and occupying Spanish territory in Gibraltar. War with England, however, cost a great deal more than anyone anticipated. The English navy cut Spain off from America, especially after the destruction of the Spanish fleet at Trafalgar in 1805, initiating the decolonization of Spain's overseas possessions. The loss of revenue from the silver ships and customs wrecked government finances, and declining trade erased the economic growth of the eighteenth century, as the most advanced areas of Spain were cut off from overseas markets and sources of raw materials.[12] Spaniards were, of course, aware of the evil times that had overtaken the country. Some had identified the alliance with France and war with England as a major source of the evil, and a pro-English cabal had formed around the Bourbon heir, Prince Ferdinand.[13] Yet, against popular anti-English sentiment and against the overwhelming force of Napoleon, the Spanish government had little choice but to remain friendly toward France.

The emperor exacted a high price from his friends: an embargo on trade with England and the provision of men and money to the imperial war effort. The Spanish contribution to this alliance, or Continental System, was heavy. First its navy, and then a force of 15,000 infantry, was placed at the disposal of France. After the disaster of Trafalgar, even the submissive Godoy began to chafe at the cost of the French alliance. In 1806 France began what most observers anticipated would be a difficult campaign against Prussia, and Godoy took advantage of the moment to try to break with Napoleon. Godoy ordered a general mobilization against France. Unfortunately, Napoleon made quick work of the Prussians, finishing them off at Jena even as he became aware of the Spanish betrayal. Godoy tried to patch up relations with the emperor, but the damage was done. The Spanish government had shown that it was an unreliable ally. When Napoleon knocked Russia out of the war at Friedland in 1807, the day of reckoning was at hand for Godoy and Spain. In secret protocols attached to the Treaty of Tilsit, the Russians agreed to allow Napoleon to take over Spain, Portugal, and Gibraltar in exchange for a free hand in Turkey.[14]

Napoleon needed a pretext to place troops on the soil of his Spanish allies, and he found it in the problem of Portugal. Portugal was England's last ally in western Europe and the only piece missing in Napoleon's Continental System. If France could take Lisbon, England would be isolated from the Continent and the hegemony of France sealed. Given England's dominance at sea, the only way to place French troops in Portugal was to march them overland through Spain. Napoleon gained the frightened approval of the Spanish government for this project by the Treaty of Fontainebleau, signed on 27 October 1807.[15] Within a few months, 30,000 French troops had driven the Portuguese royal family, together with English nationals, from Lisbon. Yet, the imperial divisions continued to pour across the Pyrenees. By February 1808 there were 100,000 French soldiers in the peninsula, most of them in Spain for "security" against an English attack. For Napoleon, it was an irresistible step to use these troops to occupy strategic points inside Spain, above all the northern fortresses and Madrid. This was the background to the seizure of the Ciudadela and the other Spanish fortresses in the spring of 1808.

Napoleon expected the conquest of Spain to be a quick affair of a few marches, little more than a "military promenade."[16] The Spanish government was in Napoleon's pocket, and even if Spain's armies resisted, they could never keep the field against the French. In late March, however, events in Spain took an unexpected turn. The inaction of the king and Godoy in the face of injuries like those suffered at Pamplona had given further impetus to an undercurrent of dissatisfaction with the government. It had long been rumored that Godoy had insinuated himself into the queen's bed and even into the royal succession. This added to Godoy's unpopularity, not least with Prince Ferdinand. At last, the faction grouped around Ferdinand became exasperated with the weakness of Charles and Godoy. On 18 March a crowd led by members of Ferdinand's cabal and supported by the royal guard carried out a bloodless palace coup in Aranjuez, where the government had relocated to escape French scrutiny. A mob invaded the royal residence and forced Charles to dismiss Godoy and to abdicate in favor of Ferdinand. All across Spain, people tore down public portraits of Godoy in celebration. The new object of the crowd's affection, Ferdinand VII, "the desired one," was proclaimed king amid millenarian expectations.[17]

The March revolution surprised Napoleon and filled him with foreboding for the future of his enterprise in Spain. The "people" had shown itself less somnolent than the government and army. Roads suddenly became unsafe, and French soldiers were instructed to act as if they were in hostile territory. Around the western Pyrenees it was as if war had already been declared.[18] The irony of Aranjuez, however, was that it placed on the throne a prince no less subservient to Napoleon than Godoy and Charles had been. For the past year, Ferdinand had been trying to gain Napoleon's friendship, and he redoubled these efforts once he came to power, despite the opposition of many of his supporters, who would have liked to see him steer Spain's foreign policy on a more independent course. Thus, when Napoleon summoned Ferdinand to Bayonne for a conference in early April, the young king decided to make the trip against the wishes of his advisers. Ferdinand departed Madrid on 10 April, leaving behind a junta to govern in his absence. When he arrived in Bayonne on 20 April, he was arrested and told of the emperor's intention to take possession of Spain.

Over the next two weeks, Napoleon pressured Ferdinand to abdicate the throne back to his father. Charles had already declared the events at Aranjuez illegal. On 30 April Napoleon arranged a meeting between father and son at which Charles, following a script prepared in Paris, demanded that Ferdinand relinquish the throne. María Luisa applied additional pressure, but Ferdinand refused to step aside.[19] A few days later, impelled by a dangerous turn of events in Madrid, Napoleon personally asked for Ferdinand's abdication, but again the young king proved unwilling. According to witnesses, the emperor's "request" then took a more direct form. "It is necessary," he told Ferdinand, "to choose between abdication and death."[20] On 5 May, Ferdinand chose to abdicate to his father. Charles then abdicated to Napoleon, and the emperor turned Spain over to his brother, Joseph Bonaparte.

As this drama in Bayonne unfolded, events in Spain once again outpaced Napoleon's capacity for planning. The revolt at Aranjuez had raised hopes of long overdue change, and Spaniards, as a result, became more truculent and less willing to accept the insults of French troops stationed in the country. In Madrid there was a wave of violence in the streets between French soldiers and Spaniards that threatened to degenerate into open warfare.[21] On the night of 25 March Spanish troops killed one French soldier and wounded two others as the three tried to force their way into a brothel on the rough Calle de San Antonio. In early April a French soldier refused to remove his hat for a religious procession, and the devout beat him severely. The violence escalated further when rumors of Ferdinand's arrest in Bayonne reached Madrid in late April. On 26 April three soldiers assassinated and robbed a civilian, and in the evening one of Murat's aides killed another Madrileño in a street battle. The next day a merchant stabbed and gravely wounded a soldier, and that evening seven French soldiers were set upon by patrons of a cabaret they were attending. Three fell seriously wounded. In all, according to General Grouchy's reports, the French troops garrisoning Madrid suffered twenty-three casualties in March and April.

By the end of April things had come to a head. The violence had provoked Joachim Murat, Napoleon's supreme commander in Spain, to mobilize his troops. On 30 April Murat, ignoring the objections of the governing junta, ordered Francisco de Paula, the last Bourbon heir, shipped to Bayonne. That day and the next, people filled the streets and milled about the royal palace, waiting for a signal. Some begged members of the junta to distribute arms, but this they refused to do. Even in the supreme crisis, giving arms to the mob was instinctively abhorrent to Ferdinand's supporters. Instead, they ordered Spanish troops to their barracks to prevent them from joining popular demonstrations and circulated a proclamation calling for an end to disorderly gatherings in the Puerta del Sol and other public places. This order had no effect, however, and on the morning of 2 May the crowds in the streets were larger than ever.

The rising of *dos de Mayo* began at nine o'clock. A small group of Ferdinand's supporters raised the cry that the French were about to cart off the last members of the royal family. A crowd formed at the royal palace, stopping the carriage intended to transport Francisco de Paula to France. To cries of "death to the French," the growing mob surged through the streets looking for victims. A number of French soldiers were killed in the first instants, but Murat counterattacked with overwhelming force. The people of Madrid fought with the weapons available to them—knives, scissors, awls, stones, and some firearms—but French grapeshot and cavalry quickly cleared the streets. Meanwhile, a pocket of resistance by Spanish regulars in the artillery park of Monteleón was taken. By midafternoon, the revolt was over.

The rising of 2 May was doomed to fail from the start. Madrid had a population of 176,000 people, but Spanish troops in the capital numbered only 3,000. The French had in or around the city 36,000 soldiers. Indeed, it is possible that the French had wanted an uprising all along so that they could set an example by crushing it.[22] The rebellion of 2 May developed beyond French expectations, however, and led to heavy losses on both sides. According to Grouchy, between 400 and 500 Madrileños died in the fighting.[23] Among these were 80 civilians executed by the French during the night of 2 May and the morning of 3 May.[24]

The French also suffered casualties. A French eyewitness claimed the loss of 500 men, but this is probably too high.[25] Grouchy reported only 150 casualties, 14 of them fatal. Moreover, a third of the injuries were light wounds from tiles and rocks. Most of the deaths and the most serious casualties occurred during the assault on the Spanish artillery park, while the action of the mob in the streets was not terribly devastating. For example, the legendary horror of boiling water poured down upon the French troops apparently resulted in only one superficial burn.[26]

The rising was a military failure but a political turning point. It was news of the events of 2 May that persuaded Napoleon to drop all niceties and force Ferdinand to abdicate. The French show of power on 2 May convinced Ferdinand's junta, the Council of Castile, and the municipal government of Madrid to accept Joseph as their new king and to participate in the pacification of the country.[27] During May Napoleon matured plans for a constitutional assembly in Bayonne to be opened on 15 June. Invitations were extended to some 150 Spanish notables. Ultimately, ninety delegates arrived to pledge fidelity to Joseph and to discuss and ratify a constitutional statute drafted beforehand by the French. Many of the provisions of the statute, such as the abolition of torture and the suppression of the Inquisition, were long overdue in Spain and met with little opposition. Others, like the threat to regional autonomies, promised to subvert the most sacred Spanish traditions. On such matters as these, the deputies were not willing to act merely as ciphers. Some warned Joseph and Napoleon that they would meet stiff resistance unless certain demands were met. These included the preservation of the church and its property, a guarantee of the territorial integrity of Spain, the protection of noble and regional privileges, and the lowering of taxes.

In effect, the Spanish representatives succeeded in modifying some of the most revolutionary aspects of the document, expanding the original 68 articles to 146, with additions securing the status of the church, the statist structure of the national Cortes, and the protection of noble and regional vested interests.[28] The final statute was probably an adequate compromise whose provisions could have formed the basis for Spain's transition from feudal monarchy to constitutional government. The weakness of the Bayonne constitution, however, lay in the nature of its origin, powerfully symbolized for Spaniards in the conspicuous presence of French infantry at the ratifying ceremony.[29] The fact that the statute was forced upon the nation by a foreign power working through an extraordinary and unrepresentative body condemned the work completed at Bayonne from the beginning. Bayonne did not set the stage for a new era of constitutional government. Rather, it revealed the imperial rhetoric of progress and rational government for what it was: a cover for French dominion in Spain.

The statute of Bayonne was, in any case, rendered irrelevant by a pandemic of rebellion that swept Spain in late May and early June 1808. The abdication of Ferdinand, coming on the heels of news of the dos de Mayo in Madrid, touched a central nerve in the body of Spain causing a nationwide revolt against French rule. In cities all over the country, mobs demanded that their officials step down or join them in proclaiming Ferdinand king. Provincial governments that proved too wedded to Godoy and the old order or too timid to oppose Napoleon were swept aside and replaced by revolutionary juntas. In other areas, the old elites were co-opted into or even led the revolution. This was the case in Asturias, one of the first provinces to rise against France.

The governor-general of Asturias, Alvaro Flórez Estrada, one of the greatest leaders of the generation of 1808, had been in Madrid on 2 May and returned to the provincial capital, Oviedo, on 9 May with an eyewitness report of the uprising. News of the abdication in Bayonne arrived shortly afterward. Pressured by a riotous crowd in Oviedo, but also backed by elements of the local nobility and bourgeoisie, which had a reputation for liberalism and Anglophilia, Flórez Estrada and his friends declared Ferdinand king on 23 May, formed a junta of resistance, and established relations with England. Thus, in Asturias, local leaders absorbed the revolutionary impulse and guided it along an orderly path.[30]

In Valencia, news of Ferdinand's abdication arrived early on 23 May and led to the formation of a revolutionary junta later that same day. In Valencia, however, the process was much more violent than in Asturias. A mob several thousand strong marched through the streets on 23 May wearing red cockades and carrying banners painted with the image of the

Virgin Mary, a mixture of revolutionary and traditional symbols reveal-
ing the dual nature of the Revolution of 1808. The demonstration started
peacefully, but turned ugly when civic leaders, who feared the working-
class crowd more than they feared the French, refused to declare Ferdinand the rightful king. In response, a popular coalition swept aside the
old government, and public order quickly degenerated. According to
one of the leaders of the revolt, "the entire nobility" was suspected of
treason for the "apathy and egoism" with which they had initially responded to the crisis. The result was a butchery of over 300 suspected
collaborators and French nationals that nearly sidetracked the resistance.
In the end, however, Valencians succeeded in mobilizing themselves for
war. The guilds were formed into militias, regular and secular clergy
were mobilized, and deserters, smugglers, and convicts were granted
amnesty if they agreed to enlist.[31]

In Cádiz, too, the mob seized power when the Marqués del Socorro,
captain general of Cádiz, hesitated to declare Ferdinand king. Exasperated rebels took over the artillery park and armory, stormed the house
of the marqués, dragged him to the center of town, and executed him.
They trained the artillery on the fashionable homes of the Calle de la
Caleta, and the violence might have gone further but for the intervention
of Capuchin monks, who succeeded in quieting the crowd. By then,
however, the rebels had established a new junta in the city and had
proclaimed war against France. During the next six years the people of
Cádiz were principal actors in the defense of the city and nation.[32]

On 24 May new juntas took control in Zaragoza, Cartagena, and
Badajoz. And in the following week Seville, Córdoba, León, Mallorca,
Granada, and La Coruña, among the major population centers in Spain,
formed governments of resistance. By mid-June, each province was governed by its own revolutionary junta, and by summer's end these sent
representatives to a Central Junta for all Spain. The mobilization against
France brought new men into government. These men, through the juntas, conceived the idea that the Spanish nation, through the process of
resistance, had recovered its primitive sovereignty. The juntas were the
first popularly chosen authorities in Spain, and they placed new ideals
and programs on the political agenda, from which they would never
be entirely erased, even during the darkest moments of reaction in the
nineteenth and twentieth centuries. The juntas gave birth to liberal, constitutional government and to the modern concept of nationhood in

Spain. This was the Revolution of 1808, the beginning of contemporary Spanish history.[33]

The revolutionary climate brought out the best and the worst instincts in people. The nation had been prepared for a xenophobic explosion by a century of French cultural and political domination, and when Spain woke in 1808, it was to the sound of hateful tirades against France. The Central Junta engaged in the most inflammatory rhetoric in proclamations intended to mobilize the Spanish people:

> What sort of thing is a Frenchman? A being monstrous and indefinable: a being half created. There is nobody who does not have the right to kill these ferocious animals. Therefore, fellow countrymen, let us hunt these creatures; let us pursue them day and night by sea and on land through many years of blood and fire until we rid the universe of this barbarous, brutal, lascivious, and libertine people, along with its wicked leader, until we are purified of this damnable race of monsters so noxious to the human species.[34]

The ugly propaganda produced results. Anyone who had been associated with the pro-French regime of Godoy or who chose to support Joseph, anyone who even dressed or acted French, was liable to become the victim of popular wrath. Yet, without this climate of national chauvinism, the explosion of popular energy and the reforging of the Spanish nation in the summer of 1808 would have been inconceivable.

The fall of the old regime and the breakdown of order also led to a significant degree of class and regional conflict. In each provincial revolution patriots had first to deal with collaborators and shirkers among the local elites before they could mobilize people to the resistance. The class warfare of the summer of 1808, evident in places like Valencia and Cádiz, less obvious in the case of Asturias, preceded the national war and was its precondition. When local notables could not be enrolled in the popular cause, they had to be circumvented or replaced. The collaboration and inaction of the Spanish elites created the opportunity for numerous incidents of popular violence. The Conde de Aguila, the Conde de Torre del Frasno, and the Marqués de Perales were among the prominent nobles who lost their lives to the popular revolution. Generals Borja, Trujillo, Saavedra, Filangieri, and San Juan and Colonel Cevallos were among the military officials who died at the hands of their compatriots. The revolution claimed the captains general of Cartagena and Cádiz, the governors of Tortosa and Castellón de la Plana, and the intendants in Cuenca and Salamanca. City officials were sacrificed in Cuenca, Reinosa, Jaen, La Carolina, Talavera de la Reina, and many other municipalities.[35]

At times, rebellion against France and French sympathizers spilled over into a general hostility toward all government, all nobility, all elites, even those who stood at the heart of the revolutionary impulse. The Cádiz newspaper, *El Robespierre español*, expressed the class animosity felt by many in the patriot movement. Spaniards fighting for the French should be captured, burned alive, their ashes scattered, and their goods confiscated, wrote the editors. Grandees who were merely sympathetic with the French should suffer the same fate. Neutral nobles might be spared, but their property should be taken anyway, and even nobles fighting with the patriots should have three-fourths of their land expropriated.[36] Thus, the revolution threatened to destroy itself, in a massacre or alienation of some of the very people who were needed to give it direction.[37]

Even in Galicia, where the uprising seemed nearly unanimous to the French, the insurgency received little help from the bourgeoisie and almost none at all from ecclesiastics and nobles. One Galician patriot recalled that the resistance in Mondoñedo in 1809 was made difficult due to the lack of cooperation by local elites: "I will not say that the nobility has generally distinguished itself here, nor supplied aid, nor inspired anyone as patriotic examples. . . . Also, generally speaking, members of the clergy haven't lent themselves [to the resistance]."[38] Officials in Galicia tried to impede the rebellion. In El Ferrol, the governor-general refused to recognize Ferdinand until a mob of women burst into his quarters on 1 June, seized the armory, distributed 30,000 rifles and other weapons to the people, and forced the general to declare himself willing to die for Ferdinand.[39]

Ecclesiastics were specially suspect in Galicia, and the local junta kept a watch on them to prevent them from aiding the French.[40] This detail is an important feature of the uprising, because the Spanish war is perceived by many, especially in France, to have been a religious crusade led by priests and monks.[41] The clergy did play a leading role in mobilizing people in some places, but not everywhere. The activity of clerics in Valencia has been mentioned. In Logroño on 31 May a mob drove the mayor from power and handed the city over to the archbishop. When Logroño fell a week later almost all of the regular clergy were taken with arms in hand, according to D'Agoult's information, and the general predicted that France would have to do something about the "frocked canaille" of Spain.[42] Priests in the Basque country circulated missives calling for war against France, and in Madrid after 2 May clergymen began propagandizing among Spanish and Portuguese troops attached to imperial armies, encouraging them to desert or sell their weapons, apparently with a degree of success.[43] On the other hand, the bishop of Pamplona collaborated willingly with the French, as did many others.[44] Even the bishop of Calahorra, who had been acclaimed leader of the Logroño insurrection, had actually been forced into accepting the position after the crowd had flushed him out of hiding.[45] In Cádiz, the Capuchins aided the revolution, but by demobilizing the mob rather than joining it. In the end, a majority of the church hierarchy in Spain sided with the Bonaparte regime, either out of necessity or out of preference, but the incidence of collaboration varied greatly from province to province.[46] It is evident, therefore, that the role of the church and of religion in the insurgency was complex and must be handled with great care.

Another feature of the urban risings of 1808 was the reign of local patriotism over national unity, a harbinger of the cantonalism that would continue to undermine national revolutionary movements in Spain, as it did in 1868–74 and 1934–39. In the early days of the insurrection, the juntas of Asturias, Valencia, and Seville declared themselves sovereign. The Sevillan junta narrowly rejected a proposal to invade and subdue Granada, which had refused to recognize the superiority of the Sevillans.[47] In the province of Murcia juntas in Lorca, Cartagena, and Mazarrán simply ignored orders from the junta of Murcia, for a time effectively eliminating concerted government at the provincial level.[48] In the North, Puigcerda practically came to blows with Urgel in a battle over which junta should claim precedence.[49] Local juntas fought not just among themselves but also with the military commanders and representatives of the Central Junta.[50]

Yet, the particularism that threatened to dissolve patriotic unity in 1808 was also, in a strange way, one of the great strengths of the patriots. For centuries, neither the Hapsburgs nor the Bourbons had been able fully to implement the absolutist program in Spain. Resistance to central control was an honored tradition that took on various and complex forms, from movements for outright provincial or regional independence, to the squirreling by peasants of their savings in hollow walls and false rooms hidden from the tax collectors, to the smuggling and brigandage endemic to mountainous and border regions of the country. The Spanish people, especially in some peripheral provinces, including Navarre, had been left with a freedom and autonomy surprising to foreigners accustomed to thinking of Spain as a nation under the yoke of despotism. Napoleon's troops contrasted their experience in Spain with that in the occupied countries of northern Europe. Germans and Austrians, conditioned by militarism and centralization, had proved unable or unwilling to act without the permission of their superiors. Against the German princes and against Prussia and Austria it had been enough to win a major battle to gain a favorable peace.[51] Even the vaunted mobilization of the German people in 1813 was at best partial and anemic. In Spain, however, Madrid had never entirely succeeded in gaining control over provincial and municipal bases of power and leadership. This dispersal of authority gave Spaniards the ability to generate resistance from dozens of separate centers in a whirlwind uprising that effectively isolated the French in a few major capitals and military encampments.

Thus, despite the threat of federalist dissolution and class violence, the revolutionary juntas survived, prospered, and, by the fall of 1808, constituted a unified national government in the Central Junta. The Central Junta contained some of the finest minds and greatest leaders in Spain, and men like Blanco White, Cienfuegos, Martínez de la Rosa, and Quintana projected a radical vision of Spanish society into the plans and pronouncements of the revolutionary government. "Providence" had created an opportunity for the nation to recover the freedoms lost to the Hapsburgs in the sixteenth century. But to the Liberals of 1808 the revolt was about more than just the recovery of ancient dignity. Spain would achieve a new degree of liberty even as it struggled for independence, and it would become "the envy and admiration of the world." In this new Spain, laws would be based on the consent of the governed, people would be free to publish and worship as they wished, and the structures of feudal society would be eliminated. The "paralysis of arbitrary rule" that had consumed the country from within would be replaced by a government based on the "general utility" of the majority.[52] Over the next six years, the Liberals wrote these ideals into legislation, first within the Central Junta and after 1810 within the Cortes of Cádiz, where the Spanish Enlightenment would achieve its highest political expression. In the summer of 1808, however, the more pressing requirement was to mobilize the nation against the Bonapartes.

The French forces in Spain were placed in immediate jeopardy by the risings in the provinces. In June armed peasants began to patrol highways and to watch city gates even in regions occupied by French troops. The period in which an individual French officer or an unescorted stage could travel freely through the country was over.[53] The spirit of resistance returned even to Madrid, which had seemed cowed after the defeat of 2 May. Once again, Madrileños congregated in the public squares, now sporting the red cockade of revolution.[54]

In addition to a sullen capital and a hostile countryside, the French also faced a growing military threat from Spanish regular forces. During May and June the juntas began piecing together an army from remaining Bourbon units and from new conscripts. The junta of Cádiz captured the French squadron in the harbor and with it an important arsenal that included 442 cannon, 830 tons of powder, 1,429 muskets, 100,000 balls, 1,000 swords, and almost 4,000 prisoners.[55] In June the juntas of Seville and Granada raised large, if untried, armies of recruits, reinforced with veterans who had deserted their units. How dangerous these armies were the French could not guess. Certainly, General Dupont, entrusted with the invasion of Andalusia, did not perceive the peril of leading 20,000 troops over the Sierra Morena and into the valley of the Guadalquivir. In late June Dupont wrote from Córdoba that he did not believe stories of insurgent armies in Seville and Granada.[56] Dupont learned the extent of his error on 19 July when he ran into 35,000 Andalusian troops at Bailén. After a desultory series of maneuvers in unbearable heat, the French placed themselves in an untenable position, and the Spanish made prisoners of the entire force after having done battle with less than half of it.

The Spanish victory at Bailén proved to be of enormous importance. It was the first time an imperial army had surrendered. Bailén, even if it was a fluke, dispelled the aura of invincibility that had come to surround imperial troops. Napoleon's supporters in Spain wavered, and some found their patriotism.[57] News of the battle caused an exodus from Madrid, as people flocked to join the insurrection.[58] On 24 July the Royal Council informed Joseph that it considered the statute of Bayonne a dead letter.[59] After Bailén, growing Spanish armies began moving north to threaten Madrid, and the exposed position of the French forces in Iberia became evident. In Lisbon Junot's army of some 25,000 negotiated terms of surrender at Cintra and was evacuated, courtesy of the British Navy, to the French Atlantic ports. Moncey's army of 9,000, impossibly bogged down in the Valencia plain, which had been flooded to protect the city, abandoned its mission in the Southeast. Valencia would not fall until 1812. Joseph evacuated Madrid on 30 July, earning the nickname "King of the Eleven Nights," and French troops, government officials, and collaborators crowded the northern routes, retreating to a position behind the Ebro River and reconcentrating in the Basque provinces and Navarre.

4 ✸ The Failure of Revolution in Navarre

D URING THE SUMMER of revolution in 1808 Navarre was one of the quietest provinces in all Spain. The city of Pamplona was incapable of producing a revolt like the dos de Mayo in Madrid or a revolutionary movement like that in Valencia. The conservative bourgeoisie, resident nobility, and rich clergy of the viceregal capital made spontaneous disorder of any kind difficult to sustain.[1] In addition, the presence of some 2,400 French troops and their Spanish auxiliaries entrenched in the Ciudadela discouraged resistance.[2] Finally, the collaboration of government officials in Pamplona robbed the rebellion in Navarre of any central direction. The viceroy and provincial government, or Diputación, followed French directives with unnecessary relish in 1808, functioning as the nexus between the occupying power and the people and calling for cooperation with France in achieving the "regeneration" of the nation.[3]

Outside of the capital, there were some signs of resistance. The town of Estella, in particular, was the scene of an early uprising against the French. On 25 April Estella learned of Ferdinand's predicament in Bayonne. Crowds appeared in the streets wearing the red cockade, but, as elsewhere, it was news of Ferdinand's abdication that precipitated open rebellion. On 1 June a mob forced the city council to dissolve, and two days later a new council purged of collaborators circulated a proclamation to the surrounding countryside calling on people to rally to the defense of Estella.[4] The viceroy in Pamplona sent in constables to arrest the rebel leaders, but they were driven off, after a short skirmish in which one of the constables was killed.

Meanwhile, Estella's plea for support from its neighbors received little response. In Viana, a special junta of priests and other leaders sidetracked popular demands for a distribution of arms.[5] In Corella, the "lower orders of the city" and "people without education" tried to overthrow the municipal government in the first week of June, but a group of "enlightened subjects" was able to reestablish order. The role of Corella's clergy in calming the populace was especially noteworthy, once again illustrating the ambiguous role of the church in the Spanish resistance.[6] Officials in a number of other towns also took active measures "to impede the mobilization and arming proposed by the city of Estella" and proudly reported the fact in letters to Pamplona.[7]

The failure of revolution in the rest of Navarre condemned the efforts of Estella to isolation and collapse. Estella finally raised three companies of men, armed with shepherds' hooks, old swords, and some rusty firearms. Barricades were erected in the streets, and all was made ready for a French response.[8] By itself, however, Estella was not a worthy military target, and the French ignored the city. Thus, there was no revolution of 1808 in Navarre, and effective rebel leadership had to come initially from outside the province, especially from nearby Zaragoza.

The situation in the Aragonese capital was very different from that in Navarre. In the first place, Zaragoza was still free of French troops in the spring of 1808. Also, Zaragoza had long been a bastion of support for Ferdinand, and the city had greeted the fall of Godoy and Charles at Aranjuez with jubilation.[9] In late April and early May, news of Ferdinand's mistreatment in Bayonne produced profound resentment in Zaragoza and generated an insurrectionary climate in the city.

Zaragoza, like much of Spain, was gripped by a millenarian mood, rooted in a profound sense of national decadence, the result of economic contraction, bad harvests, and military and political humiliation.[10] People believed that evil was afoot and that only Ferdinand, like a modern Moses, could lead the country to better times. On 17 May a miracle in the cathedral of Zaragoza galvanized the city. At the midday mass a crown appeared—some said out of a cloud above the cathedral, others said surrounded by palms above the altar—with the unlikely inscription: "God supports Ferdinand." The clergy took advantage of the miracle to incite the populace to insurrection. They proclaimed the miracle a sign that the Holy Virgin of the Pilar of Zaragoza had granted protection to patriots. Any soldier wounded fighting the French was ensured 100 years relief from purgatory. Anyone killed would be reborn three days later in paradise. Murat was said to have been arrested in Madrid, and Ferdinand was rumored to have returned in disguise to lead a holy war against France. The day of deliverance was apparently at hand.[11]

On 24 May Ferdinand's abdication became public knowledge in Zaragoza. Students and clerics called for an uprising, and a mob wearing cockades and led by a local surgeon took the military governor hostage and seized the castle of the Aljafería, which contained an enormous arsenal of 25,000 rifles and 80 pieces of artillery. On 26 May the armed crowd marched to the country estate of José Palafox y Melcí, a long-time supporter of Ferdinand, and brought him back to Zaragoza as their leader. Palafox was installed at the head of a governing junta drawn from members of the old government, the military, and the clergy. The junta adopted the red cockade, defusing its revolutionary symbolism and identifying the new government with the insurrection. During the following days retired officers and soldiers as well as new recruits poured into Zaragoza. By 29 May 4,500 troops were drilling on the outskirts of town, and thousands more joined this force in the first days of June.

Meanwhile, the French had prepared a force of some 4,000 men under General Lefèbvre-Desnöettes to deal with the Zaragozan rebels. To reach Zaragoza, the French had to pass through Tudela, the second city of Navarre, located on the Ebro River fifteen miles north of the border with Aragon. Palafox hoped to check the French advance at Tudela, and on 31 May he offered to send men and arms to the city. The gift was at first rejected by the municipal government, which had no wish to be sacrificed for the good of Zaragoza.[12] There were some in Tudela, however, who desired a battle, and when the details of Palafox's offer leaked to the public on 2 June, a crowd formed in the streets and demanded that the municipality put up a fight.[13] The mob forced city officials to retreat to the house of a town notable, José Yangüas y Miranda. There a special junta of community leaders was convened. On 3 June this junta apparently yielded to the revolutionaries and promised to accept Palafox's aid and attempt to block the passage of the Ebro.

The city had exactly three days to prepare a plan of battle, not much time in any case, but the junta dragged its feet, and Tudela was left almost defenseless. On 6 June peasants reported a French column just a few miles away. This was Lefèbvre-Desnöettes's force, which had just crushed the rebels in Logroño on 4 June. At the last minute, 2,000 recruits from Zaragoza arrived, joining a thousand ill-armed young men from Tudela and its hinterland behind hastily erected barricades. Just before the battle, the junta tried to sue for peace, but its efforts were spoiled by the Zaragozans, who initiated the firefight on 8 June. Once the battle started, the French swept the Spaniards aside and quickly forced the city to surrender. Lefèbvre reported only two French soldiers killed and a few wounded. The Spanish suffered twenty-four casualties, with most of the defenders escaping to Zaragoza. The junta of Tudela quickly went over to the French and reestablished calm.

The conditions of both the resistance and the surrender of Tudela reflected the incomplete development of the revolutionary forces. According to the governor of Aragon, Tudelans "lay indolent" during the crisis and their leaders were "debased by intrigue." In fact, Tudelan patriots, unlike those in Zaragoza, had failed fully to overthrow or co-opt the existing government, dooming all efforts at mobilization. Lukewarm leaders like Yangüas maintained the real power in Tudela and never intended to offer resistance. As in Madrid on 1 May the junta refused to distribute arms. Five hundred rifles that had arrived from Zaragoza just before the French attack were never distributed. Thus, the French faced a poorly armed opponent that had, with the exception of the Zaragozan troops, received no training. On 8 June the Tudelans simply melted away, and officials were able to do what they had been waiting days to do—hand over the town to the French. Tudela was rewarded with a thorough sacking.[14]

With the fall of Tudela, the insurrection in Navarre, such as it was, collapsed. There were several reasons for the lack of initiative and success by Navarrese rebels during this early phase of the war. The first was the province's strategic importance. The security of the whole French operation in the peninsula depended on the domination of Navarre, since the French used the passes of the western Pyrenees to resupply and reinforce their armies in Portugal and in most of Spain. The French took special pains, therefore, to prevent resistance from gaining a foothold in the region.[15] This was easy to do in 1808, when it was a matter of dealing with isolated urban revolutions, as in Logroño and Tudela. Thus, until the middle of 1809 and the rise of the first important guerrillas in the countryside, Navarre was relatively quiet, and French soldiers considered themselves lucky to draw duty in Navarre, which reminded some of their experiences in the easily pacified Rhineland.[16]

The second factor working against the Navarrese was, ironically, the Spanish victory at Bailén and the subsequent French withdrawal north of the Ebro. From August to November, when most of Spain was liberated, Navarre and the Basque provinces became Napoleon's staging ground for the reconquest of the peninsula in the winter of 1808–9. In the last half of 1808, therefore, the French had 100,000 troops in Navarre, making resistance impossible.

Finally, the government in Pamplona showed itself an eager participant in the suppression of rebellion. In other provinces battles had first been fought with local elites, either to co-opt them into new power structures or to oust them entirely from the government, before revolutionary juntas could be installed. In Navarre this civil struggle was resolved in favor of old Godoyites and supporters of the French regime, as in Corella and Tudela, due to the presence of French troops and the successful action of collaborating officials, or *afrancesados*. As a result, no alternative leadership developed in Navarre until the middle of 1809, when guerrilla armies learned to act on their own authority. In the meantime, however, the initiative to resist France had to come from outside Navarre, especially from Zaragoza.

After the fall of Tudela, Zaragoza was the only center of serious resistance in north-central Spain. From mid-June to mid-August, French troops laid siege to the city. Zaragozans knew that the key to raising the siege lay in Navarre. The forces sent against Zaragoza entered Spain through the Navarrese towns of Irún and Roncesvalles and fed upon the rich grain lands of Navarre before descending to the Ebro River valley. To interdict these supply lines, the junta of Aragon tried to organize guerrilla resistance in Navarre.

In the mountains of Roncal and Valcarlos there had already been signs of unrest, triggered by mounting French requisitions. Working the western Pyrenees and the Aragonese border around Sangüesa were half a dozen armed bands, led by men with colorful pseudonyms like the Pesoduro and the Malcarado.[17] None of the Navarrese parties was strong enough, however, to accomplish more than hit-and-run operations against French stragglers and small convoys, and the junta of Aragon decided to send its own agents to Navarre to try to provide the rebels with better leadership.

In July the Aragonese junta dispatched Andrés Eguaguirre and Luís Gil to organize Navarrese volunteers whose task would be to divert

French troops from the siege of Zaragoza.[18] Gil conducted a small operation in Ujüé, near Sangüesa. Ujüé, a remote village atop a dry plateau in
eastern Navarre, was especially suited to Gil's purposes. The place had
become an unlikely center of rebellion after a group of peasants from
Ujüé robbed a French officer and his wife near Tafalla. Later, the officer's description of the crude mountain people he had seen and of their
coarse language left no doubt that he had been accosted by people from
Ujüé. On 17 July a French column arrived to punish the village. However, the local population had escaped into the deserted mountains that
surround the village. Remaining behind was the priest of Ujüé, Casimiro Javier de Miguel, who used his knowledge of the French language
to preserve himself from harm and to persuade the French not to set
fire to the village. He was not, however, able to protect five other individuals, people too old or too sick to flee. Four were run through and
killed and one wounded by the French troops, who were infuriated by
the desolation that greeted them in Ujüé.

The village had been denuded of everything useful to an army. In a
practice that other villages would follow when faced with the approach
of French forces, the people of Ujüé had stripped their homes of all livestock and food. Even the water supplies in the houses had been dumped
into the streets, making the village, situated on top of a hill in the middle
of an arid highland, uninhabitable for any extended period of time. As
a result, the French were unable to tarry or rest. Could they have foreseen the village's and Miguel's later active role in the guerrilla war, they
would surely have burned Ujüé and arrested its priest.

Thus, at the point Gil entered the stage, Ujüé was already mobilized.
Gil ordered the men of Ujüé to Carcastillo, at the southern foot of the
plateau on which the village was situated. There they were to be assigned to units of a volunteer army that was being gathered from villages
throughout the region of Sangüesa. A band of armed peasants led by
the regidor of Ujüé duly marched into Carcastillo. Once this force had
assembled, however, Gil found that he had too many people for his resources and that they were too poorly trained to undertake a regular
action against the French. Gil was unable to envision or lead a guerrilla
campaign. Instead, he sent the volunteers back to their villages, each
group accompanied by a regular soldier who was to provide training to
the peasants. The impact of this decision by Gil has never received the
praise it merits. By sparing untrained peasants from the certain destruc-

tion of a regular battle with French troops and by providing for their training, Gil helped to create a reservoir of personnel for Mina, who would later recruit heavily in the Ujüé-Sangüesa region.

The second official sent to Navarre, Andrés Eguaguirre, attempted a more ambitious project than Gil. Despite Eguaguirre's lack of military experience, General Palafox had granted him the rank of colonel with the authority to organize an army in occupied Navarre. In July Eguaguirre headed to Estella, which he judged a propitious area in which to begin recruiting for his so-called Volunteer Mobile Musketeers of Navarre. Estella had been the most enthusiastic city in the aborted revolution of May and June. Many Estellans had fought in Tudela and had returned home with arms and a taste of combat. At first Eguaguirre achieved some measure of success, at one point commanding an army of some 800 men. Now, after weeks of rebelling in a vacuum, Estella finally attracted a French response. After driving off the first French assault, Eguaguirre retreated into the mountains northwest of Estella in order to avoid a second, more serious attack by the French. For the next two months, Eguaguirre's army operated in the rugged country northwest of Estella, with its center of command in the remote hermitage of Santiago de Lóquiz. Estella secretly continued to supply this force, which otherwise would have starved in the mountains of Allín, until it was driven out of hiding on 9 September.[19]

Despite an initial period of rapid enlistment into the Mobile Musketeers, Eguaguirre's unit soon disintegrated. Eguaguirre was too weak to face the French and he responded to attacks by hiding in mountains too barren to support his troops. The formula had still not been discovered that would allow irregular forces to disperse and hide in their homes when faced with superior French numbers and to reassemble as quickly when the time was right. Eguaguirre could not send his troops home, because he had no confidence that they would ever return. Indeed, his men had come to hate Eguaguirre almost as much as they hated the French.

Eguaguirre created enemies of the Navarrese because he relied on force to obtain supplies from villagers and terror to enlist men into his army. The use of violence and terror against civilians who show a preference for the enemy or who remain neutral is a necessary component of guerrilla warfare. However, this violence must be combined with a demonstrated ability to defeat enemy forces, defend friendly territory, and protect villages from the troops and tax collectors of the occupying power. The Mobile Musketeers, however, could barely protect themselves much less the civilian population. As a result, most Navarrese were unwilling to offer Eguaguirre their support, which Eguaguirre interpreted as treason.[20] Finally, terror became Eguaguirre's preferred method for enforcing his authority, a sign of the imminent dissolution of the movement. Some towns even sought French aid against the Mobile Musketeers.[21]

On 11 July Eguaguirre attempted to enlist the city of Tafalla in the patriot cause. Tafalla had shown no interest in resisting France, probably due essentially to its location on the main north-south route through Navarre and the concomitant heavy presence of French troops.[22] After meeting with officials from Tafalla in a hermitage located outside of town, Eguaguirre found that the city was unwilling to offer him any support. Eguaguirre expressed his disgust with the "complete lack of energy" on the part of the city and threatened: "what I request today through political channels I may achieve when I return in a few days time through the use of force."[23] The town of Leiza went so far as to betray the Mobile Musketeers to nearby French forces. Eguaguirre caught wind of the treason and, before his troops were driven off by the French, shot up the town. Eguaguirre promised the leading citizens that he would return, that Leiza would be burned down and that many "heads would roll."[24] Fortunately for Leiza, the colonel's days as the commander of Navarre were numbered.

With little support in Navarre, Eguaguirre turned to robbery and extortion to supply his needs, becoming, finally, what the French claimed every guerrilla was, a bandit. Even larceny proved insufficient to satisfy Eguaguirre's wants, however, and throughout the life of the Mobile Musketeers troops were poorly clothed, underfed, and unpaid. The colonel soon faced widespread insubordination and desertion. He attempted to maintain control over his recruits through rituals of public humiliation, forcing volunteers to kneel and swear oaths while he had guns pointed at their heads.[25] These methods naturally proved unproductive. By the end of September his force had declined to a mere 280 individuals. The first inauspicious experiment with guerrilla warfare in Navarre came to an end in October, when the Mobile Musketeers were trapped and defeated in Sangüesa. After the battle, those who escaped fled across the border into Aragon, where some were incorporated into regular Spanish units, which had by then advanced into the region.[26]

In the aftermath of Bailén, with Spanish armies in Aragon and southern Navarre, it became possible for members of the Navarrese Diputación, who had by then become disgusted with French rule, to flee behind the Spanish lines drawn up north of Tudela.[27] Soon after arriving in Tudela, the deputies rediscovered their patriotism. In October and November the Diputación proclaimed a return to that "happy epoch" in which the "valiant and generous Navarrese" could speak in "the language of honor." Defense of religion, king, and nation "demanded revenge," while the "constitution of Navarre and the venerable authority of its ancient Fuero" required the arming of all able-bodied men.[28]

The Diputación even flirted with the idea of forming its own volunteer army, projecting four battalions of 1,200 men each. Municipal officials in liberated southern Navarre formed lists of men eligible for military duty. However, fewer than 1,800 names were submitted, and some of these individuals were listed as cripples, missing persons, and men already enlisted with the Aragonese.[29] Ultimately it did not matter how limited the number of eligible men was. The Diputación did not have the resources with which to organize even a fraction of them. Three things made the Diputación's project impossible. First, most of Navarre still lay in French hands, and by mid-October there were some 100,000 French troops in Navarre preparing to retake Spain.[30] Second, liberated southern Navarre suffered from a swarm of Spanish units that exacted arbitrary requisitions as burdensome as those of the French. Third, both occupied and unoccupied Navarre had already suffered the devastation of over six months of war. The usual sources for taxes, loans, and gifts in a province used to exemption from contributions had run dry. In the end, the Diputación scraped together 250,764 reales in loans and 72,366 reales in gifts, less than 4 percent of the government's usual haul from customs tariffs before the war and certainly not enough to equip an army. In any case, the "battalion" of volunteers that joined the deputies in Tudela consisted of only eleven men and six chaplains.[31]

The legitimate government of Navarre, already tainted by months of collaboration, was quite evidently not equipped to rouse the province. Municipal officials, with the exception of those in Estella, where a new junta had been created, feared the revolutionaries more than they feared French reforms and were also incapable of leading a rebellion. Outside agitation from Aragon alienated rather than inspired the Navarrese. The revolutionary potential of Navarre did not lay in volunteer armies organized by the Aragonese and the Diputación, nor could it be found in Pamplona and the other cities of Navarre, where a stupor reigned after the defeat at Tudela. The power of Navarre was in its villages, and it would take a new kind of military leadership and strategy to mobilize it.[32] Beyond the reach of the Diputación, the urban elites, or, indeed, the French, profound disturbances were brewing in rural Navarre, as the peasantry prepared to enter the political and military stage. First, however, Spain's regular armies were to experience the humiliation of utter defeat at the hands of Napoleon, who personally led the reconquest of Spain in the late fall of 1808.

IN NOVEMBER 1808 Napoleon intervened in Spain with his veteran troops and soon erased the shame of Bailén. The French took Biscay in a few days and entered Burgos on 11 November, dispersing Joaquín Blake's Army of the Left. In late November the French recaptured Tudela and drove the Army of the Center under Castaños out of the Ebro valley, while Palafox was forced back inside Zaragoza, which faced another siege. On 3 December Napoleon entered Madrid. The rapid defeat of Spain's armies imperiled the 34,000-man English expeditionary force in Spain, which was compelled to make an epic retreat through the snow-covered mountains of Galicia to escape encirclement by General Soult. On the morning of 18 January the last of the English army was evacuated.[1]

With the defeat of the Allied regular forces, Spaniards turned in 1809 to guerrilla warfare as the only available means of resistance. Galicia became the setting for the first widespread guerrilla insurgency in Spain. After driving the English from Galicia, Soult found himself in the midst of a hostile population. It seemed that everyone in Galicia, groaning from the depredations of retreating English and victorious French troops, was disposed to resist. When the French approached villages, peasants fled to the hills with their livestock and goods, returning to their homes only after the French had departed. French officers likened the march through Galicia to "the progress of a ship on the high seas: she cleaves the waves, but they close behind her, and in a few moments all trace of her passage has disappeared."[2]

The people of Galicia seemed to take up guerrilla warfare by second nature.[3] The priest of Couto, Mauricio Troncoso y Sotomayor, fled before Soult's men on 9 February 1809, gathered a small band of supporters, and that same day attacked a French detachment, killing fifteen and capturing fifty-one. Within a month, Sotomayor stood at the head of the "Division of the Mino," an army of several thousand peasants. This force came to dominate the Galician countryside, and even captured the French-held city of Vigo, together with 1,300 prisoners.

By late spring, the guerrillas in Galicia came under the command of General La Romana, who still had a few thousand regular troops around Astorga. In June La Romana led this combined force to victory at the bridge of San Payo, ejecting the French from the region of Santiago de Compostella. Marshal Ney, who had been left with half of Soult's original force, while Soult himself advanced into Portugal, was incapable of pacifying Galicia. Indeed, by late June Ney had lost half of his men. Meanwhile, Soult had insufficient numbers to fight the English and the Portuguese in Oporto. Thus, both Ney and Soult were outmatched, and they had to abandon Portugal and Galicia.[4]

The events in Galicia taught Spanish leaders a new respect for the effectiveness of guerrilla warfare. In concert with Wellington's and La Romana's regulars, guerrillas had helped to liberate Galicia and Portugal. The Spanish government learned that, despite the loss of urban centers and the destruction of its armies, rural Spain could still be defended. Through the strategy of guerrilla warfare, it was possible to spread French forces so thinly that they became vulnerable to attack. And by eliminating collaboration, the guerrillas confined the occupation to areas physically controlled by French troops.[5]

It was also Galicia that first opened the eyes of some French commanders to the difficulty of their situation in Spain. Marshal Soult left an eloquent testimonial as to what he faced in Galicia. "This province is in constant ferment," wrote Soult. The resistance of civilians promised to "make warfare in this country extremely bloody, infinitely disagreeable, and seemingly endless." A long struggle would be necessary, Soult informed Joseph, before anything of value could be gained in Galicia.[6]

The success of the Galician campaign convinced the Spanish government to embrace guerrilla warfare as the means to national salvation. In the summer and fall of 1808, when Spain still had ostensibly strong armies to field, the Central Junta had discouraged the formation of guerrilla parties.[7] The junta had feared that the existence of guerrillas would encourage desertion from regular units. By December 1808, however, it had become clear that Spain could not keep an army in the field against the French. The ambush of French stragglers and small detachments, the isolation of enemy garrisons, and the disruption of French administration were the most effective means of resistance available after December 1808.

Accordingly, the Central Junta issued a series of decrees giving legal existence to the guerrillas. On 28 December 1808 the junta passed its first "Reglamento de Partidas," establishing procedures for the organization of guerrilla parties throughout Spain. On 1 January 1809 the junta issued a "Manifesto of the Spanish Nation to Europe" justifying the mobilization of civilians. The manifesto described acts of incredible savagery perpetrated by French troops against Spaniards. French soldiers had profaned Spanish homes "with the rape of mothers and daughters, who had to suffer all the excesses of this brutality in sight of their dismembered fathers and husbands, [while] their children were pierced with bayonets and carried in triumph as military trophies." Convents and monasteries had been sacked, and the rape of nuns and murder of monks had become routinized. Religious houses and churches were converted into barracks and brothels. The French were discovered to be "bandits not soldiers, ferocious monsters not men, against whom every means of vengeance, every method of extermination, no matter how horrible or unprecedented they might seem, were authorized."[8] On 17 April 1809 the Central Junta authorized the formation of the *corso terrestre*, or "land pirates," and ordered all able-bodied males in occupied territory to form guerrilla bands.

Many of the guerrilla parties in 1809 were formed by dispersed regular troops and led by officers from the defeated Spanish armies. In the area southwest of Zaragoza, three officers, José Joaquín Durán, Ramón Gayán, and Pedro Villacampa, commanded 3,000 to 4,000 troops by the winter of 1809.[9] General Juan Díaz Porlier, "the little Marqués," was authorized by General La Romana and the junta in Oviedo to begin operations with two regiments in Asturias.[10] Julián Sánchez, who would operate a guerrilla party in the mountains of León, got his start as a cavalry sergeant fighting around Salamanca with General Del Parque.[11] Yet, most of the units formed of dispersed regulars were reintegrated into the Spanish army by the spring of 1810.[12]

More promising, in the long run, were guerrilla parties formed by civilians. It is true that in 1809 many civilian guerrillas were barely distinguishable from bandits. One of the most infamous of the privateers of 1809, Don Antonio Temprano, a monk of the order of Mercenarios Calzados, openly disavowed higher motives. He assiduously avoided French troops, preferring instead to terrorize and loot villages around Madrid, telling his men that the nation had entered an "epoch of every man for himself." Temprano's career was not an isolated exception. Saornil in Zamora, Piloti near Madrid, and a number of others also degenerated into mere criminals.[13]

It is also true that in most of Spain, guerrilla parties were small and of little military value.[14] In northern Spain, however, some of the guerrillas did raise large and effective forces as early as 1809. The priest Merino, after killing a French soldier in revenge for a slight suffered in the first days of the occupation, took to the hills to escape French justice and formed a guerrilla band in Biscay. Julián Sánchez, after failing to stop French soldiers from murdering his family, took up arms in the region of Salamanca. Juan Martín, the famous "Empecinado," raised an army in Old Castile.[15]

Guerrilla warfare also reappeared in Navarre in 1809. Zaragoza capitulated on 23 February, and some of the Navarrese fighting in Aragon returned to Navarre. On 21 March the French took the fortress at Jaca, eliminating the last regular force within striking distance of Navarre. The night before Jaca fell a group of Navarrese who had formed part of the city's garrison escaped over the walls. Among the refugees was a very new recruit named Francisco Espoz Ilundáin, the future Espoz y Mina. In Jaca and Zaragoza men like Mina had learned the use of arms, how to load and fire in twelve counts, and how to face the enemy. Now they returned to Navarre and became the basis for a new guerrilla movement.[16]

Soon there were dozens of small bands roaming the countryside, sometimes attacking French stragglers and mail couriers, but for the most part offering little challenge to the occupation. In the far North the priest of Valcarlos had a small following. In Baztán Antonio Zabaleta operated a band that roamed as far south as Estella. Bands under Sarto, Fidalgo, Marcaláin, Juan Ochotorena, Manuel Gurrea, Félix Sarasa, Juan de Villanueva, Vicente Carrasco, Pascual Echeverría, and the priest Hermenegildo Garcés de los Fayos were just some of the other guerrillas harrying the French. Yet, none of these bands was large enough to have much effect. And some were falling into Eguaguirre's trap, alienating rather than gaining adherents. Others began to act like Temprano's men, avoiding conflict with the French and robbing Spanish civilians instead.[17]

What Navarre required was a unified command to establish discipline among the guerrillas. The Central Junta tried to provide it by appointing the priest of Ujüé, Casimiro Javier de Miguel é Irujo, to organize Navarre. Miguel had saved Ujüé from French troops in June 1808 and had aided Gil in July. In 1809, with the help of the priest of Alaiz and the priest of Lárraga, he set up an intelligence network of agents (who were often also priests) in Pamplona, Zaragoza, Paris, Bayonne, and in villages on both sides of the national frontier. Miguel's system of espionage was facilitated by the common Basque language of the peasants on both sides of the Pyrenees. It was said that Miguel knew "by noon each day all that had been said the night before at the table of General D'Agoult," the French military governor of Pamplona.

Miguel was not, however, a good choice to lead the resistance. He could not inspire others to fight, because he himself did not participate in combat. Military leadership fell to others.[18] For a time, it seemed that the Roncalese might provide that leadership. Already in late 1808, the wealthy Gambra brothers had formed a band of some fifty men in the valley of Roncal that engaged the French on several occasions and even succeeded in chasing off a small garrison stationed in Aoiz. In March 1809 the Roncalese attacked a French convoy of prisoners being transported from Zaragoza to internment in France. Among the men they liberated were Navarrese who had fought in Aragon and a recently elevated brigadier general, Mariano Renovales. Renovales took charge of the Gambra band and galvanized a spectacular rising in Roncal. His army of peasants sealed the valley off from the rest of Navarre, beating off successive French invasions and inflicting over 1,000 casualties on the French. In July the French in Pamplona made a truce with Roncal, promising to leave the valley alone in exchange for a contribution in sheep and a pledge of nonbelligerency.[19] Having successfully defended their valley, the Roncalese appeared uninterested in taking the war to the French in the rest of Navarre. This task was left to Javier Mina, the younger relative of the more famous Espoz y Mina.

Martín Javier Mina y Larrea was the son of prosperous small farmers living in Otano, a small village at the foot of the Sierra of Alaiz, about half way between Ujüé and Pamplona.[20] When the French took the

Ciudadela, Javier was an eighteen-year-old seminary student who had just transferred his studies from Pamplona to Zaragoza. Javier had demonstrated with the other students in favor of Ferdinand when the news reached them of the coup at Aranjuez.[21] After participating in the uprising of Zaragoza, Javier returned to Navarre and began working as a spy for Miguel.

In the fall and winter of 1808 Javier joined the resistance in Aragon, and in February 1809, he witnessed the final tragedy of Zaragoza from the heights outside the city.[22] Returning to Navarre, Javier joined a handful of close friends in Pamplona. With the blessing of Miguel, he decided that he would set about unifying some of the existing guerrilla bands under his authority. By August, Javier Mina had succeeded admirably in his project and stood at the head of his own corso terrestre.

Javier Mina's initial following included Don Félix Sarasa, a well-to-do farmer from a village just outside Pamplona and the "most closed-minded Basque that ever lived." Sarasa could neither write, read, nor speak Castilian, but in the Basque villages around the capital, he was known as a shrewd merchant, who never missed an opportunity to sell the produce of his ample farm at every market and fair. Sarasa eventually took over the customs operations set up by Espoz y Mina in 1810.[23]

Also joining Javier Mina were Lucas Górriz, who would become a regimental commander under Espoz y Mina, and his brother José, who headed the Treasury of the Division of Navarre, again despite an inability to read anything more than a catechism, which he "read" from memory. Espoz y Mina himself, whose native Idocín lay only a few miles east of Otano and who was therefore in close contact with his nephew in the summer of 1809, also followed Javier from the first day. Espoz y Mina later recalled this group with some regret: Lucas Górriz was killed in action during the war; José Górriz was shot by the forces of the Restoration for defending the Constitution of 1812; Sarasa was imprisoned by the Restoration from 1816 to 1820, lost his fortune, and saw his children reduced to poverty. Mina was captured by the French in 1810, imprisoned in France until the end of the war, exiled by the Restoration, and eventually killed in action fighting for the independence of Mexico. Espoz y Mina was condemned by the Restoration to spend a third of his life in exile, although his reputation, unlike that of the other four, was ultimately rehabilitated. During the summer of 1809 these men, three of whom knew nothing beyond the use of the laya and pruning knife, embarked on a career that would for a time give them almost absolute power in Navarre.[24]

Javier Mina promised volunteers eight reales a day in wages, far more than the one real that Gil and Eguaguirre had been able to offer in the previous year. These wages were paid from the tithe, which the corso appropriated wherever it went, demonstrating how little the guerrillas were motivated by a desire to defend church property against the French "atheists." Soldiers were also promised daily rations of bread, meat, and wine, and the right to profit from booty and the ransom of prisoners. In every village and town in Navarre Javier and the priest of Ujüé appointed spies, often the priest or mayor, who received regular wages, some as much as the volunteers themselves.[25]

On 7 August 1809 with just twelve men the corso engaged in its first action, capturing ten French artillerymen foolish enough to travel alone on the road from Tafalla to Pamplona. With the captured arms, Javier doubled his following. By the end of the month, uniting a few of the smaller bands in Monreal, halfway between Idocín and Otano, Javier already stood at the head of some 200 volunteers.

Javier's activities at first centered on capturing convoys and small detachments. The guerrillas traveled from one end of Navarre to another to obtain arms, munitions, horses, and money. In early September the corso raided sixty mules from the garrison of Puente la Reina just southwest of the capital. In the middle of the month, now with 300 men, Javier shifted his operation to the region of Irún, where he captured a convoy transporting Spanish prisoners of war to France. Some of these prisoners joined the corso, and with his augmented force, Javier returned to the familiar territory east of Pamplona. There some of the men of Roncal, breaking their armistice with the French, joined the corso. Among these recruits was Gregorio Cruchaga, who would become Javier's second in command.

Most of the weapons and uniforms used by the volunteers in these early months were captured from the French, but Pamplona also supplied clothing manufactured in the city and smuggled out by the undertaker, Miguel Iriarte, and the vicar of the hospital, Clemente Espoz, Francisco Espoz y Mina's older brother. These two hid the uniforms beneath the bodies carted from the hospital to the cemetery outside of the city gates. The clothing was then taken to Badostáin, a village just east of Pamplona, where the priest Andrés Martín, who became the first historian of the Division of Navarre, saw that they were delivered to the guerrillas.[26] These details are significant, because both English and French sources often assumed that the guerrillas were created and sustained by English money and supplies. In Navarre, the greatest center of guerrilla warfare, this was never the case.

Mounts were more difficult to acquire. The unwritten rules of guerrilla war said that any foot soldier who could procure a horse automatically entered the cavalry. The guerrillas became consummate horse thieves, stealing from the French, from each other, and from private citizens. Entering the valley of Aézcoa in October, the corso "liberated" eighty-five horses.[27] With these a cavalry force of some 100 men was added to the 300 infantrymen under Javier. In late October the corso headed back to the region south and east of Pamplona. There the guerrillas seized a munitions convoy, captured a mail courier, and took thirty-seven French prisoners. These were transported, as usual, by secret paths to Lérida, thence to Valencia, the patriot stronghold in southeastern Spain.

The old Diputación, now in hiding outside of Navarre, reacted with horror to Javier's success. "Gangs of armed peasants," complained the deputies, "under the name of guerrilla parties" had entered Navarre and had "trampled over people of distinction and insulted many whom even the most rebellious soldier would venerate." The guerrillas compromised Navarrese towns and their officials, and this led to French reprisals and the demoralization of local leaders. Worse still, in the eyes of the former governors of Navarre, these guerrilla bands had begun to requisition goods, something not to be tolerated in peasants. The deputies saw the guerrillas as little more than bandits and predicted their destruction by the French.[28]

The attitude of the Diputación toward the insurgents revealed the limits of the deputies' patriotism and imagination. Their main concerns remained the maintenance of social order and the protection of private property. The deposed government, incapable of mobilizing Navarre itself, had clearly not grasped the nature of guerrilla warfare.[29] In this they were not alone. Neither the French nor the Central Junta had yet fully realized the importance of the guerrillas. That compromising municipal authorities and elites and exposing them to the possibility of French reprisal might be one of the essential preconditions of successful guerrilla warfare—so long as this were combined with victories over the occupation forces—had not entered the military consciousness.

In November Javier joined up with guerrillas from Rioja under Cuevillas, a smuggler of some fame in the area, to attack 800 French troops stationed in Los Arcos. This was the first large-scale engagement of guerrilla forces in Navarre outside of Roncal. Altogether Javier commanded some 700 troops reinforced by hundreds of local peasants, which he used to drive the French back to Estella after a sharp engagement in the mountains of Sansol on 20 November. The French lost 50 dead and 100 wounded, while the guerrillas lost 8 dead and 40 wounded, according to a Spanish source.[30]

The casualty figures from this first major action serve to indicate the effectiveness of partisan tactics. The French possessed two major advantages over the guerrillas. They had an effective cavalry, and they brought superior firepower, especially field artillery, into battle. The guerrillas could neutralize these advantages, however, by avoiding battle except under the most ideal circumstances.

The first requirement for guerrilla victory was proper terrain. In a set battle on flat land, French armies, with their excellent cavalry and artillery, could overcome even experienced infantry. For the untrained insurgents, lacking sufficient screening cavalry, with no artillery, and short of lances, muskets, and munitions, to be caught in open country would have meant instant annihilation. The guerrillas therefore traversed plains at night, on the run, and only when in dire need. On the few occasions when the guerrillas were trapped in open terrain, French victory was the inevitable result, as will be seen.

The second requirement for the guerrillas was superior numbers in any given engagement. The corso had neither the training nor the munitions to hold off a force larger than itself in a lengthy, ordered retreat should a battle develop unfavorably. Therefore, when the French approached with large columns, the guerrillas avoided battle by dispersing or hiding in the mountains, making use of their knowledge of the country and of the sympathy of the populace to escape.

Attacks were normally ordered only when a numerical advantage could be ensured. The insurgency had to make up for a lack of munitions by using its excellent intelligence network and mobility to achieve surprise. The dispersed insurgents were given the message to descend by various routes upon a prearranged point, where Javier expected some convoy or French detachment would pass. The guerrillas massed superior numbers, positioned themselves for ambush, fired a single volley, and charged immediately with the bayonet. The spirit behind this style of fighting is often associated with French Republican armies, but by the time Napoleon had occupied Spain, the élan was all on the Spanish side. For this reason, there was always a disproportionate number of dead among the French casualties, and the guerrillas took large numbers of prisoners by overcoming their opponents in hand-to-hand combat. Casualties in battle on the Navarrese side were customarily low, although the French made good this deficit by executing civilians and captured guerrillas and by the horrendous slaughter that occurred on the few occasions when the guerrillas were surprised by overwhelming forces of mounted enemies in the plains of southern Navarre and Castile.

On 28 November, soon after the battle of Sansol, Javier united his corso once again with Cuevillas and, reinforced by one of Porlier's cavalry squadrons, invaded Tudela. The garrison took refuge behind fortifications, but the Tudelans were not so lucky. Despite the efforts of Cuevillas to control Javier's undisciplined peasants, the soldiers of the corso devoted themselves to plundering the population rather than to engaging the French. The guerrillas took horses and a large number of sheep. They stuffed their pockets and knapsacks with money, silver, and anything they could find of value in the houses and retired to nearby Corella, where they fought over the spoils and ultimately disbanded. On 29 November General Buget—the garrison commander in Tudela— rode into Corella with his cavalry and killed twelve of Javier's men who had tarried there.

It was as important for the French as it was for the guerrillas to demonstrate that they could protect the towns and villages that had shown adhesion or at least acquiescence to their rule. This the French had failed to do at Tudela. As a result of the corso's incursion, Suchet began to lobby for the dismissal of D'Agoult, who was officially relieved at the end of December, though his replacement wasn't appointed until the end of January. During the next six months a succession of four generals ruled Navarre, as Napoleon searched vainly for the right commander to pacify the province. General Reynier took command of Navarre and the three Basque provinces at the end of January. In February Reynier was replaced by Dufour, who was relieved on 28 July by General Reille, Napoleon's aide-de-camp. Since each new appointee altered and countermanded his predecessors' policies, however, the rapid turnover merely served further to hamper antiinsurgency efforts in the province.

In December 1809 Javier set up headquarters in Los Arcos, a hilly area in southwestern Navarre little frequented by French troops. The interval gave his men a needed respite. The corso numbered some 500 infantry and 150 cavalry, but many were new recruits who lacked military training. In Los Arcos Javier saw that they received rudimentary instruction, organized the corso into companies, selected a staff of officers, and created the flag that would remain in use for the next five years. Gregorio Cruchaga was made second in command, Lorenzo Calvo, a former infantry sergeant, was placed in charge of the infantry, and Severino Iriarte, an ex-cavalryman, took command of the cavalry. Javier's force was rapidly passing from a small, irregular formation struggling to survive, into an ordered and disciplined body made up partly of dispersed or retired soldiers and operating, at least part of the time, on instructions from a regular commander, General Areizaga.[31]

The interval in Los Arcos lasted only a short time, until late December, when Suchet took charge of coordinating a new round of persecution against the corso. The enemy forces occupying Navarre had already been increased substantially. The French had reinforced churches, convents, and caseríos of robust construction with earthworks, ditches, and wooden palisades, converting them into small fortresses stocked with supplies. In April 1809 D'Agoult had fewer than 2,500 troops in Navarre, but by midsummer that total had gone up to nearly 4,500 to counter the growing guerrilla threat, and by December thousands more were added. Some of these troops were, of course, dispersed in garrison duty.[32] Their absence was made up, however, by the presence of thousands of troops from outside Navarre who joined the hunt for Javier in December 1809. All told, by January 1810, some 10,000 French troops were attempting to corner Javier's elusive "land pirates."

Among the generals who intervened in Navarre were Suchet and Harispe. Harispe would be one of the guerrillas' most determined and successful opponents throughout the war. He was a native of the border town of Baigorry, making him practically Navarrese. Since he spoke Basque, he was able to gain the confidence of some of the villages in the Montaña, something no other French commander succeeded in doing.

With such strong forces pursuing him, Javier Mina began the new year running from one end of Navarre to another, from Los Arcos, to Lumbier, to Roncal. In the fastness of the mountains, Javier learned that Suchet had brought up troops from Aragon and from the garrisons in the

Ebro valley to work in concert with Harispe and D'Agoult in order to seal off the Roncal valley. Throughout the war, it was the great fortune of the guerrillas that they could usually avoid pursuit merely by passing into a neighboring province. Communications were too poor and French commanders were too jealous of their autonomy to undertake joint operations. The concerted persecution of January 1810 left Javier puzzled. This was the first time French forces under separate commands worked together against the corso. Javier narrowly escaped encirclement in Roncal and passed quickly to the other side of Navarre, to the mountains of Dicastillo, pursued closely by the French. Finally, with enemies swarming all around, Javier dispersed his forces, hiding his armaments in the mountains and sending most of his troops back to their homes. A few remained united in small bands hidden in the mountains west of Estella. Javier Mina himself, with six bodyguards, took cover in the mountains of Álava and western Navarre. The numerous French columns thus found themselves operating in a void and had to let up in their persecution.

A military solution having failed, the French government again attempted to enlist civil officials in the destruction of the insurgents. On 10 January 1810 the Duke of Mahón, who had replaced Vallesantoro as Joseph's viceroy during the previous year, offered rewards for information leading to the arrest of the guerrillas. When this failed to produce results, the royal court at Pamplona joined its voice with Mahón's in a more threatening circular dated 25 January. Municipal officials were directed to produce lists of those who had left their houses vacant or who had recently returned, along with the names of all of their relatives. Towns were to inform the government whether the clergy had preached in favor of order and peace or had served to inflame the inhabitants against the French. Those who failed to carry out this order or who were found protecting insurgents would be taken to Pamplona for execution.[33]

This was a critical moment for the insurgency in Navarre, and the French knew it. They attempted to exploit the corso's discomfiture to make their presence felt once again at the village level. Yet, they could not come to grips with Javier's band itself, and they did not have sufficient forces to maintain such a heavy presence in Navarre indefinitely. Suchet's troops returned to Aragon, D'Agoult's men to Pamplona, and Javier took advantage of the respite to reunite a portion of his followers.

Reynier, shortly to be given authority over Navarre, was already the commander in Álava. He had just congratulated himself that the Navarrese had not been able to disturb his troops in Vitoria, when Javier decided to extend the war into that province. In mid-January, based upon information that a column of some 300 French troops from Vitoria would seek to requisition supplies in villages near the Navarrese border, Javier ordered his troops to reassemble in Santa Cruz de Campezo, in Álava. There, he drove the enemy back to Vitoria, killing 50 and wounding 100, before ordering another dispersion in anticipation of renewed French pursuit.

Reynier sent 20,000 men after the corso, but far from catching it, they ended up spending the next month in vain pursuit, delaying their real mission to reinforce French troops in western Spain.[34] Reynier's forces were joined by those under Suchet, who entered Pamplona on 20 January determined finally to come to grips with Javier after the disgrace at Santa Cruz. The two commanders intended to pacify Navarre with overwhelming force. Javier responded by ordering some of his dispersed troops to take secret paths to Aibar, on the other side of Navarre, where a small force was again reunited. In Aibar Javier learned that he was required to appear in Lérida to receive instructions from the Spanish government. In early February, therefore, Javier departed for Catalonia, and command of the guerrillas was turned over to Gregorio Cruchaga.

Cruchaga, due to the presence of so many enemy troops, had no alternative but to order another complete dispersion of the corso. During the first three weeks of February, therefore, the corso did nothing. Toward the end of the month, however, Cruchaga reunited 300 troops and attacked the 100-man garrison of Burguete, causing 28 casualties, taking 30 prisoners, and forcing the remainder to flee to Roncesvalles. On 6 March Cruchaga turned south again and attacked the garrison of Lumbier, forcing the entire force of seventy troops to surrender. The prisoners were sent to Lérida just as Javier Mina made his return.

The reappearance of Javier caused general excitement among the men. Unfortunately, the return of their leader, now a captain in the army, coincided with the departure of Miguel, the spy-priest of Ujüé, who was the secret power behind the corso. Miguel's status as the head of the corso's espionage and supply system had become common knowledge within Navarre, and inevitably the French began to hear rumors about a priest who was running a ring of spies. With his position compromised, Miguel found it necessary to abandon Navarre. He sought and obtained selection to represent the province in the national Cortes scheduled to assemble in Cádiz. On 2 March Miguel left Navarre. Less than a month later, and as a result of a failure of intelligence, something that had never happened under Miguel, Javier fell into French hands.[35]

During the short time left to him, Javier continued to operate in the region of Aibar and in northwestern Aragon. Reuniting 600 infantry and 100 cavalry, the corso battled the garrisons in Ejea and Zuera and attacked French columns traveling between Pamplona and Aragon before running out of ammunition and seeking refuge once again in the region just east of the capital. During these last engagements, Javier's troops killed eighty of the enemy, according to the records of the second regiment. In Labiano and Aranguren, Javier rested his forces.

On the morning of 28 March Javier received notice that French troops had discovered his position and were fast approaching from Pamplona. Whether he had come to believe overmuch in his own legend of invulnerability, or whether he had misjudged the capacity of his new adversary, Dufour, Javier remained in Labiano until the last moment. Not knowing that the French had already occupied the heights behind Labiano before entering the village, Mina attempted to escape into the hills on horseback with only a few men. There he was surprised, had his horse shot from under him, received a saber wound, and was taken prisoner.

Javier Mina's career may be assessed from several different perspectives. On the one hand, the toll he took on French troops was not that high. According to the records of the second regiment, during the life of the corso, the guerrillas killed 211 French soldiers, wounded 280, and captured 114. During the same period the guerrillas lost 34 killed and 129 wounded.[36] While these numbers seem unimpressive, it is still notable that the French considered Navarre unpacified territory in March 1810 and that men dreaded duty against the Navarrese guerrillas.[37] In addition, the guerrillas had diverted French troops from the western front, contributing to the stalemate in Portugal and western Spain. In December 1809 and January 1810 some 10,000 troops were occupied chasing the guerrillas from the Estella region to Sangüesa and into the eastern Pyrenees. For a time in late January and early February 1810 there were perhaps 20,000 troops holding down Navarre, which had not seen regular Spanish soldiers since October 1808. In March additional units of French gendarmes received permanent assignment in Navarre. (Other companies were sent to the neighboring Basque provinces and Upper

Aragon, also heavily affected by Mina and other guerrillas). Meanwhile, the French did not have sufficient numbers to take Valencia, and an army wasted away in Portugal for lack of reinforcement.

Finally, guerrilla resistance caused the French to spend a great deal of money on Navarre. Until the spring of 1810 Paris paid the cost of occupation, but as the guerrilla war heated up, the growing drain on his finances infuriated Napoleon, and he directed his lieutenants in Navarre to do whatever was necessary to make the war feed itself. This directive resulted in punitive new taxes in March 1810, as will be seen. These taxes were so high that villagers simply could not meet their allotments. To avoid imprisonment, they fled to the guerrillas, becoming "patriots" by default. Thus the guerrillas indirectly ensured that more and more Navarrese would join the resistance out of exasperation with the fiscal policies of the French regime.

If one traces the movements and battles of the corso, one can obtain a good picture of the "home base" maintained by the guerrillas and, conversely, of the areas they considered too dangerous to remain in for long. The places most frequented by Javier's troops were in three regions. Most important was the area between Sangüesa and Pamplona. When pressed by the French, this base was extended north into the Pyrenees, especially into the valley of Roncal, but sometimes as far west as Burguete and Roncesvalles. This was the region best known to Javier, Espoz y Mina, and Cruchaga, and all of the recruits from Ujüé to Roncal. The second most frequented area was Estella and the country west of Estella, both an important scene of operations and one of the regions most supportive of the corso. The guerrillas were saved more than once by hiding in the mountains of Lóquiz and Andía. The third area was less a home base than a convenient point of attack. The region of the Carrascal, a narrow place in the Pamplona road south of the French garrison at Tiebas, was the site of numerous guerrilla ambushes, and remained a dangerous stretch of road throughout the course of the war. On only one occasion did the corso penetrate the heart of the Ribera, but the foray into Tudela in the fall of 1809 was only partly successful, and the guerrillas actually suffered more losses than they inflicted in the action.

This orientation toward the Montaña is further illustrated by a consideration of the geographic origin of the guerrillas. A detailed study of the personnel in the guerrilla army of Navarre will be undertaken in chapter 9. It is appropriate at this point, however, to note that the chroniclers of the Division of Navarre identified Ujüé, Roncal, the Lumbier basin, Estella, Los Arcos, and the Pamplona basin as the regions that contributed the most men to the corso. This confirms a picture of the guerrillas as men of the Montaña.

Despite Javier Mina's capture in March 1810, it was clear to the French that the occupation of Navarre was not going well. Navarre had been forced during the first two years of warfare to contribute over 12 million reales in taxation.[38] Yet, the government in Pamplona still required subsidies from Paris, and the military governor was forced to resort to ad hoc requisitions, which inflamed the resistance more. The failure of the occupation was a sign of Javier's success and of the impossibility of governing Navarre from Madrid or from Paris. Napoleon therefore set up in Navarre an autonomous government by the measures of 8 February 1810. (At the same time, the French also created independent military districts in Álava, Catalonia, Guipúzcoa, and Vizcaya.) A month later Napoleon sent Navarre a new governor-general, Georges Dufour.

Napoleon asked Dufour to accomplish two interconnected objectives within his new satrapy: to make an end of the resistance and to generate more revenue. Although he was destined to succeed in neither task for very long, Dufour did disrupt the insurgency as long as he ruled Navarre. Only three weeks into his tenure, on 28 March, his troops wounded and captured Javier Mina in Labiano. Dufour was one of the most formidable opponents, and certainly the most fortunate, that the Navarrese would face.[39]

Dufour proclaimed civilian resistance to be the work of a few rabblerousers and criminals. If only these could be captured, he thought, then the misguided peasants who had followed them would lay down their arms. Already during the previous summer, D'Agoult had offered a prize for the capture of Javier Mina, hoping to achieve through the betrayal of the guerrilla chieftain what he had not been able to do in battle.[40] D'Agoult had gained nothing by this tactic, but Javier's capture in Labiano made Dufour optimistic that Navarre might finally be pacified.

There were some in the French administration, including Napoleon, who called for Javier Mina's blood. Suchet announced the guerrilla leader's capture with a casual mixture of inaccuracies, lies, and imperial barbarism: "The highwayman Mina has been made prisoner in the woods of the Carrascal [Labiano is far north of the Carrascal]," wrote Suchet.

"He thought to make his escape by offering a sack of gold and an expensive watch, but it had no effect on our valiant soldiers. The people have demonstrated their happiness at seeing the province freed from such a scourge. A trial will be held, and . . . he will be hanged, drawn and quartered, and exposed on the public roads."[41]

Fortunately for Javier, the desire for revenge was not consistent with Dufour's strategy for pacification. The new governor realized that he could turn Javier's capture to greater profit if he could induce the guerrillas to lay down their arms in exchange for their leader's life and a general amnesty. On 2 April Dufour offered amnesty for anyone who gave up his weapons or joined a French militia.[42] Some of the volunteers, according to Espoz y Mina's recollections, accepted the offer, though most simply evaporated (with their weapons) into the general population.[43]

Similar French initiatives to disarm or to enlist civilians had met some success elsewhere in Spain.[44] In New Castile, La Mancha, and Andalusia Joseph Bonaparte had been able to "seduce the people" by sending collaborators to enlist local officials in the French cause or to set up new municipal corporations. Joseph even formed several imperial regiments from Spanish recruits.[45] The French also succeeded for a time in organizing some civil guards and counterguerrilla units made up of Spanish traitors, especially in Andalusia, Aragon, and Catalonia.[46]

In Navarre, none of these measures to gain collaborators had much effect. For example, when the French tried to raise a civic guard in Estella, the municipal government simply delayed supplying lists of people eligible for duty until the guerrillas liberated the town.[47] There was no way to protect sympathizers where the population was dispersed among more than 700 villages. And without the promise of French protection, very few individuals proved willing to work with the French. Indeed, outside of the Ribera, every attempt in Navarre to raise an urban militia failed.

When Dufour could not gain adherents in Navarre, he turned to terror in order to command obedience. In truth, Dufour inherited a system of terror begun by his predecessor, General D'Agoult. In July 1809 D'Agoult had required municipal officials to procure the names of those absent from their homes. If the French captured some "bandit, or so-called volunteer of the people," who had not been reported missing, then a fine of 4,000 reales would be levied against the municipality failing to report.[48] D'Agoult had also decreed that anyone with a son fighting for the insurgents would have to present at his cost a man fit for service in the French army, and anyone discovered absent from his home for an unauthorized period of time would have his goods and property confiscated.[49]

The effectiveness of these regulations can be guessed from the Dufour administration's need to reiterate substantially the same code in March 1810. Under Dufour, however, the penalties for violating the regulations were severer. Those absent from their homes were assumed to be guerrillas and were subject to execution upon capture. Priests and *alcaldes* (mayors) who did not supply names were turned over to military commissions, specially formed for the purpose, to undergo deportation proceedings. Clerics suspected of stirring up resistance were arrested and deported.[50] Fortunately, Dufour was able to enforce these measures only in areas either occupied by or within easy reach of a garrison.

D'Agoult had passed strict regulations against political activity and had created a new police force to back them up. Under D'Agoult, Pamplona and the other towns of Navarre became deserted and somber places. Beginning in 1809 the Navarrese were signed into government registers and required to take an oath of allegiance to the new regime. The French prohibited meetings of more than a few people and suspended public holidays. Handball courts and bull rings were closed. In each venue the French detected, under the guise of sport and spectacle, the occasion for a volatile mixing of people from different social classes and political persuasions in a patriotic ambience.[51] Under the watchful eye of the police the population of Pamplona had even abandoned its daily *paseo*, or promenade.[52] One French eyewitness took the desertion of the streets as an indication of the "superstition, fanaticism, and enslavement" of the people, though it indicated only the latter. Indeed, the city had taken on the air of a prison camp. Those who ran public houses or rented rooms were required to report the names, professions, places of birth and residence, and the purpose and length of their guests' presence in Pamplona. Travel anywhere required a passport, which had to be presented to city officials and to innkeepers.[53] All of these practices, begun by D'Agoult, were continued by Dufour.

D'Agoult had reserved the harshest treatment for captured insurgents, and here too Dufour continued his predecessor's practices. Because the French viewed the guerrillas as bandits, they felt no compunction about denying Spanish captives the rights due to prisoners of war. For example, in the struggle for Roncal in the summer of 1809, captured Roncalese were taken to Pamplona and executed without trial. Their bodies were left to hang for days in trees outside the eastern city gate, facing the valley of Roncal, so that anyone approaching from that direction might be reminded of the fate awaiting captives.[54] Roncal's response was the simple "no importa" that was to become the watchword of the Spanish resistance. Indeed, that autumn Roncal contributed Javier's second in command, Cruchaga, to the corso terrestre, along with one of its largest and most experienced contingents of troops.[55]

Thus, the French attempt to terrorize civilians backfired from the start. Even in Pamplona, French "justice" served only to fan the fires of resistance. In October 1809 the French shot three men discovered manufacturing cartridges in a church and hung them up for public view in Pamplona. This act was intended to humble the city, but instead it caused a riot that briefly threatened the French hold on Pamplona. On the night of the hangings, three grenadiers failed to make it back to their billets in the Ciudadela. The next morning they were discovered hanging in place of the three executed patriots, and on the chest of one of the soldiers was attached the following notice: "Vous pendez les notres. Nous pendons les votres." (You hang ours. We hang yours.) In response, D'Agoult ordered fifteen monks, selected for their popularity and influence, from among the fifty-seven then imprisoned in Pamplona, to be executed and strung up in public view for twenty-four hours. The people of Pamplona collected 20,000 francs to ransom back the condemned men, and an unruly crowd surrounded the French governor's house to force his hand. Their cries for clemency were ignored, however, and the fifteen men died on the scaffold after French troops twice drove back an ugly mob with their bayonets.[56]

Dufour continued the work of D'Agoult, collecting data on men absent from their homes and suppressing political dissent. Dufour had the heads of families who could not account for absent children and grandchildren arrested and fined. The penalty for any such absence was set at a minimum of 200 reales a month. Failure to pay resulted in deportation. Every Sunday priests were required to read these regulations from their pulpits, failing which they too were arrested and deported.[57] Dufour, having received a lukewarm response to his offer of amnesty, gave his commanders orders to execute guerrillas upon capture, without trial, and to hang their bodies in trees along the nearest main roads.[58]

These measures, combined with the military defeat of the corso, brought the French in the spring of 1810 as close as they would ever come to pacifying Navarre. Villages were repeopled by inhabitants who had earlier fled to the guerrillas. Officials "ventured at last to give open support" to the government. Towns began to accept the protection of French troops, to inform on insurgents, and to solicit and obtain arms with which to defend themselves.[59]

The winter and spring of 1810 was the low point of the guerrilla resistance everywhere. The French used information supplied by civilians to catch and destroy a band led by the Estellan Carrasco.[60] French cavalry overtook the Empecinado in the plains near Cuenca and killed 180 of his men.[61] Suchet practically cleared Aragon of guerrillas, and Lérida, the last focus of resistance in Catalonia, was taken.[62] Suchet formed six Spanish companies to fight against the guerrillas, and the Aragonese began to look on a "steady and regular occupation" as a way to escape the vigilance of the guerrillas.[63] In Fuentes and Huesca the garrison commander Marc Desboeufs even became popular. Desboeufs "played cards with the bourgeois and the priests and handball with the peasants." The poor called him "father" and the children "cried with joy" at the sight of him. It was as close as the French came to a welcome in the lands north of the Ebro River.[64]

Dufour's strength in Navarre was at its height. In addition to the thousands of troops under his command, he had companies of French gendarmes at his disposal, and he could call on Suchet's garrisons in Upper Aragon and in the upper Ebro valley.[65] The collapse of the corso allowed Dufour to send forces into areas that had been guerrilla preserves under Javier Mina. Villages that had been too loyal to Javier or that continued to show signs of resistance were burned with resin torches that the French carried for this purpose.[66]

Dufour also felt strong enough to embark on the second part of his mandate—the fuller exploitation of Navarre's economic resources. In March and April Dufour decreed a series of new taxes to raise over 22 million reales, almost one-fourth of Navarre's gross agricultural production. The enforcement of these exactions was not automatic, however, and it is unclear how much was actually collected. Of Dufour's first tax of 3.3 million reales, almost a third still remained uncollected in 1811.[67] Despite these difficulties, French prospects seemed bright in April 1810. As a result of the application of terror, military force, and a dose of good luck, the guerrilla movement in Navarre had been reduced to a low state not seen since the collapse of Eguaguirre's Mobile Musketeers in 1808.

In April 1810 Navarre entered a period of anarchy and civil war. The province was covered by dozens of marauding bands, hardly worthy of the name of guerrilla armies, which fought each other and the civilian population for the decreasing pile of loot represented by Navarre's over-taxed economy. In truth, the anarchy of civil war and brigandage had always lain just below the surface of the movement, despite Javier Mina's attempts to impose order.[68] After the capture of Javier Mina, the great-est check to anarchy was removed. Petty tyrants roamed the province grabbing whatever they could from churches, monasteries, municipal buildings, and private residences, and in some cases forcing young men to join their parties, a practice that neither Javier Mina nor Espoz y Mina ever had to adopt. It was, to borrow Temprano's phrase, the era of "every man for himself."[69]

Bandit chieftains elevated their robberies to the status of a (not very sophisticated) theoretical system: they called the new pattern of indi-vidualized "warfare" by the simple name of the "Idea." Andrés Martín chronicled the breakdown of the movement and the birth of the "Idea" in the spring of 1810. "There were some," wrote Martín, "who wanted to preserve their liberty and their idea. Hence they took their name— the Men of the Idea. These men wanted one thing but destroyed it with another. They wanted to fight for their country without submission; they wanted to conquer without obedience; they wanted a perfect militia without discipline. This was impossible and contradictory."[70]

The Men of the Idea believed that in nature no person was subor-dinated to another. In their view, all power structures that subverted the natural equality of men were equally corrupt and contemptible. Guerrillas who believed in the Idea therefore opposed village, province, and nation almost as much as they did the French government. In the matter of warfare, the Men of the Idea believed that the energy of the people could best be harnessed by giving each individual free reign to grab whatever portion of power and territory he could forcefully domi-nate. The French would be faced with a hundred separate bands moving like shadows across Navarre and subsisting entirely on spoils of battle. This "perfect militia" would melt into the hills at the approach of the enemy to emerge later in harassing operations against stragglers and lines of communications.

The collapse of Spain's regular armies in 1808–9 meant that the Spanish road to victory would not be trod by conventional forces. Yet, anarchic guerrilla warfare was never much more than a nuisance to the occupation. Guerrilla parties everywhere in Spain only became really effective to the degree that they established discipline and order. In 1810, the Navarrese Men of the Idea lacked discipline, and they had little military impact as a result.

The discipline of Javier's corso had been rooted in the social background of its personnel. The rank and file comprised "honorable farmers" from the villages around Pamplona, which was their main theater of operations, rather than Ribereños.[71] The men of the Montaña tended to stay in line because they were property owners operating in their home territory. Men cannot be asked to sack their own and their neighbors' homes. Even so, Javier Mina had to work hard to establish military discipline among his troops.

In contrast, the Men of the Idea who succeeded the corso were entirely lacking in discipline, indeed, opposed to it. Most of the new leaders were from the Ribera, like Pascual Echeverría, the butcher of Corella, or were "foreigners" from Aragon and Castile. Many had deserted their regular formations or were running from personal difficulties and were primarily intent on enriching themselves at the expense of the population. The most infamous of such bands was run by Echeverría, a man who "never sought battle with the French" and who was filled with every vice imaginable, according to Mina.[72] With his praetorian guard of deserters from the imperial armies, Echeverría became as feared a presence as the French, even in Estella, a region that had already proved its loyalties.[73] Two other important figures from this period were Miguel Sádaba, who ran a band partially dependent upon Echeverría, and Juan Hernández, who had taken with him the greater portion of the cavalry of the former corso. These were the figures most wedded to the "Idea" of 1810, for it gave them an excuse for their inability to face the French in combat and a justification for their attacks on civilians.

The Central Junta in Cádiz investigated the "Idea" and tried to stop the guerrilla parties inspired by it. The junta discovered that such parties had no other purpose than to "frighten and sack villages according to a well-arranged formula." The guerrillas would choose a village in the path of French troops, and, "shooting off their guns and riding through the streets," they would pose as an "advance guard of the enemy." The guerrillas would then establish a cordon to prevent inhabitants from escaping to save themselves or to seek French help. These security measures fulfilled, the guerrillas would proceed to attack the village. In one incident a band sacked at least seven towns and villages according to this pattern in a single night. The guerrillas "instead of being the support and consolation of the people were taking advantage of the conflict and desperate situation" created by the occupation to rival the French in "barbarism and ferocity."[74]

As a result of this situation, popular support for the war was faltering precisely in regions dominated by the Men of the Idea.[75] This was certainly the case in Navarre in the spring of 1810. In addition to the crimes committed by Echeverría and other local guerrilla chieftains, the province was also infiltrated by numerous such bands roaming north from Castile and Aragon. The Empecinado, the Capuchino, Cuevillas, and other less savory guerrilla chiefs brought their forces into the vacuum left by the destruction of the corso. The province, in the words of Mina, was a "picture of horrible demoralization" and chaos.[76] The Navarrese quite naturally began to accept the French view of the partisans as bandits and sought French aid against guerrillas like Echeverría.[77]

Two events from this period indicate the depths to which the resistance had sunk. The Marqués de Ayerbe, an aristocratic relative of Palafox and a patriot of unimpeachable integrity, had formed an ill-starred conspiracy for the rescue of Ferdinand in Valençay as early as the summer of 1809. After receiving little encouragement from the junta, Ayerbe suffered the loss of the ship that was supposed to deposit him secretly on the western coast of France. Ayerbe had no choice but to risk a crossing of the Pyrenees in Navarre.

In the early summer of 1810 (the exact date is not known), Ayerbe and a captain in the Spanish army entered Navarre traveling as two peasants, "Tío Lorenzo" and "José." They were stopped, however, around Tafalla by a detachment of guerrillas of uncertain connections. Because Ayerbe and his aide carried French passports to facilitate their mission, they were suspected as traitors. Their disguises, intended to fool the French, probably incensed their captors. The bearing and accent of Ayerbe also suggested the possibility of an easy prize in the ample saddlebags. And in fact, the marqués was carrying a large sum of money that he hoped would help secure the release of Ferdinand. This money was his undoing. Ayerbe and his aide were taken to Andosilla, where they were stabbed to death and buried in a shallow grave dug in a corral and covered over with a dung pile. Their bodies were discovered after the war and returned to Zaragoza. Thus did the resistance lose a capable leader to the Men of the Idea.[78]

Shortly afterward, an even more horrible incident showed how literally demoralized the guerrillas had become. A guerrilla band, possibly a detachment from the Empecinado's party, entered Villafranca in August 1810, during the period when Mina was still far from having established his ascendancy in Navarre after the capture of Javier. The guerrillas captured five of the fifteen grenadiers stationed in the town along with a local woman who had made the mistake of marrying one of the French soldiers. The woman was stripped, tarred, and beaten as she was led, mounted backward on a mule, through the town with a notice attached to her back reading "whore of the French." On the following day she was placed in a wooden cage in the town square to witness the death of the five grenadiers. The unlucky captives were buried alive with only their heads above the ground, while the Spanish troops took turns trying to hit their heads with a large wooden ball. When the last "goal" had ceased to cry out, the game was over. The poor woman, after having one of her ears cut off—a torture commonly practiced by both sides—was carted to Puente la Reina, where she was nailed to the church door until she bled to death.[79] Two years of seeing men shot, hanged, and impaled in roadside trees had led to a complete breakdown of ethical norms of conduct. And the terror was to become much worse and more systematic before things improved.

I N APRIL 1810, of the 900 soldiers who had been serving in
the corso, only Francisco Espoz y Mina (at the time still going
by his given name, Francisco Espoz Ilundáin) and 6 others remained to call themselves the "partida of Mina." The rest had returned
to their homes or joined one of the other bands fighting in Navarre and
neighboring provinces.[1] In his memoirs Espoz y Mina identified four of
these initial followers: Manuel Gurrea, natural of Olite, who early in
1809 had operated his own party supplied out of Ujüé; Tomás Ciriza,
a labrador from the village of Azcarate on the Guipúzcoa border; Luís
Gastón, a youth from Tafalla and a close friend of Espoz y Mina during
and after the war; and Pedro Miguel Sarasa, a wealthy labrador from
Aibar, a village situated between Ujüé and Sangüesa. These men from
the Montaña met near Idocín and agreed that Francisco Espoz should
succeed to the command of a revived corso terrestre and that he should
adopt the name of Mina as a sign to everyone of his intention to follow in
the footsteps of his famous "nephew."[2] From that time forward, Espoz
became known as Espoz y Mina, or simply as Mina.

Mina first needed to reenlist troops. The quickest way to do this was
by taking over some of the already existing bands that had been formed
out of the dissolved corso terrestre. Mina first targeted a party led by
Miguel Sádaba, with whom Mina had been friendly in the corso. Sádaba
had 120 men in the area of Echarri-Aranaz, where his name was becoming anathema due to his reliance on extortion and violence to raise
supplies. Officials in Lacunza, a village near Echarri-Aranaz, gladly in-

formed Mina of Sádaba's approach, and with only his six companions, Mina was able to ambush Sádaba as he rode in ahead of his troops. With Sádaba in custody, Mina harangued his rival's troops, condemning them for the crimes they had committed against the peasants. Through bluff, not letting on that his own following amounted to a mere handful, Mina gained the allegiance of Sádaba and his entire band. Mina stood at the head of his own small army for the first time.[3]

This success was an early indication of two factors that worked in Mina's favor. First, Mina enjoyed the collaboration of municipal authorities and parish priests against the pretensions of other rivals. By Mina's account, village elders supported him because he scrupulously avoided direct taxation, in contrast to other guerrillas, and because he requisitioned goods and services only in areas that he had some hope of defending from the French. The second factor working in favor of Mina at Lacunza was his capacity for bluff. Over the course of the war, Mina blustered his way through a number of similarly tense situations, and his personal bravery, which bordered on a fanatic belief in his own invulnerability, turned many an opponent into a devotee.[4]

After Lacunza Mina circulated a notice of his "appointment" as chief of the revived corso. In fact, Mina did not receive official recognition from any higher authority until 13 May, when the junta of Aragon recognized his preeminence. By then, however, his circular had achieved the desired effect, causing a number of guerrilla parties superior in size to his own to submit to Mina's rule. Among these parties was that of Lucas Górriz, a labrador from Subiza (near Otano) and the eldest of three Górriz brothers who would serve under Mina. Górriz was the first important leader to join Mina voluntarily, and he was rewarded with the command of the third of three battalions that were formed later that year.[5]

Of even more importance than the adherence of Górriz, was Mina's absorption of Cruchaga's band from Roncal and Salazar, which had become by mid-April the most effective of the parties then left in Navarre. Cruchaga was the only man whose military prowess had rivaled that of Javier. Because of his reputation for fair dealing, he was also the only leader who had been as popular as Javier. Cruchaga, with some 100 followers, met Mina, escorted by 50 foot soldiers and his small cavalry, in early May in the town of Aoiz, the site of the corso's disintegration in March. There they decided that Mina should continue as head of the corso, with Cruchaga as his second in command. The addition of Cruchaga's men brought Mina's force to 500 troops, the largest concentration of guerrillas in Navarre at the time.[6]

At first glance, the rise of Mina to the command of the largest guerrilla party in Navarre within such a short time appears inexplicable. Mina had attained only a subaltern rank in Javier's cavalry, and upon the dissolution of the corso he had a mere six backers compared with the hundreds who had remained loyal to Echeverría, Hernández, Sádaba, and Cruchaga. What impelled Mina into the spotlight?

Mina suffered scurrilous attacks from the moment he began his military career until his death on Christmas Eve in 1836. It is difficult to separate the truth about Mina from the lies spread by his detractors and from his own propaganda. Mina's greatest literary enemies, Puigblanch and Saint-Yon, believed he was a brute, whose great leadership qualities amounted to ruthlessness combined with a generous portion of luck.[7] There was some truth in this assessment, though these two qualities need not detract from the reputation of a soldier. Mina promoted an image of himself as a simple peasant who had fame thrust upon him. There is also some truth in this. Yet, Mina's ability to turn an unruly mob of half bandits into a disciplined army suggests that underneath the simple and rustic peasant from Idocín there lay dormant a complex and powerful individual in charge of his own destiny.

Mina was born in 1781, the youngest of four children. His family, well-to-do peasants, lived in Idocín, a small village of eleven houses huddled in the narrow cleft of the Ibargoiti River, surrounded by mountains, and lying halfway between Sangüesa and Pamplona. In 1800 the family estate encompassed eighty-four acres of arable planted in wheat, oats, maize, alfalfa, and beans, a garden of one acre, and just over four acres of vineyards. The house, with communal rights attached to it, included corrals, granaries, a large wine cellar and press, and an impressive stock of furniture: eight benches, twenty-four chairs, seven tables, eleven beds, and an array of linens and kitchen utensils that included an antique set of silver. There were pictures and laminations in each bedroom and a statue of Christ in the main room. One of the clearest indications of the family's wealth was its livestock. The Mina estate counted 6 oxen, 6 mules, 10 pigs, and 143 sheep and goats.[8] Thus Francisco and his family were not quite the simple rustics portrayed in memoirs and admiring biographies.

Nevertheless, Francisco's life in Idocín was hard. His father died in 1796. His older brother, Clemente, left home for Pamplona and the priesthood when Francisco was a child. As the only male remaining in the house, Francisco would have had a disproportionate burden placed upon him to help support his mother, María Theresa Ilundáin, and his two sisters, Vicenta and Simona.

In 1800 Vicenta married. As the eldest child in the family, she inherited the house and lands. Simona, the youngest, married soon after and removed to Pamplona. Francisco was still just eighteen years old when these events passed, and he remained in the house working for Vicenta, his new brother-in-law, and his mother, who maintained usufruct rights until her death. This was customary in Navarre. A young man like Francisco was likely to spend his life working in a subordinate position within the household of his extended family. For Francisco, therefore, the French invasion presented an opportunity as well as a threat.[9]

Mina's early life was hard in another way too. As a child he witnessed a dramatic crisis in Idocín. In the 1790s the population of the village declined from 107 to 71 individuals. Idocín suffered cruelly in the war with the French Republic, and recovery was slow. Idocín was one of the richest villages in the region, but in a subsistence economy, where there was no wage work, there was nothing to attract new residents.[10]

Despite these difficulties, Mina remembered Idocín as a happy place, where he enjoyed "the most profound peace and perfect tranquillity" until the French invasion of 1808.[11] However, his was not the nostalgia of a false pastoralism, for Mina was personally acquainted with the hard work required of a peasant farmer. As Mina later recalled, he and his associates were men who "knew nothing more than the use of the laya, the hoe, and the pruning knife, and no more business than that of gathering in the fruits" produced by their lands.[12] It is hard to know how seriously to take Mina's characterization of himself. Mina understood the value of propaganda to his own legend. As governor-general of Galicia in 1821, Mina took time out to help the peasants with the harvest, or at least made certain that such stories circulated among his troops. And in his last years he secured his personal layas for preservation in museums in Madrid and Pamplona.[13] Certainly, Mina was not above self-conscious posing, but there was also clearly some truth in the legend of the *layador*, even if the Mina family never suffered from real poverty.

The market was Mina's connection to the larger life of the city and kingdom. Saturdays Mina sold produce in the capital. Unlike his brother or his relation, Javier Mina, however, Francisco was not meant for the university. In fact, he must have appeared the least adventurous member of his family, for he had been entirely devoted, from a very early age, to the labors of the farm.

Mina could neither read nor write Castilian and was truly fluent only in Basque, the language spoken in the Mina household. Not that this was a liability. Indeed, Mina's followers would likely have seen it as an asset, since they too were mostly illiterate Basque peasants. Francisco learned well enough how to sign his name with a flourish during the war, but in many respects he was something of the bumpkin depicted by both his enemies and supporters.[14]

Mina was not a dominant figure in the life of Idocín before the war. He had, after all, only just come of age in 1806 and had no inheritance.[15] Indeed, Mina's name showed up only once in records generated by the local notary before the war. On the other hand, this one citation is extremely significant. Mina, immediately before the French invasion, led a group of six youths in an attack on Don Eusebio Garcés de los Fayos, señor of nearby Lecáun. Unfortunately, the records are silent on the precise outcome of these events. Mina's band was apprehended, and he certainly spent time in jail in Monreal, but the length of the incarceration and the sort of judgment rendered are unknown. It is possible that these events indicate some leadership qualities not apparent in other historical records. The gang of six Mina led against los Fayos prefigured the gang of like number from which Mina reconstituted the guerrillas of Navarre, and it is possible that he already exercised some charismatic attraction on his peers. This may help to explain the willingness in 1810 of superior military talents like Cruchaga and Lucas Górriz, the latter known to Mina since before the war, to accept his leadership with such alacrity.[16]

Another personal characteristic that aided Mina was his personal integrity, which seems to have spread to his followers. It is well known that, despite enjoying full authority to collect church rents, custom duties, taxes, and requisitions, neither Mina nor his lieutenants came out of the war with anything more than the humble means with which they entered it.[17] In many ways, Mina was even puritanical. For example, neither during the war nor in his later career did he allow anything like a camp following to develop.[18]

Another quality that gave Mina the ability to lead the Navarrese guerrillas was his cruelty. A partisan war like that fought in Navarre led to the sacrifice of many innocent victims. The French were old hands at using terror to intimidate subject populations. To survive, the guerrillas had to outdo the French, executing captured Spanish "renegades" and punishing anyone who tried to remain neutral. By 1812, as we shall see, Mina was able practically to eliminate collaboration. Men who had entered the French service carrying messages, carting food, driving animals, or enforcing edicts were killed, kidnapped, mutilated, or despoiled of their property. The French found that nothing they could do inspired as much fear as Mina did. Even when the French threatened prison and death for cooperating with Mina, men forced to carry messages for the occupation ran immediately to the guerrillas once out of the enemy's grasp. This sort of control over the civilian population was one of the keys to Mina's success. Yet, to dominate the population in this way required a person who could enforce his will in an unswerving and brutal manner. This came easily to Mina.

The general revealed more than he intended about this side of his personality in a story he related as an aside in his memoirs. Throughout the war, but especially during the first year, it was the practice of the guerrillas to retain any captured military prize. Capturing a lance qualified one to be a lancer; taking a good musket increased one's status in the infantry; the most coveted prize was a horse, since it meant immediate entry into the cavalry, a more prestigious, safer, and less physically demanding branch of military service. While still serving as a common soldier under Javier, Mina captured a French mount better than any then in the corso's cavalry. One of Mina's superiors, neglectful of the "Idea" which must have animated even Mina in that early epoch, decided that the horse should be his. Mina was offered an exchange of any horse in the corso, but "between the debt owed by a subordinate and my own desire for the animal, I decided to incapacitate the horse in order not to suffer constantly by seeing it the property of another."[19] Mina recalled the episode as a lesson of how a commander should not act toward a subordinate, but we need not limit ourselves to this interpretation. The horse was a victim, like many others to come, of Mina's cruel pride. On the other hand, it was this kind of clear-cut action taken without remorse that helped Mina to rise from an obscure follower of Javier to ruler of all the guerrillas of Navarre in a few months' time.

The situation in April 1810 placed a premium on these character traits. What the guerrillas needed was order, someone who could discipline men who had abandoned the patriotic war to engage in robbery. The Men of the Idea whom Mina inherited were a dangerous lot, forcing Mina to maintain a constant ring of bodyguards around his person. But Mina was temperamentally suited to this situation. If anyone could succeed with such men, it was the layador from Idocín.

In addition, the very name of Mina, which Espoz now added to his own, recalled the success of Javier's corso. Javier had brought order to Navarre, and some Navarrese had begun to wish for nothing more than order, even if it had to be imposed by the French. This was the great danger for the insurgency. It was crucial that Mina eliminate his less idealistic rivals to avoid alienating the population. The men who rallied to Mina in May no doubt understood the psychology of the moment and the suitability of Mina to resolve the situation. However, even with the men of Sádaba, Górriz, and Cruchaga, Mina was still too weak to proceed immediately against the strongest of his rivals. Instead, he began his first tentative campaign against the French.

At the head of a small but growing band from April to July, Mina engaged the French three times in the region between Pamplona and the Guipúzcoa border, once near Sangüesa, and four times in the area around the Carrascal. Mina's theater of operations thus coincided with that of his predecessor, except for the increased activity in the far northwest. In these encounters, the French lost 201 killed or captured according to the records kept by Mina, and the guerrillas lost 40 killed and 93 wounded.[20] French records confirm the plausibility of these numbers. Indeed, they suggest that losses to the guerrillas were much higher than Mina ever suspected. Dufour reported 77 killed, 235 prisoners of war, and 54 deserters in the three-month period, as well as a rising number of troops in hospital beds.[21]

Already Mina's combat record rivaled that of the old corso. As the new band's fame spread, Mina began to attract recruits. From a following of some 500 in early May, Mina's party increased to nearly 1,200 infantry and 200 cavalry by early July, surpassing the maximum force ever gathered by Javier. The principal points of recruitment, following the readherence of Cruchaga's Roncalese and of the band raised by the Górriz brothers, were Lumbier and Echauri, which the guerrillas used as bases during much of June and July.[22]

Mina's strategy derived from Javier's. The ambush of convoys accounted for six of the eight battles that occurred during these three months. Such encounters, by their very nature, almost never went awry. One French convoy of 105 men gave up without offering resistance near the Carrascal. Another, composed of sixty men, was wiped out after seeking cover in a hermitage in the mountains north of Pamplona. As the guerrillas had learned, most of these French escorts were too exhausted, ill-prepared, and undermanned to resist a surprise attack.

At about this time Mina discovered, almost by accident, a tactic ideally suited to this kind of warfare and one which almost always ensured success. In his earliest battles, a shortage of ammunition forced Mina to engage the French immediately in hand-to-hand combat. The first time such a tactic was used, in one of the Carrascal ambushes of June 1810, Mina had only one cartridge per man. Dividing his force in half, he had one group fire and charge with the bayonet, while the others stood in reserve in case it became necessary to cover a retreat with another volley. Much later, even during times when the Division was well-supplied, Mina continued to use this procedure in his ambushes of French columns and convoys. It produced two desired results. First, casualties against better-armed but less enthusiastic French conscripts could be held to a minimum by proceeding immediately to the bayonet. Second, engagements could be terminated rapidly, an important consideration, since the presence of additional enemy forces in nearby garrisons meant that the French might always turn a defeat into a victory or a rout into an ordered retreat.[23]

It was important to the guerrilla strategy to eliminate enemy garrisons. In the early summer of 1810, however, this was a task still beyond the means of the corso, which possessed no artillery. The one attack on a garrison in this period ended disastrously. When Mina surrounded the garrison at Oyarzún, the French simply remained inside picking off twenty-four killed and fifty wounded before Mina realized the futility of the venture.

The French had many such fortified places. They had taken over convents and caseríos at every strategic point, and had constructed their own forts along the remoter stretches of road between Pamplona and the French or Guipúzcoan border. Once the guerrillas acquired artillery, these latter sorts of garrisons were the first to fall. In 1810, however, the French could not be challenged inside their forts.[24]

Mina was finally powerful enough by July to embark upon the elimination of his last rivals. Pascual Echeverría was the first victim. Echeverría, with a following of 400 men, was still the corso's main competition in the summer of 1810.[25] But Echeverría, like Eguaguirre and Sádaba before him, had made the mistake of alienating civilian support without offering any protection from French troops. His band was particularly loathsome to the people of Estella, who had been forced not only to provide daily rations to Echeverría's soldiers but also to turn over resources from the town's shops and industries.[26] It was as a welcome guest, therefore, that Mina entered Estella on 13 July to meet with Echeverría, who was cantoned there. After a brief encounter in Echeverría's lodgings, Mina had his rival taken prisoner before any of his band could respond to save him. Together with five of his most devoted followers, Echeverría was escorted to the monastery of Irache, where all six men were shot by a firing squad. The people of Estella poured into the streets to celebrate Echeverría's demise, while his troops served to swell Mina's own following. At this time also, 136 Aragonese guerrillas arrived, drawn by Mina's fame, to join the corso.[27]

Another rival, Juan Hernández, who had emerged from the breakup of Mina's army with the bulk of the cavalry, fled to Rioja in order to escape a similar fate. Within a few months, though, Mina arrested and executed Hernández, who had foolishly moved north with thoughts of making peace with the ruthless layador. Hernández's men thereafter formed the core of Mina's cavalry.[28]

No sooner had Mina eliminated Echeverría than an even more dangerous rival arrived on the scene. In the first week of August, Casimiro Javier de Miguel, the former priest of Ujué, returned after a long absence carrying orders from the government in Cádiz to take command of the guerrillas in Navarre.[29] Ever since April, when his brother, Clemente, had been dispatched as an emissary to Cádiz, Mina had been trying to gain the approval of the government. During the summer of 1810, however, Mina was entirely cut off from the rest of Spain. His only contact outside Navarre, and that back in May, had been with the junta of Aragon, which had named him to head the guerrillas even though it had no mandate in Navarre. As for his brother, Mina received news much later that he had been killed by bandits in Portugal without successfully completing his mission. It was therefore a severe blow when Miguel, now made a colonel, arrived to relieve him of a position so recently consolidated. With the presence of Miguel, Mina no longer had a legitimate claim to authority.

Initially, Mina's followers were filled with enthusiasm. The priest of Ujüé had some reputation in the province; he brought official standing to the guerrillas; and he might just succeed in convincing the new French commander, General Honoré Charles Reille, to stop the summary executions of captured guerrillas; finally, Miguel promised to get economic assistance from the government in Cádiz. Outmaneuvered, Mina was forced to recognize the legitimacy of Miguel's claims and turn over command of the corso.[30]

On 4 August, just as Miguel arrived, the guerrillas were camped in the area of Estella, while French troops, recently increased to the levels of the previous winter, approached from several directions. In this situation, the priest's lack of military experience was quickly manifest. Miguel panicked and ran to Estella along with a dozen followers. There he decreed a monthly tax on Navarre and attempted to collect the first payment from the city.[31] In this situation, Mina reassumed command, and extricated the troops from encirclement. Later he arrested Miguel and deported him to Valencia, where in 1812 he fell sick and died.[32]

In the month of September Mina's emergence as the "little king" of Navarre received formal recognition from the Regency in Cádiz. Ironically, it arrived during one of the most difficult moments for the guerrillas. After the successes of the summer, the corso found itself hounded from one end of Navarre to another beginning in September.

Mina's success in the summer of 1810 drew the attention of Napoleon in Paris. The guerrillas' ability to penetrate the French border had forced Napoleon to reinforce the frontier troops and to raise the number of gendarmes in Biscay, Navarre, and Aragon.[33] Dufour, who had assumed command in March with such high hopes, had taken to skulking in Pamplona, as Napoleon saw it, and had displeased the emperor by failing to make an end of the "banditti." So Napoleon replaced Dufour with his aide-de-camp, General Reille.[34] Reille arrived on 27 July with 8,000 men determined to pacify the province.[35]

Reille's first act was to assess the situation in Navarre. His initial dispatch from Pamplona is worth some attention, since it describes the mood of gloom that had descended upon the French occupation that summer.[36] The situation, he wrote, was "worse than he had imagined." Two days before his arrival, a convoy of 360 men had been wiped out in the Carrascal with almost 200 men captured by Mina. The guerrillas numbered 2,500 infantry and 300 to 400 cavalry. Worse still, Mina had obtained so many weapons from French deserters and prisoners that the size of his army was expected to grow even more rapidly in the months ahead. Guerrilla successes had emboldened them and raised the spirit of the province. In contrast, French troops were so discouraged that they hardly had the heart to fight.

The guerrillas had destroyed the customs system and disrupted tax collection, so that the French could "obtain nothing except by armed force." This further alienated the population. And even people who longed for pacification could not be induced to cooperate with the French because the insurgents had "inspired terror everywhere."

In combat, Mina gained an advantage by knowing French troop movements perfectly from the intelligence sent by "the young men in the villages." When pursued, the insurgents could divide up and take to the mountains, so that they fought only when they had the advantage. In marching Mina's men made twelve leagues in the time the French made six. The guerrillas were "really the masters of the country," while the French mastered only the "points they actually occupied." In six months of fighting, at times using 12,000 troops, the French had captured just "four men" and succeeded above all in feeding the rebellion through random violence fed by frustration. To do anything Reille said he would need 12,000 infantry, preferably Basques or other troops used to mountain fighting, and 1,000 horse.

Reille's recommendations could not be acted upon in time to save him from two humiliating defeats during the first week of his command. On 31 July near the Carrascal pass the men of the corso surprised a French column of 2,560 and drove it back to Pamplona. In the encounter, the guerrillas killed forty and captured thirty, while losing seven dead and thirty-five wounded. Of the captives, nineteen were "renegade" Navarrese, who were executed on the spot.[37] It was this practice that moved the French governor to continue the routine execution of captured guerrillas.[38]

The next engagement was even more costly to Reille's forces. On

3 August the corso attacked the 300-man garrison in Puente. Charac-
teristically, most of Reille's forces were in the wrong place. On this
occasion, they were far to the west scouring the mountains of Urbasa
and Andía, which the guerrillas had just evacuated. Mina and his men
had left the mountains during the night and had marched until dawn
to catch the garrison in Puente unaware. Still having no artillery but
safe in the knowledge that the nearest French troops were many miles
away, the guerrillas leisurely collected dried vines and brush to burn
out the garrison. The fire killed 70 before the remaining 230 men surrendered.[39] Reille's account of the event differed slightly: he reckoned
the loss at 50 killed and 198 captured.[40] In all, through August, Mina
caused some 1,570 French casualties while studiously avoiding serious
losses himself.[41]

By this time, Mina's army numbered 3,000 men, too unwieldy a force
to operate always together under the conditions imposed by guerrilla
warfare. Therefore, on 8 August Mina created three battalions, the first
commanded by himself, the second by Cruchaga, and the third by Lucas
Górriz. As yet, however, these commanders had neither official recognition of their rank nor subordinate officers through which they issued
orders. Instead of a chain of command, each battalion chief depended
on his own prestige with the troops for his authority.[42] This almost
tribal organization had terrible disadvantages, above all when one of the
leaders was hurt. In May 1812 Mina was shot in the leg while returning
from an expedition to get supplies on the Cantabrian coast. Mina kept
vital information, like the names of spies and the location of caches to
himself. More important, his personal influence was crucial to the fighting spirit of the troops. As a result of his absence, therefore, the corso
was crippled from May to July 1812. As will be seen, whenever one of
the guerrilla leaders was injured or killed, it caused confusion or even
dissolution.

Reille finally got the fillip of troops he had requested when Pannetier joined him in August and some of Marshal Masséna's troops were
diverted from the Army of Portugal in September. Reille had almost
15,000 men prepared to battle the 3,000 men of the corso, about the odds
regular troops require to deal effectively with guerrillas. As a result,
Mina's men became so hard pressed that they scarcely stopped running
from late August to December.[43] By following their movements, we can
appreciate, aside from the sheer stamina of the men under Mina, the

areas that served as refuge to the guerrillas when they were forced into a defensive posture.

From Puente, the insurgents escaped to their favorite base of operations, the region around Lumbier and Sangüesa. There they were forced to separate into battalions in order to divide their pursuers. The first battalion under Mina moved a few miles west to Monreal, a village known to Mina from childhood. The second battalion went south to Ujüé and the third back to the Andía mountains north of Estella, two other favorite bases of the guerrillas. On 28 August the corso reunited in the mountains of Ulzama, north of Pamplona. Pursued closely, they fled further north to Baztán, and from there west to the rough country along the Guipúzcoa border.[44] In all this time, Mina was able to avoid battle. As Reille complained, "the great difficulty [was] not fighting them but finding them."[45]

September brought the corso back to the mountains of Andía, where the men were finally able to rest for four days. At the end of this time, they discovered that they were hemmed in by 12,000 enemy troops. French columns had occupied Estella and the valleys west of Estella; Echauri and Puente to the east were guarded; the region of Echarri-Aranaz to the north was under firm control; and the Vitoria plain to the west was a death trap for unsupported infantry. The commander of the third battalion recalled thinking that his military career had come to an end. However, superior knowledge of the country and the collusion of the population allowed the corso to escape unharmed even from this trap. The French were fed false intelligence that the guerrillas were planning to break out in the direction of Estella, and they left the strategic bridge over the Arga in the valley of Echauri lightly guarded. The corso passed over, taking seven prisoners in Belascoáin before marching all night to the other side of Navarre and the mountains of Alaiz. The French pursued and again surrounded the guerrillas by occupying Unzüé, Monreal, and Lumbier. Once again, however, false information caused the French in Monreal to march east, while the body of the corso, under the command of Cruchaga, passed north right through Monreal to the refuge of the Salazar valley and the high Pyrenees. Meanwhile, the cavalry and 200 infantry led by Mina were sent to Soria in the hope of diverting French pursuit from Cruchaga.

The French ignored Mina and the cavalry, however, and brought 13,000 troops to the valley of Salazar, where they thought to bottle up

Cruchaga. But the north-south valleys that run to the French frontier and that seem to an outsider isolated one from another had their secret exits known only to local inhabitants, and Cruchaga and his Roncalese knew this part of Navarre well. Passing over high paths that had, in Mina's words, scarcely ever been traversed by man, Cruchaga escaped encirclement and returned to the mountains west of Sangüesa. After a short night's rest, the troops were moved again, marching for a day and a night without stopping. The guerrillas had traveled 116 miles in two days. By this feat of endurance, Cruchaga had created enough space between his men and the French to cross the plains of southern Navarre, ford the Ebro, and join Mina in Soria. The French cavalry caught up just as the last guerrillas reached the other side of the river, where Mina was waiting. Here the exhausted French abandoned the chase. During the remainder of the month of September, the corso stayed in the mountains of Soria before retreating on 28 September farther south to Molina in Aragon.

With all of his forces resting in Molina, Mina further elaborated the command structure of the corso. First, he renamed it the Division of Navarre. Second, he created subordinate officers within each of the three battalions into which he divided his army. Mina dispatched messengers to Cádiz with the news of his deeds and asked for formal recognition of his Division. He did not receive a reply for almost a year.[46]

In the second week of October 1810, Mina decided to emerge from hiding to attack the garrison at Tarrazona, a few miles from Tudela. Here, on 11 October, the Division suffered a significant defeat that prepared the way for its near destruction at Belorado a month later. Because of the terrain and the quality of their cavalry, the French at Tarrazona were able to force the Division to adopt a regular line. Mina's small cavalry was asked to hold off 1,200 French hussars in open country while the infantry sought high ground and a back door. The result was a slaughter of the insurgents. Among the many wounded were Cruchaga and Mina, the first slashed in the skull, the second shot through the leg. The fighting degenerated into an Iliadic struggle by the Navarrese to save their fallen leaders. The result was a confused and precipitous retreat, with the stragglers mopped up by the French cavalry. It was not to be the last time that the misfortunes of a captain destroyed the order and resolve of the Division.[47]

From mid-August to mid-October the Division had shrunk by half.

Many men had purposely stayed behind in Navarre to wait for a more propitious juncture. After Tarrazona, Mina returned home with the remnants of the cavalry. His object was to reunite some of his dispersed men and reopen the war in the Montaña of Navarre. The bulk of the infantry that he left behind hid in the mountains of Aragon, Soria, and Rioja, trying merely to survive by avoiding contact with the thousands of troops pursuing them and sealing them off from Navarre.

In mid-November, as the guerrillas attempted to reenter Navarre at Logroño, they were sighted by a column of 7,000 French infantry and 1,100 cavalry, which chased them deep into Old Castile and cornered them there. In the fields of Belorado the Division lost almost 500 killed, a third of the troops remaining active at that date. Many of those killed were bayoneted as they lay wounded or were taken prisoner and executed later. It was the greatest French victory yet over a guerrilla force.[48]

It may be asked what Mina was doing operating outside of Navarre at this time. Guerrilla armies in Galicia and elsewhere had shown themselves notoriously incompetent and rebellious outside of their home provinces, and the south bank of the Ebro was not well known to Mina or to any of his officers, who were all men from the Montaña. Tarrazona, the object of the one offensive operation in the midst of months of retreating, had a strongly fortified garrison, lay within striking distance of thousands of troops stationed in Tudela, and was situated in a plain affording perfect conditions for French cavalry and artillery. Despite all this, Mina attacked.

It was a piece of news Mina received while in Molina that caused him to risk a frontal attack on Tarrazona. In the first communication he had received in months from Cádiz, Mina learned that he had been granted the rank of colonel, even though his troops were not yet accorded the status of regulars. At the same time, he was also informed that the troops chasing him were intended for the relief of Masséna in Portugal and that more of Masséna's men would be passing through Navarre during the weeks to come. By diverting these forces, Mina could contribute dramatically, in his first action as a colonel, to the wider Allied strategy. Such a prospect no doubt appeared irresistible to Mina. It was a constant struggle to convince the politicians in Cádiz, most of whom were skeptical of or downright opposed to guerrilla operations, that the Navarrese volunteers should be recognized as a regular division. What better way to persuade them than to thin the ranks of Wellington's opponents? For political reasons, therefore, Mina attempted to convert his guerrillas into a regular force. His men could do many things, but unfortunately for Mina they could not fight a regular campaign in strange, open country. Thus, Tarrazona and Belorado were the result of Mina's loss of faith in the guerrilla strategy. Only after rededicating his force to a guerrilla campaign inside Navarre was he able to rebuild the movement.

GENERAL REILLE TRIED to make the most of his victory over the Division at Belorado by publicly trumpeting news of the slaughter. "Navarros," proclaimed Reille, "your volunteers were destroyed in Castile. The fields of Belorado are stained with their blood, and their sad bodies remain behind as sustenance for birds. The principal chiefs were mortally wounded in Tarrazona, and the miserable relics of these bands, wandering through remote mountains, will surrender at last or fall into our hands. Awaken from your error. Join our side, and declare your obedience to the government." [1]

For once, a French proclamation was not far from the truth. In fact, the disaster in Castile completed a long process of disintegration that had been affecting the guerrilla movement since September. By the end of October, the Division had virtually ceased to exist. Many of Mina's men had been disabled with the fatigue of constantly hiding in the mountains. Many more had simply abandoned the cause, some at Mina's instructions, to wait for better times. As the remnants of the Division scurried through the mountains of Aragon and Castile, inside Navarre enthusiasm for the war waned, and civilian authorities began to seek a modus vivendi with the occupier.

The reasons for the decline of the Division and of civilian support in this period are not difficult to discover. Reille had brought great political resources as well as military might to bear against the guerrillas. One of his first acts, on 4 August, had been to abolish the French-style Council of State that Dufour had established and to replace it with a re-vamped Diputación. Reille, evidently appreciating the importance that the Navarrese placed on the preservation of their traditional autonomous institutions, publicized these new arrangements widely.

However, Reille appointed the members of his new Diputación, considerably mitigating his claim to have reestablished a "national representation" for Navarre.[2] There were six deputies, one from each merindad and one for commerce, but in fact all six had important ties to the world of trade. The mercantile interests of the new deputies corresponded well to their function, which was spelled out for them in instructions received from Reille. The Diputación was simply meant to assess and collect taxes.[3] It was significant that four days after the establishment of the new body, Reille decreed an additional tax of 8,621,000 reales.[4] In the months to come, the deputies showed themselves worthy of Reille's trust, for they proved infinitely more capable of levying and collecting taxes than Dufour's council had been.[5] Thus, the new Diputación, by regularizing revenue collections, contributed to the relative pacification that was achieved during the first months of Reille's tenure.

Along with a more efficient administration came a more liberal use of terror. Reille had captive insurgents routinely hanged along roadsides in order to demoralize the population. On 11 October two guerrillas were executed in this manner. Two days later the French found two of their own hanging in trees on the outskirts of Pamplona. Reille answered this reprisal with one of his own, replacing the French corpses with eight freshly executed insurgents whom he had been holding. In his commentary on the episode, Reille noted that he had declared his intention to hang four brigands for every French soldier killed. And when he ran out of captured guerrillas, he promised that he would find a new supply of victims among the noncombatants, a promise he was soon to fulfill.[6]

To carry the terror to civilians, Reille required a more effective police force and military tribunal. He established both under the direction of Jean Mendiry. On 18 August 1810 Mendiry's competence was outlined in a decree published and posted throughout the province. Mendiry was to have authority over "crimes against the state," which covered a broad range of activities, including the expression of opinions or the publication of works antithetical to the regime. Cooperation with the insurgents or communication with them in any form also came under the purview of the new organization, as did the "seduction" of imperial troops and "any deed or word" that denoted "disaffection, disapproval, or disobedience" to the government.[7] Mendiry placed agents in churches, taverns, handball courts, and street corners. He became the most hated symbol of the occupation.[8]

Reille put his new mechanism of repression to work immediately in a series of punitive expeditions against civilians. Reille had two sources of intelligence to aid him in this project. He benefited from the returns of the demographic and economic surveys begun under his predecessors. As one would expect, the surveys were never completed for every locale, but they nevertheless constituted powerful tools in the hands of the police. An even more important source of information, one of Reille's own projects, was a community-level survey of men who had been absent from their homes without explanation. These lists, again missing for most communities, began to reach Reille's hands in late 1810 and early 1811. The arrest of civilians by the French police followed.

There are two sources of information that make it possible to quantify the police repression to a certain extent. The first is the prison entry book kept in Pamplona's Recoletas convent, which had been converted into a prison during the war. This book showed that 2 percent of the population of Navarre had passed through the Recoletas. Almost 80 percent of the prisoners were eventually released, 17 percent were deported to France, and 2 percent died in jail or were executed. The jailer recorded the place of origin for 48 percent of the inmates. Most (82 percent) of these prisoners came from the Montaña. The French hit especially hard in Estella, Falces, Huarte, Lárraga, Mendigorría, Olite, Pamplona, Puente la Reina, and Sangüesa. Only 2 percent of the prisoners came from the merindad of Tudela.[9]

As large as the total number (3,323) of prisoners is from the Recoletas, it represents only a fraction of those detained by the French. Suspects were sent not only to the Recoletas but to prisons located in Logroño and Zaragoza, and it is likely that some Ribereños, in particular, would have been incarcerated there. There were also a number of smaller jails in places like Irurzún. Fortunately, the Recoletas data can be supplemented by a second source of information. In 1817 communities in Navarre were asked to complete a survey indicating, among other things, the numbers of civilians arrested by the French during the war. The responses are startling.[10] We know, for example, that in the valley of Echauri, which showed only 8 inmates in the Recoletas, the French actually imprisoned, deported, or killed 259 people.[11] Similarly, Erroz was supposed to have lost 7 of its residents to the Recoletas, but local data show that 38 people were actually incarcerated either in Pamplona or Irurzún.[12]

If such proportions were to hold for other areas not represented in the Recoletas data, then the global numbers for people imprisoned or deported by the French would be enormous indeed. Unfortunately, compliance with the survey was uneven. In the merindad of Pamplona 56 percent of the communes responded, representing 53 percent of the population. In Estella 49 percent of the population was represented in the responses, in Sangüesa 44 percent, in Tudela 42 percent, and in Olite only 31 percent. Flawed though the survey was, careful handling of the data on its own terms does produce certain trends and conclusions about the nature of the French repression.

The essential feature of the repression, like the intelligence upon which it was based, was its unevenness. Some areas, like the region of small villages along the Araquil River and its tributaries northwest of Pamplona, saw almost a third of their population carted off by the military police. In most towns and villages, however, the number of detainees was small. If the French suspected a village of helping the Division, they usually detained only the priest, regidor, or some other community leader. Even if an area was merely in arrears on its taxes, it was cause enough to arrest the regidor, and most communities that reported civilian incarcerations noted the loss of at least one regidor. As targets of the police, priests came in a close second to regidores. The French removed dozens of priests for reading Mina's proclamations to their parishioners or for sheltering wounded guerrillas.[13] Yet, the constant threat of guerrilla attack prevented Mendiry from maintaining a regular police presence outside Pamplona and a few other towns. As a result, much of rural Navarre escaped the French terror.

However, regidores, and less frequently priests, were also subject to reprisals by the guerrillas, for Mina expected local officials to act as adjuncts to the Division, ready to sacrifice their persons and property to the cause. When he was disappointed in his expectations, Mina was not reluctant to brand, blind, cut ears from, or kill collaborating regidores. Thus, local elites who escaped Reille's terror might still be caught by Mina's.

Although the mass of the population was not, of course, normally subject to imprisonment, there were significant exceptions. Mass detentions were carried out by Reille as a last resort against municipalities that had proved themselves committed to the insurgency. Mass arrests took place mainly in the merindad of Pamplona, to a degree in Sangüesa, Estella, and Olite, and hardly at all in Tudela. It is also apparent from the responses that the towns and villages that suffered most from mass arrests were those that had repeatedly given information and supplies to the guerrillas or those known to have contributed a large number of volunteers. If a French force was ambushed in or around a particular village or town, all of its inhabitants were liable to suffer for not having given warning of the presence of the guerrillas. Cáseda was sacked in December 1810 because the guerrillas had surprised a detachment near the town.[14] In Monreal, one of the insurgent strongholds near Idocín, the French burned down the houses of seventeen patriots in a town of eighty-four houses.[15] Elsewhere, the French were less selective. Noáin, strategically located midway between the Carrascal, Pamplona, and Monreal, was completely destroyed by the French in 1812.[16] And the valley of Roncal must have produced an almost continuous plume of smoke. The French burned 311 houses in Roncal during the course of the war. Isaba, which lost 153 houses, and Burguí, which lost 126, were at times practically erased.[17]

The detentions also tended to occur in waves, normally when the French captured a town defended by the guerrillas or when they decided to act on the lists of volunteers and their relatives that local officials and collaborators had been ordered to supply. It was in the smaller localities near the capital that the French used these lists to enact their vengeance fully. In the village of Erroz, located on the main road from Pamplona to Guipúzcoa, the French killed, deported, or imprisoned 28 percent of the population, and nearby Beasoáin lost 30 percent of its people.[18] Belascoáin, with some 220 inhabitants had 80 people taken away to prison and 2 deported, the equivalent of 37 percent of its population.[19] These villages, located in the strategic and vulnerable region west of Pamplona, straddled the routes taken by the guerrillas between Andía (or the Basque provinces) and the Pamplona basin. As a result, they came to supply resources, intelligence, and, as shall be seen in chapter 9, a great number of volunteers to the Division. However, they paid a heavy price in the form of French terrorism. In similar fashion, Lorca, on the royal road between Puente and Estella, saw almost 20 percent of its people sent to prison.[20] In general, these trends reinforce what we know from the Recoletas data and what we have learned about Mina's choice of battle sites and about the regions in which the Division sought refuge. Guerrilla country lay in north-central Navarre and it was in this region that civilians suffered most from the actions of the French police.

Scrutinizing the data in another way reinforces this conclusion. It is notable that in the merindad of Tudela, Fitero was the only city to report the imprisonment or deportation of a significant number of civilians. While this seems an unlikely circumstance, it is supported by the scarcity of prisoners from Tudela in the Recoletas.[21] Moreover, even Fitero's losses pale next to that of any number of small villages in Echauri, Olza, or certain other mountain valleys. Again, of the deaths reported in the merindad of Tudela, most occurred in the city of Tudela as a result of the battles fought there on 8 June and 23 November 1808. They were not actually associated with the terrorism of the counterinsurgency.[22] Thus we are confirmed in the belief that the resistance, at least judging by the tangible evidence of police repression against it, hardly made itself felt in the Ebro valley.

In the merindad of Olite, the towns most affected by the police measures of the French were Mendigorría, Olite, Santacara, and Ujüé. The last of these municipalities ought to be grouped from a geographic, social, and economic point of view with other villages of the Montaña. The first lies along the northern fringe of the Ribera and, moreover, became a common stopping point for the guerrillas in their journeys from the mountains of Estella to those of Sangüesa. Only Olite and Santacara appear somewhat surprising. This trend is duplicated in the Recoletas data, where most of the inmates from the merindad of Olite came from the battle zone between Ujüé and Estella.

No doubt complete data that included returns from Tafalla, Corella, and some of the other big Ribera towns would show that a larger number of Ribereños suffered the consequences of the French terror. We know from the Recoletas data that at least forty-six people from Tafalla went to prison in Pamplona who were not reported in the 1817 survey. Yet, the absence of data from cities like Corella and Tafalla, which were not notably involved in the fighting at any point during the war, is more than made up by the lack of information on places like Baztán, Salazar, and Valcarlos, the last being one of the earliest centers of the resistance. Thus, while complete returns would have shown a much larger number of civilian casualties and incarcerations in Navarre as a whole, it is unlikely that the proportions would have changed much between the merindades or between the Montaña and Ribera.

The effect of Reille's repression, combined with the absence of the Division as it ran from the remotest regions of Navarre to the mountains of Castile and Aragon, was that the ardor of the civilian population cooled in the fall of 1810. Reille's peroration to civilians after Belorado to join the French cause produced a number of defections from the patriot side. The chronicler of the third battalion recorded the mood of the time. Along with the military defeat of the Division, the continuous persecution of civilians had "cowed the spirit" of Navarre. Officials had succumbed to the French by turning in weapons and informing on young men who had taken up arms. Apparently, many believed that the guerrillas would never return.[23]

Already in mid-October 1810, however, Mina was back in Navarre recovering from the wounds he had received at Tarrazona. He soon discovered that his absence in Castile had caused civilian confidence in the guerrillas to wane. Mina gave one of his officers, Ramón Ulzurrún, the task of locating and reenlisting demobilized and disheartened troops to let civilians know that the guerrilla movement had not been entirely destroyed in Castile. In late October Ulzurrún was able to bring Mina a small band of men reconstituted from dispersed volunteers.[24] With these men Mina returned to his original hit-and-run tactics.

A French detachment penetrated Monreal in late October to arrest demobilized volunteers and their families. Mina received news of this French action in time to warn Monreal, and the result was that the demobilized guerrillas in the town were forced by the anticipated French crackdown to reenlist in the Division. In this way, Reille's terrorism backfired and resulted in a fillip of new troops for Mina, which he used to defend Monreal. The French detachment was easily driven off. Another French force had been given a similar mission in Aibar and had succeeded in making some arrests. Mina attacked this detachment on its return to Pamplona and freed all of the prisoners, again incorporating them into his Division. These actions rejuvenated the spirits of patriots and caused collaborators to waiver.[25]

On 17 November Mina attacked a group of thirty-three gendarmes escorting cartloads of munitions through the pass at Carrascal. While Mina's previous actions were greater symbolic coups and certainly contributed to his ability to reinitiate recruitment, the capture of this munitions convoy was in many ways the most important achievement in this period. The guerrillas had almost no ammunition. In fact, the magnitude of the loss at Belorado had stemmed, in part, from a shortage of shot and powder. As the unarmed and dispirited remnants of the Division filtered back into Navarre and rejoined the Division, it became imperative to find arms and ammunition to equip them. The ambush in the Carrascal occurred just at the perfect moment and allowed Mina to reoutfit his men.[26]

Mina spent late November and December rebuilding his shattered force. The enemy troops that had harassed the Division since August finally departed for Portugal, too late, however, to have an impact on events there. Reille's own forces were as exhausted as the guerrillas and unable to continue the war. As a result, Mina succeeded in establishing a headquarters in Lumbier and attracting hundreds of new recruits as well as volunteers dispersed in September and October. This pattern repeated itself several times during the next two years: intense periods of persecution by the French were followed by periods of inactivity in which the insurgency was allowed to revive.

Mina used the respite to eliminate his rivals and to chasten his more unruly troops. He executed Juan Hernández, his old cavalry commander in the corso terrestre, who (according to Mina) had continued to alienate the civilian population with his "ferocious brutality."[27] He also rid himself of "Belza," one of the first guerrillas to operate in the far northwest.[28] However cruel and unjust, the Belza operation did allow Mina to begin recruiting heavily in Baztán, Cinco Villas, and the Guipúzcoa borderlands. Within a month he raised a fourth battalion of 800 men in the region.

Mina also gained the confidence of his rebellious followers through less violent means than those used against Belza and Hernández. It was the style at that time for men pretending to independence and authority to wear their hair long. A closely shaved head was a sign of humility. Army conscripts had their hair shorn; officers kept their hair long. Naturally, for the Men of the Idea only long hair would do, braided or held behind the ears and sometimes complemented by muttonchop sideburns. By his own admission, Mina was as devoted as anyone in the corso to this vogue, which must have made the unwashed volunteers as lice-ridden as they were picturesque.

In early December 1810, when the morale of the guerrillas had reached its nadir, Mina employed a brilliant exercise in authority to clean up the appearance of the men, reimpose their submission, and instill confidence. Against the protests of his subalterns, who worried that they might not be able to control the troops, Mina ordered everyone under his command to receive a haircut. Once the mutinous troops had been shorn and their submission assured, Mina allowed his own hair to be cut in a public ceremony. Afterward, his troops were given new clothes and embarked on one of the most successful campaigns of the war.[29] The result of Mina's efforts was that by the end of December the Division once again numbered 3,000 men, and in January Mina added the 800 men of the fourth battalion. Despite all of the hardships of the war, the Navarrese had rallied once again to the resistance.

In late December Mina finally drew the attention of General Reille again. Reille sent one column of 700 men from the west and a second of 1,700, many of them drawn from Suchet's garrisons along the Ebro, from the southeast to trap Mina in Lumbier. However, this force, which in November could have overwhelmed Mina's men, was already too small to do the job in December. Mina ambushed the first column in Idocín on Christmas Eve, killing forty-eight and capturing seventy, twenty of whom were shot as renegade Spaniards. On the day after Christmas, Mina ambushed the second column in a gorge near Lumbier. The guerrillas, aided by dozens of local peasants, rained stones and shot upon the enemy and chased them all the way back to Caparroso on the northern fringe of the Ebro plain. The French reported the loss of 112 men killed and captured in these battles in the official report of 1 January 1811, with another 46 dying in the hospital in Pamplona during the following two weeks. An unofficial French source came up with a similar estimate of 162 men lost, while Spanish sources claim to have killed and captured 200 men. Navarrese losses in both ambushes were small. With these two engagements, the guerrillas announced their complete recovery to the world.[30]

For almost two weeks Reille again allowed the guerrillas to rest in Lumbier. Mina used the time to establish hospitals in the valleys of Roncal, Salazar, and Aézcoa in the Pyrenees. He sent the fourth battalion to Echarri-Aranaz and the Araquil valley to train and to recruit more men. It has already been noted that the fourth battalion drew heavily on the populations of the northwest. The battalion's commanders, Ramón Ulzurrún and Francisco de Asura, were themselves from the villages of Asiáin and Amezqueta, respectively. Asiáin was located a few miles north of Echauri, and Amezqueta was the last Guipúzcoan village before the Navarrese border and the mountains of Aralar. It was in these areas that the battalion sought to fill out its ranks.

The other battalions had been recruited in a similar fashion. The first battalion, led by Mina, relied heavily on Monreal and the villages west of Sangüesa, Mina's backyard. The second battalion was commanded by Cruchaga and later by Antonio Barrena, the first from Roncal and the second from Salazar, and it drew on those populations. Finally, the third battalion was commanded by the Górriz brothers, from the village of Subiza, located south of the capital not far from the Carrascal. This battalion included many men from the Pamplona basin and Estella. Mina also set up, or rather absorbed, a fifth battalion in the month of January 1811. This battalion consisted mostly of Alavese who were already integrated into the guerrilla party run by the Alavese patriot Sebastián Fernández. All of the battalions were thus made up of men from the Montaña. When united, which it never was at this time, the full Division could well have approached the mark of 5,000 men.[31]

In the middle of January, however, there began another round of pursuit. The French had recently cleared Upper Aragon of guerrillas, and Suchet, who had just seen some of his troops massacred at Lumbier, decided to intervene again in Navarre. He dispatched General Harispe to hunt down Mina. On 12 January 5,000 French approached Lumbier only to find the bridge into the city cut and the far bank of the river Irati defended. Mina held an advantageous position, and his men defended the city until their ammunition ran out and they had to flee into the Pyrenees. Losses on both sides were minimal, the French suffering twenty-three deaths and the Navarrese four, according to Andrés Martín. The French reports recorded greater losses than the Navarrese: eighteen killed, thirty-one taken prisoner, and five deserted.[32] After chasing Mina a short way into the mountains, the French returned to Lumbier, sacked the town, and killed sixteen civilians who had been foolish enough to remain behind.[33]

From 24 December through January the Division altogether killed or captured 341 French combatants and wounded hundreds, especially in the battles of 24 and 26 December. French totals do not differ significantly, showing 338 killed, captured, or deserted, with no estimate of the numbers wounded. In return, the French had been really effective only against the unfortunate civilians in Lumbier. Such a stain on French military honor had to be rectified, and the French once again poured overwhelming forces into Navarre beginning in the middle of January. Generals Cafarelli and Chlopiski joined Harispe and Reille in the pursuit of Mina. Together they had some 13,000 troops, reinforced in Aragon and the Ebro valley by another 9,000 troops, forcing Mina once again to disperse his Division in order to save it.[34] Mina took the bulk of his troops across Navarre to the mountains of Andía in early February. There they were divided further. The first and second battalions fled to the relative safety of the Pyrenees and were cantoned in the valleys of Roncal, Salazar, and Aézcoa in the east and Baztán in the west. The third and fourth battalions occupied the mountains of Estella and Santa Cruz de Campezo on the border with Álava. Reille's information coincides roughly with that provided by the guerrillas and again supports the idea that the guerrillas were men of the Montaña. On 1 March Reille's spies placed the guerrillas in four bases: Goñi, Lecumberri, and Baztán, all in the northwest, and Aoiz, in the eastern Pyrenees.[35]

The Division remained in this dispersed state in the Montaña until the end of May, with the following exceptions. In the space of one week in late March, the guerrillas united to kill or capture 46 men of the Estella garrison without suffering any loss, fought off a column of 3,300 stationed in Los Arcos, inflicting 38 casualties, and surprised and captured a requisition party of 90 men in Aragon. They then melted away before the French could respond.[36] In April Mina again united part of his force, captured ninety-eight muskets and a convoy of munitions in Azagra, and surprised the 150-man garrison at Exea de los Caballeros in Aragon, which he took after killing 71 French troops and capturing the rest.[37]

In May, after months spent in fruitless pursuit of the Division, Harispe and his men evacuated Navarre. Still, Reille counted 4,700 men under his command together with 2,400 men under General Cafarelli. Mina's full Division came to some 5,000 men at this time, each of five battalions counting approximately 1,000 troops and the cavalry about 150. However, the fifth "Alavese" battalion rarely operated in conjunction with the first four Navarrese battalions. The French thus enjoyed a significant numerical advantage over the guerrillas. However, this apparent advantage was eliminated by the requirements of garrisoning the countryside. Of Reille's troops, 2,700 were in permanent garrison duty, leaving him a field force of 2,000 men. Even when united with Cafarelli's 2,400 men, therefore, Reille could only match numbers with the guerrillas.[38] The dispersion of enemy resources in occupation duties is, of course, one of the desired results of guerrilla warfare. In the peninsula as a whole, it was what allowed Spanish and English regular armies to survive against the French. Inside Navarre, it gave Mina the ability to unite his troops for campaigns in the knowledge that Reille, without Harispe or some other outside help, could not overwhelm the Division.

Mina responded to this situation by reuniting his four Navarrese battalions in late May in Estella. Mina heard from Fernández in Álava that a column made up of 100 carriages of French wounded and sick, 1,070 Spanish and 58 English prisoners, and an enormous amount of booty, including personal effects of Marshal Masséna and possibly the one-eyed marshal himself, was to depart Vitoria on 25 May. Mina decided to strike. In two days he marched his men fifty-three miles to the pass at Arlabán, on the Álava-Guipúzcoa border, where the French column had to pass. At Arlabán Mina employed his usual tactic, firing once and attacking with the bayonet. The results were familiar. Of the 1,650 men who made up the escort, 240 were killed and 160 taken prisoner. The rest fled to Vitoria, warning Masséna, who had lagged behind in the city. The money, weapons, and other goods captured provided the biggest payday ever enjoyed by the guerrillas. Arlabán was Mina's Bailén. It was the greatest single victory yet by a guerrilla army. Most important was the rescue of all but 150 of the Allied prisoners, for it spread the fame of Mina and the Division of Navarre throughout Spain.[39]

The surprise at Arlabán finally forced Cádiz to alter its perception of Mina. The government had repeatedly denied recognition to the Division. Although Mina had sent representatives to Cádiz, they had been dismissed. The government felt that the Navarrese troops were still half bandits, and Mina was forced to keep the content of the rejection letters he received from Cádiz secret in order not to demoralize his men.[40] It is true that there were some inside the government who had become disgusted with the performance of the regular Spanish armies and who had begun to listen with sympathy to Mina's case. The junta of La Mancha, in hiding at this time, argued in favor of Mina in the first number of its official organ: "This Navarrese hero knows the art of winning battles and not being beaten," wrote the editors of the junta's newspaper, alluding to the failure of Spanish armies to protect La Mancha. "It matters nothing to the nation that he is ignorant of the tactics of the [military] academies."[41] After Arlabán the Regency agreed with those who advocated guerrilla war as the path to liberation, finally recognizing the personnel of the Division as regular troops on 5 June 1811.[42]

Mina quickly evacuated his troops from Arlabán to avoid pursuit by a column dispatched from Vitoria. The fifth battalion remained in eastern Álava. The third and fourth battalions were sent north, where they drove the force stationed in Irún across the Bidasoa to Hendaye, briefly sealing the French border and seizing a valuable stockpile of cotton cloth and indigo before retreating south into the Pyrenees. The rest of the Division crossed Navarre to the Carrascal.[43]

The French tried everything to control the guerrillas. They set up a system of fortifications and towers in Álava and Navarre to link the cities of the interior to the coast. Ten towers were erected between Vitoria and Irún, and others were created on the Irún/Pamplona/Tudela highway. The towers communicated with each other through a semaphore system "to give notice of what is going on in the mountains" to the forces in Vitoria, Irún, and Pamplona before they ventured out into guerrilla territory. Ideally, the forts would both warn columns of the presence of guerrillas and serve as refuges for ambushed convoys and detachments. The forts were never effective in carrying out the first task. As islands of darkness in a countryside dominated by the insurgents, they received no intelligence and were no help to the garrisons in the cities. They did, however, afford secure havens to French troops isolated in the mountains. One fort built in the fateful pass at Arlabán saved hundreds of French soldiers in 1812, though it could not prevent a recurrence of another surprise attack.[44]

The French decided after the humiliation in Álava to act in concert once again. General Bessières, who commanded the military district of Biscay, loaned Navarre thousands of troops. In all, as many as 20,000 men, under the veteran generals Cafarelli, Harispe, Pannetier, Arnaud, Severoli, Abbé, and Bertholet, entered Navarre.[45] On 13 June the first four battalions of the Division were intercepted and surrounded in the plains north of Tafalla by two columns of a combined strength of 7,000 infantry and 800 cavalry. Mina lost 200 killed and wounded, and his men set out in a dozen directions to return to their homes and fields.[46] Others found refuge where they could. The second battalion was divided among Roncesvalles, Salazar, Roncal, and Upper Aragon. The fourth battalion remained in the northwest, near Guipúzcoa, where most of its personnel originated. The first and third battalions sent some elements west to the region of Echauri, some east to Lumbier. The Division was not able to reunite again until the end of July.[47]

Facing no challenge from the guerrillas, the French police were able, in the summer of 1811, to vent their rage over Arlabán. Mendiry sent hordes of civilians to the jails of Pamplona and executed dozens of "spies" and parents of the guerrillas. Reille described these measures in a letter of 11 July. "Three days ago," he wrote, "I had 40 of the brigands held in the Ciudadela shot, and I have declared that the 170 still there will be held hostage" in case further object lessons became necessary.[48] Andrés Martín described with more emotion the atmosphere this terror produced in the city of Pamplona.

> In the streets people hear the heartrending cries of their friends taken to prison and torture. If they flee the city, they see the high gallows on which innocent Spaniards hang. Everywhere, there is nothing but prison, exile, and death. And in this terrible situation, the expression of grief is forbidden. A simple complaint or glance of compassion is cause enough for imprisonment. People lose their humor. They avoid gatherings, are deprived of friendship, and give themselves over to silence and pain.[49]

One unintended result of Reille's focus on the repression of civilians was that it gave Mina another needed respite. And Mina used this time to extend his presence more deeply into Álava and even into Guipúzcoa and Vizcaya. Since 5 June Mina's Division had become nominally integrated into the Seventh Army, under General Mendizábal. With the only effective division in the region, Mina was given sway over Álava (which he already partially controlled through the fifth battalion) and was authorized to support the incipient guerrilla army of Antonio Jaureguí, "el Pastor," in Guipúzcoa. He was also directed to coordinate his efforts with those of the Vizcayan guerrilla Longa, and for all of these reasons he absented himself in Vizcaya from 4 July until 21 or 22 July.[50]

When Mina returned, he called all of his troops together for an attack on a French column moving through Piedramillera, in the foothills west of Estella. On 23 and 24 July Mina's 4,000 men drove Pannetier's 2,000 men back into Estella, after killing 150 and capturing 16. The Spanish had fewer casualties, according to Mina, but many were wounded, including Gregorio Cruchaga, who suffered his third serious injury since the beginning of the war.[51]

Now, however, the coordination and resolve of the French in the aftermath of Arlabán caught the guerrillas by surprise. Mina had learned that a column of 2,000 French was stationed just across the Alavese border in Santa Cruz de Campezo, and he set out in pursuit. But this force was nothing more than bait, and as Mina marched his men further into Álava, he became aware that Pannetier had not remained in Estella but, after receiving reinforcements, had begun to close on the Division from the rear. Following his usual methods, Mina sought to escape the difficulty by doubling back in order to cross the plains of central Navarre at night to reach the mountains of Sangüesa.

On this occasion, however, a misfortune of nature thwarted Mina's plans. During the night march, the weather became so bad that his men could see only by the flashes of lightning. Mud sucked the shoes from their feet, and heavy rains rendered their weapons useless. The Division, which had set prodigious records for endurance, marching some eighty miles in twenty-four hours on one occasion, made only a few miles the entire night, placing it underneath the noses of Reille's column of 5,000 infantry and 500 cavalry in Los Arcos.

For reasons perhaps associated with Cruchaga's injuries, Mina, Cruchaga, and a small escort abandoned the Division in this hour of desperation and fled to the north. They left it to the third in command, Barrena, to cross the plains of Navarre with the barefoot and disarmed men under the eyes of a far superior enemy well supplied with artillery and horse. In the hills near the city of Lerín, the guerrillas were surrounded and annihilated. The French killed 400 and captured 200, while losing very few against the defenseless Navarrese. Many who escaped smashed their useless weapons and returned to civilian life.[52]

After Lerín Reille attempted to divide the guerrillas by renewing offers of amnesty, by placing prices on the heads of Mina, Cruchaga, and the other commanders, and even by attempting to bribe Mina. This last effort resulted in a peculiar episode in which Mina seemed for a while on the verge of accepting a French offer of employment in exchange for demobilizing the Division. After an exchange of letters with the government, Mina agreed to meet a party of two Navarrese merchants and a Frenchman sent by Reille in a safe village chosen by Mina. Once the parties had come together, though, Mina promptly took them hostage. Perhaps he had sensed a trap. More likely, however, Mina had only agreed to the charade in order to obtain a cease-fire as a condition for negotiation. This he achieved, and the Division, or what remained of it after Lerín, gained a much needed rest from pursuit. The fact that the envoys, some of whom were later revealed to have performed services on the sly for Mina during the war, were quickly allowed to "escape" from their captors, demonstrates that Mina did not suspect their patriotism or hold the affair a failure.[53]

Until the middle of October what remained of the Division was sent, in the last great dispersion before the end of the war, to the Pyrenees and the mountains west of Estella, and to Álava and Guipúzcoa, where the guerrillas began to make the life of Thouvenot, the commander in Álava, miserable. Recovery began almost immediately. In early October, the Division counted only 950 men.[54] The battalions were soon filled out, however, from two sources. First, the complete destruction of organized resistance in Catalonia and most of Aragon during 1811 resulted in a flood of men from these areas joining up with Mina in the fall.[55] Second, Mina circulated an order that all of those volunteers who had returned home were required to rejoin the Division. Anyone discovered to have accepted the French amnesty would be shot together with his parents or three other relatives.[56]

Soon Mina was able to return to the offensive. During a sweep through Upper Aragon, Mina surprised and took the garrison at Exea (his own chronicles say it was the garrison of Ayerbe) and then wiped out a relief column sent out from Zaragoza. Of 800 men in the column, the guerrillas killed 197 and captured the rest, save for 3 French horsemen who escaped to report the disaster.[57] The prisoners were transferred to the third and fourth battalions who took them to the Biscay port of Motrico and handed them over to the English, along with fifty-one additional prisoners—the entire Motrico garrison—captured along the way. In exchange, the guerrillas acquired from the English a valuable cargo of weapons, including their first piece of artillery.[58]

Mina set up his headquarters in Santa Cruz de Campezo in Álava in late October, again moving east to Sangüesa in early November, where he was allowed to exist for almost two months unmolested by Reille's forces in Pamplona. During this time, the Division took no action inside Navarre, though it continued to make its presence felt in Upper Aragon, engaging the French twice and causing 270 casualties, while absorbing few losses.[59]

Even more than the previous year, when Reille's lack of activity during the late fall and winter of 1810–11 had allowed the Division a chance to recover from Belorado, the respite afforded the guerrillas in the late fall and winter of 1811–12 proved the undoing of the occupation. It was Marshal Suchet's campaign in the southeast that provided this breathing space for Mina. Suchet had borrowed Reille to command any troops that could be spared from Aragon and Navarre for the siege of Valencia. As a result, the region was left thinly garrisoned. By December 1811 there were only 6,396 troops to occupy Navarre, over half of them in garrisons and almost 800 in the hospital.[60] Aragon was even more vulnerable: the garrison inside Zaragoza had been reduced to a mere 1,600 men.[61] Once again, the symbiosis between the regular armies and the guerrillas could not be clearer. Mina knew that he would face token resistance, especially in Upper Aragon, thus his concentration on the region in this period. Suchet eventually forced Valencia to submit and was able to redirect troops to Aragon and Navarre, but by then Mina had become the master of the region.

That winter, Mina cut communications between France and Aragon. He even forced Napoleon to mobilize the national guard in order to prevent incursions into France. This was an especially sensitive matter, because some of the border settlements in France had been discovered aiding Mina, supplying him with food and even guides to help navigate the French side of the Pyrenees.[62] In December General Louis Nicolas Abbé was placed in charge of the reduced number of French troops inside Navarre. As on previous occasions, the change of command proved an advantage to Mina, because for a time Abbé had to focus on administrative matters rather than on seeking combat. The result of all this was that the guerrillas experienced their most successful recruiting drive ever in the winter of 1811–12. Thus, despite having lost about 1,000 men during the campaigns of 1811, the Division of Navarre was able in January 1812 to field more men than it had before Lerín. On the other side, the French, though they had maintained the offensive during 1811, had lost well over 2,500 men.[63] Even during the most difficult year of its existence, therefore, the insurgency had remained effective against the French. And as the year 1812 began, there were fewer occupation troops than there were guerrillas, opening the way for a Navarrese offensive.

B Y DECEMBER 1811 Mina had not only succeeded in rebuilding the Division after its discomfiture at Lerín, he had even begun to widen the war into Upper Aragon. Marshal Suchet had just cleared Upper Aragon of its main guerrilla force with the capture and execution of the partisan Larrodé, known as the Pesoduro. Larrodé's torture and death demonstrated the pathological treatment meted out by the French, and especially by Suchet, against the guerrillas. The French cut off Larrodé's hands while he was still alive and nailed them up for public viewing before dragging him to the scaffold. Then the French botched the hanging, the rope breaking several times before on the fourth try Larrodé died.[1]

Larrodé's successor, José Tris, nicknamed the Malcarado, had made himself thoroughly detested by December 1811 with his extortions.[2] Also damning were Tris's connections to the French, which became known only in April 1812, when he nearly succeeded in delivering Mina into enemy hands.[3] Mina was not yet aware of the extent of Tris's corruption, however, and when he passed into Aragon with three battalions and the cavalry in late December 1812, he tried to operate in concert with Tris.

As he had done the previous fall, Mina went after the garrisons, which had been depleted by Suchet for his campaigns in Valencia and Almería. The garrison at Zuera fled at the news of Mina's presence in the region, and on 7 January 1812 after a five-day siege the 200-man garrison at Huesca surrendered, even though the mine placed to blow up the fortress was apparently far from ready.[4] With these successes, the Navarrese spirit of resistance caught hold in Upper Aragon, and the basis was laid for an Aragonese battalion, the sixth in the Division, to be formed that spring.

During his absence in Aragon, Mina had left behind only the fourth battalion to secure Sangüesa and his return route to Navarre. General Abbé tried to take advantage of this situation by dispatching a force of some 2,000 men including a column from Aragon under Cafarelli to surprise the fourth battalion. However, Mina arrived with the first three battalions and the cavalry, some 6,000 men in all, just as Abbé approached. The presence of the united Division took Abbé by surprise, and he was forced to adopt a defensive position against an army three times the size of his own.

The battle of Rocaforte on a height just outside of Sangüesa on 11 January proved to be the most important action since the surprise at Arlabán. Not only was it an important guerrilla victory, it was also the first action witnessed by a senior officer of the Spanish army, for General Gabriel Mendizábal, the commander of the Seventh Army and Mina's immediate superior, had arrived to meet with Mina just before the battle. Mendizábal had come, in part, to communicate to Mina his promotion to brigadier general, and he just happened to be on hand to see the Division destroy Abbé's column.

For once the French possessed fewer horse, since Mina was able to use Mendizábal's cavalry in concert with his own. The guerrillas also enjoyed a decisive edge in experience, since most of the French were recent conscripts. However, Abbé had occupied a commanding height, and he possessed field pieces that initially caused confusion among the guerrillas. After almost five hours of inconclusive firing, Mina, who still lacked ammunition for a long battle, ordered a bayonet charge. This tactic, given the strong French position, surprised Mendizábal so much that he thought the Navarrese were deserting to the enemy. However, Mina's troops soon revealed their experience in hand-to-hand fighting and overran the French position, capturing the artillery. The guerrillas inflicted 600 casualties, while losing half that number. Abbé escaped to Pamplona with the remnant of his army and was unable to leave the city for several weeks.[5]

The battle of Rocaforte initiated a new phase in the guerrilla war. Operating by themselves, the French forces in Navarre could no longer take the offensive. Indeed, they could barely garrison Pamplona, Tafalla, Tudela, and the five other places they still held after abandoning the regions of Estella and Sangüesa. After Rocaforte, the French were the quarry rather than the hunters, French guards had to remain constantly alert in their posts even on the outskirts of Pamplona, and mail couriers had to be sent out with escorts of 600 men.[6]

Mendizábal was witness not just to an important victory but also to the greatest atrocity ever perpetrated against the French by Mina. There were no prisoners at Rocaforte, because Mina had them executed on the spot. The number killed in this way is not recorded, nor is Mendizábal's reaction, though judging from his subsequent enthusiasm in Mina's behalf he could not have been too dismayed. Indeed, as a result of the battle of Rocaforte and Mendizábal's lobbying for Mina, the government raised him to the rank of field marshal soon afterward.

The order to kill captives had been issued by Mina on 14 December 1811. It read, "French officers and soldiers captured with arms or without them in the course of battle or not will be hanged and left along the main roads."[7] Rocaforte was the first chance to implement this new policy. It had been common practice for the guerrillas to execute captured Spanish traitors, and the French had frequently killed captured insurgents, but the execution of French captives was not normal for Mina. Previously, captured French were taken to prisons in Valencia. Mina's new policy of rigor, however, was a response to the escalating ferocity of the French regime as it entered its death throes.

After the disaster of Lerín, the French operated with impunity against demobilized partisans and their relatives and sympathizers. On 8 July Reille had forty imprisoned volunteers executed in Pamplona in reprisal for Mina's execution of captured "chacones," as the guerrillas called Spaniards serving under French colors. In August Reille had twenty-two "brigands" and their "ferocious" captain executed in Pamplona. Larrodé's fate in Exea has been recounted already, but sixty-nine men captured with him were also executed. On 27 October sixteen guerrillas captured in Araquil were shot in the field. We will never know the true number of volunteers shot in this way by the French. The mass graves depicted in Goya's etchings suggest that many insurgents must have disappeared without a trace.[8]

Noncombatants also suffered from the terror. In Tafalla eleven "bad subjects" were shot that fall, and in Pamplona fourteen priests, monks, and other "bandits" faced the firing squad on 2 October. In Aibar the priest and five others were shot, eight died in Sangüesa on a single day in October, and twenty-two were hanged or shot in Estella, atrocities all recorded by Reille.

Many more were arrested than were executed, of course. As early as August Reille had complained that his jails were too full, that at most he needed to keep 200 prisoners on hand for public executions. But the arrests continued. From early September to mid-October Reille arrested nearly 600 parents of guerrillas, and planned to "burn their houses" and have "some of the worst shot." The jails became overcrowded, and Reille had to begin the mass deportation of prisoners. Over the next few months hundreds were sent to prisons in France. On a single day in October Reille deported 300 civilians, who he suggested should "finish their days in some distant dungeon," because they were bandits and would always be enemies of France.[9]

Abbé only increased the terror when he took command in November. On 3 December Abbé announced that twenty "bandits" held in Pamplona, together with all of the imprisoned relatives of the insurgents, would be executed. On 4 December twenty-two people were hanged in Pamplona, and on the following day eleven more were executed in Estella for the crime of being related to volunteers. Four days later Mendiry had seventeen more soldiers and seventeen relatives of insurgents shot. Their bodies were hung on either side of the Tafalla road at a point a few miles south of Pamplona.[10]

It was in response to all of this that Mina decreed his own brand of terror. Before the killings at Rocaforte, Mina had established a prison for French captives in the valley of Roncal. These men became the scapegoats of the guerrilla terror. When the French executed a Navarrese official, four French officials died. When they killed an enlisted man, Mina had twenty French soldiers executed.[11] The actual number of French prisoners killed in this way is unknown, but the atrocities, according to Mina, achieved their purpose: they caught the attention of General Abbé. Inspired no doubt by the knowledge that many more of his men were falling into the hands of the resistance than the other way around, Abbé finally stopped treating the men of the Division and their relations as if they were criminals. Mina thereafter returned to the system of giving quarter to captured enemy troops, lessening the climate of barbarity (at least between the combatants) during the last year of the war.[12]

As a result of the battle of Rocaforte, Mendizábal became a believer in Mina and his Division, obtaining for him official recognition of his growing sway over Álava and Upper Aragon.[13] With Abbé confined to Pamplona, Mina could now station his troops safely in Estella, Lumbier, and Puente la Reina, where they rested for fifteen days and attracted new recruits. Meanwhile, however, events elsewhere threatened to undermine all of these achievements.

On 9 January Suchet finally took Valencia. This was potentially a great blow to the guerrillas, for by 1811 they obtained much of their weapons and ammunition from Valencia. In the early days of the movement, in 1809 and 1810, guns and munitions stolen from the French or smuggled out of Pamplona had been enough. Shops were set up to make repairs to the weapons as needed, and Mina established "factories" in the Pyrenees to produce extra shot and powder, but the insecurity of these operations prevented them from expanding to cover the needs of the Division as it grew in late 1810 and 1811. The Spanish forces in Valencia, however, had managed to supply Mina's thirst for weapons. Indeed, Mina's contacts with Valencia were for months at a time his only connection to the wider war. Now that Valencia was in enemy hands, the supply line of both weapons and information was severed.[14]

Fortunately for Mina, he found a new source of munitions almost immediately. As early as 1810 the British Royal Navy had turned the Bay of Biscay into an English preserve, making coastal traffic almost impossible for the French.[15] The English were able to make occasional drops to the guerrillas in Asturias, Santander, and Vizcaya in exchange for prisoners. Mina had already tested this source of supplies once in 1811, and now he established regular contacts along the Biscay coast.[16] Through the small ports at Motrico and Zumaya the Division began to acquire the weapons and ammunition it needed to nearly double in size after 1812. As for clothing, the Division supplied its own picturesque uniforms throughout most of the war. The guerrillas wore brown pants and jackets and high top hats. Then in March 1813 the English also began to supply uniforms.[17]

Mina could not always exchange prisoners for supplies but had also to make cash payments to the English. The money was plentiful, though, since by 1812 Mina had nearly absolute control over the Navarrese border crossings and customhouses, except Irún, which was heavily guarded by the French. Mina estimated that he had 200 men working for him in these border posts.[18] Their initial task, under Félix Sarasa, the well-connected farmer from Artica, was to eliminate smuggling and banditry.[19] Smuggling was easily ended, because some of the guerrillas had themselves been smugglers and knew how and where to interdict illegal trade. Banditry was eliminated after Mina defeated the Men of the Idea in the spring of 1810. Indeed, it appears that Mina succeeded in controlling the borders and highways of Navarre to a degree only dreamed of by Spanish governments both before and after the war. By 1811 commerce within Navarre had become safer than anywhere in the peninsula, provided one paid Mina's tolls. The Division earned about 3 million reales a year from its tolls, enough to pay for its uniforms and ammunition as well as to pay the troops' salaries.[20]

The fall of Valencia freed up Suchet, and this was potentially a much greater threat than the loss of supplies from the city. Immediately, Suchet dispatched a column of 1,800 infantry and 50 cavalry under General Soulier, who swept into Sangüesa in early February. Soulier's column, known as the "Infernals" to denote their effectiveness in counterinsurgency, had already fought a successful campaign against the Empecinado. Soulier expected to cut down the insurgents in Navarre as he had in Castile and southern Aragon. Mina, however, could reckon almost 7,000 men by February. Even discounting those operating in Álava and Aragon, he was still able to bring 4,000 troops against Soulier. On February 5 the Division attacked the Infernals in Sangüesa, forcing them to form square and retreat to Sos, the fortified birthplace of Ferdinand the Catholic just across the border in Aragon. The French suffered 600 casualties before finding refuge inside the fortress.[21] An intercepted letter from Soulier to Suchet described the state of the Infernals after the battle, as well as the quality of the Navarrese troops. Soulier reported that his column had "lost over 600 men and is no longer able to do battle with the insurgents of Navarre. I confess to your excellency in all honesty that the brigands of this kingdom merit the name of veteran soldiers. They can compete with the best of our armies, for the continuous battles and victories have made them lose their fear of us."[22]

From Sos the Division descended on Tafalla, occupied by a French garrison of almost 500 men. The guerrillas still lacked siege weapons to take the fort, and all they could do was occupy the town for a few days, confiscating French stores and pressing the inhabitants for contributions before moving on. Nevertheless, Mina had achieved nearly complete control in Navarre.

In March, however, the French finally responded to Mina with overwhelming force. Napoleon reorganized and consolidated the military government in northern Spain under the unified command of Dorsenne, and he brought back Reille to command a special Army of the Ebro in order to clear Navarre and Upper Aragon of insurgents. Reille was assigned fifteen infantry regiments, four cavalry regiments, an artillery train and engineers, and thousands of gendarmes, for a total of over 36,000 men. In addition, he was supposed to have access to other troops in Catalonia and Aragon. In reality, however, the troops from Catalonia never participated in the venture, and Suchet, far from contributing to the Army of the Ebro, borrowed almost a third of Reille's troops for new operations south of Valencia. Even so, Reille brought 25,000 men into the chase.[23]

In a response by now familiar, Mina sent half of the Division west to the Estella region, the other half to the mountains of Roncal and Upper Aragon. This time, however, even with his main force divided and in hiding, Mina continued to dominate Navarre. There was no need to demobilize in the spring of 1812, nor was there any sign of popular disaffection as there had been in the summer of 1811. People realized that this wave of French pressure would recede, as others had, and that the guerrillas would remain. Mina had indeed become the "little king" of Navarre, dominating the province wherever the French were not physically present. His superior intelligence network made it easy for the guerrillas to avoid unfavorable encounters and to strike quickly against exposed French units. Casualties from this period, especially for the guerrillas, are impossible to calculate because of gaps in the records. It seems likely that they were low, however, since there were no major battles, despite the number of troops engaged.[24] Casualties, though, were not the only measure of the guerrillas' success. It was precisely during the spring of 1812 that the Division tightened its economic control of Navarre, blockaded Pamplona, and began the most spectacular period of recruitment in areas previously outside of its sphere of influence.

In December 1811 Mina had declared an economic blockade of Pamplona, and in the early months of 1812 the city was cut off from the rest of Navarre. Mina forbade anyone to carry money, food, or commodities to within a mile of the capital. The inhabitants of Pamplona were declared enemies for the duration of the war. People could leave the capital to take up residence in guerrilla territory, but nobody could reenter the city. Stones were fixed around Pamplona, marking the line of blockade, and Mina placed a twenty-four-hour guard on all of the roads leading into the city. Article 10 of Mina's decree read: "The detachments stationed to observe the line will, if they see anyone approaching, fire without delay, communication, or orders; and whether the culprit is wounded or not, he will be hanged immediately in a tree."[25]

By this measure, Mina required full belligerency from the civilian population. Villagers within walking distance of the capital who depended on the Pamplona market for earnings were asked to forgo this outlet. Thus, the blockade threatened economically to ruin not just the French and the Pamplonese, but everyone in the Pamplona basin. Mina was aware of the economic hardships he had created, but he did not hesitate to penalize those who broke the blockade. As he said in his memoirs, he "did not institute these measures just to see them evaded."[26] He seems to have been more lenient in practice than in his decree, at times allowing his men to cut off the ears of an offender, rather than shooting or hanging him. Mina also had violators' noses cut off or their foreheads branded with the emblem "Viva Mina." Another common penalty was tarring and feathering.[27]

These strict dealings with the civilian population were nothing new. Navarrese and other Spaniards serving in any capacity with the French had always been executed immediately upon capture. Even more passive forms of collaboration brought severe penalties. Buyers of properties seized by the French state, for example, were singled out for retribution by the insurgents.[28] And peasants in Estella, forced in 1811 to carry mail for the French garrison, were beaten, branded, shot, or lynched for a collaboration that had been forced upon them.[29] What was different in the spring of 1812 was that what had once been the threat of reprisal by the guerrillas had become a certainty.

José Yangüas y Miranda, the wealthy Tudelan afrancesado, personally attested to the insurgency's control over the province. In January 1811 Mina had tried to lay a contribution on Tudela, but the city fathers, Yangüas among them, thought they could still afford to ignore Mina's demands. On 20 May 1812 Yangüas paid for this defiance. On the Valtierra road, just north of Tudela, Yangüas and two companions were captured by Mina's men. As evidenced by the sack of Tudela in 1809, there was no love between the armed peasants of the Division and the bourgeois of Tudela.[30] Mina kept Yangüas hostage for two months, creating an inveterate enemy. Yangüas later recalled that by 1812 "the entire province, aside from the places fortified by the French, was under the absolute dominion of the guerrillas of Navarre, who had forbidden any communication with the enemy, under pain of death. . . . Justice was meted out in the field of honor, without the least formality of a trial. And there was no compromise, but only cutting off ears, execution, or complete liberty, if the accused had the fortune to persuade [the guerrillas] of his innocence."[31]

Among those who suffered the ultimate penalty were the alcaldes of Berriosuso and Orcoyen, villages located too close to Pamplona to escape French entanglement yet outside of the circle of the siege and therefore subject to Mina's law. The French ordered these villages to cart fodder into the city, but the alcaldes themselves had to fulfill the order because nobody else would. Mina could not prevent them from completing the delivery and returning home, but his watchdogs later stabbed the two men to death in their sleep in retribution.[32]

Mina's men enforced the blockade with zeal. One of the guerrillas in charge of stopping communications to Pamplona sent a note to Mina that Yangüas saw during his captivity: "My general," it read, "I have taken a poor lemon seller and I have hanged him from a tree, for certain reasons."[33] No further justification was required. Selling lemons to the weakening populace and garrison in Pamplona was punished by death, for it was only by strict adherence to the blockade that the guerrillas could deny the French any sustenance in Navarre. By April the alcaldes and regidores who had previously bowed to French pressure and carried letters for the enemy began to desert to Mina.[34] Clearly, it was preferable to risk losing one's property and family in a just cause than to face certain death or mutilation at the hands of the insurgents.

The blockade of Pamplona was one of Mina's most brilliant moves. As the noose tightened around Pamplona, the French had to send out huge forces to forage and to cut firewood. This created opportunities for the Division to surprise the French while they were exposed in nonmilitary duties. No doubt the population in Pamplona and its environs suffered greatly, especially since the harvest of 1811 had fallen short anyway. But the suffering of the capital was a sign that the Division had effectively denied the French access to the resources of the countryside.

In April 1812 Mina performed perhaps his most important coup. The Division was still vastly outnumbered and had not been reunited at full strength since early March. Mina leaked information to the French that the Division was about to reunite in Aragon, and some 15,000 French troops passed into the neighboring province to prevent it. Meanwhile, Mina concentrated his first, fourth, and fifth battalions at Arlabán, determined to deliver a surprise blow to the French, just as he had a year before.

Early on the morning of 9 April the guerrillas stationed themselves in the pass, where they surprised a convoy from Vitoria. As usual, there was a shortage of ammunition. This time, each volunteer had two cartridges, but using the usual bayonet tactics, only one shot was actually used. In less than an hour of hand-to-hand fighting the convoy was taken. The Division killed or captured 800 French and rescued 405 Spanish prisoners of war, according to Navarrese sources. French sources said the number of prisoners rescued was 300, but concurred that only 150 men of the regiment escorting the convoy escaped to the fort at Mondragón and another 55 wounded straggled back to Vitoria.[35]

Later that month, Mina did indeed pass into Aragon. On 22 April in concert with José Tris he captured a convoy containing the payroll for Pamplona valued at 80,000 reales. Soon afterward he discovered the treachery of Tris at Robres and killed his rival, the whole incident perhaps taking place as a result of fighting over the spoils from the convoy. In any case, with Tris gone, Mina reorganized the Aragonese contingent, or sixth battalion (first of Aragon). This was the real purpose of all of the trips into Upper Aragon during the past six months: to extend the influence of the Division eastward. Within a year Mina would have two battalions operating in Aragon.

After the first surprise at Arlabán, the French had quickly retaliated in Navarre with stepped up police measures and punitive fines. This time around they could do nothing. In fact, with Wellington finally making threatening movements into Castile, the French were forced practically to evacuate Navarre. Only the troops under Abbé, increasingly locked into Pamplona, Tafalla, Tudela, and the border garrisons, remained. As a result, Mina achieved perfect control over much of Navarre at this time, even appearing in the outskirts of Pamplona, now isolated in a sea of insurgency, to taunt the garrison inside.[36]

In May the Division once again sought contact with the English. Mina's men were loaded down with prisoners from Arlabán, and a flood of new recruits made it imperative to obtain rifles and ammunition.

A drop was arranged at Zumaya, but as the Division headed through Guipúzcoa to the rendezvous, Mina learned that an artillery train—a prize too important to let go—would pass near to his position on its way to Vitoria. Before the Division could engage the convoy, however, the French used their cannon to punch holes in the infantry, and one ball struck Gregorio Cruchaga, crushing both of his hands. He was evacuated to an iron foundry hidden in the mountains of Aralar. Mina completed the mission at Zumaya, but by the time he returned Cruchaga had died of gangrene.[37]

Cruchaga, second in command of the Division, was probably a more capable field officer than Mina. He had been wounded several times as a result of his insistence on leading his men in bayonet charges. His loss was a blow to the morale of the men and of Mina. Even more important than his military talents was Cruchaga's prestige with the volunteers from Roncal, who formed much of the veteran core of the Division. It was Cruchaga who had kept the volunteers together at the worst times. When he died, the despair among the soldiers caused some to desert. It was imperative that someone comparable be found to replace him as quickly as possible. It is highly significant that Mina selected Juan José, Gregorio's brother, to fill the gap.

Juan José Cruchaga was only twenty-one years old, with no previous experience in the resistance. He had spent the war years up to then caring for the family's sheep in Roncal.[38] Mina only selected him because, as he admitted in his memoirs, Juan José looked more like his dead brother than any other member of the Cruchaga clan. This incident illustrates the degree to which leadership in the Division was still based on personality rather than military rank. Gregorio Cruchaga's power to lead men stemmed from his connections to Roncal and from his own personal aura. He had become a fetish to the men of the second battalion, ensuring their victory. Only another Cruchaga could serve as replacement.[39]

In late May the Division engaged the French in three minor actions around Santa Cruz de Campezo just across the border in Álava. In the last of these occurred an event that proved once again how discipline still depended on personal influence and how this dependence could cripple the insurgency in the event one of the leaders became injured. In a fight with 2,000 French troops from Álava, Mina received a serious bullet wound to the calf. As had occurred in the past when a commander fell in combat, the battle degenerated into another Iliadic struggle for the body of the fallen hero. Similar breakdowns had occurred in the battle of Tarrazona, when both Cruchaga and Mina had been wounded, as well as in the battle in which Cruchaga lost his life. After each such incident, the guerrillas seemed to lose direction, opening the way to defeat. The defeats at Belorado and Lerín occurred when Mina and Cruchaga were absent after serious injuries to one or both of them. This time too, although the Division was able to hold its ground and continue to operate in a limited way during the month of June, the guerrilla offensive stalled.[40]

While Mina recovered in the monastery of Irache, the guerrillas skirmished with the French on numerous fronts. The French forces in Pamplona numbered some 4,000 infantry and 500 horse at this time. In addition, garrisons had been reestablished or reinforced in Arriba, Caparroso, Irurzún, Lecumberri, Tafalla, and Tudela, and there were additional garrisons stationed along the French border in Burguete, Elizondo, Fuenterrabía, Irún, Maya, Orbaiceta, Roncesvalles, Santestebán, and Urdax. However, Abbé could not easily borrow troops from these garrisons. Those stationed in the Ribera were particularly important to the occupation, since they secured Abbé's supply route to the agricultural riches of the Ebro valley. The Ribera garrisons were also frequently Abbé's only source of intelligence from the rest of Spain. As a result of these constraints, the French could place no more than 4,000 men in the field at a time, and usually the columns sent out from Pamplona numbered closer to 2,000 men.[41] Thus, even during the period of Mina's convalescence, the French were unable to retake the offensive.

In comparison, the Division numbered about 8,000 men, all of them effectives, since intelligence, supplies, and other essential services were by now provided automatically by civilians. At full strength, each infantry battalion had 1,200 troops, and the cavalry about 800. This meant that a single battalion of war-hardened Navarrese could almost match the less experienced troops normally fielded by Abbé. Accordingly, though they still lacked Mina to coordinate their actions, the battalions began to operate independently or in conjunction with companies borrowed from other battalions. During June 1812, the first, second, third, and fifth battalions were stationed in the far west, sometimes in Álava, sometimes in Estella, or along the Guipúzcoa border. These regions now became impassable to the French for long periods at a time. The third battalion with some of the cavalry beat off an attempt by a column of 2,000 French to requisition in the valley of Lana, a guerrilla stronghold of supply depots and safe houses near Estella. The fourth battalion patrolled the road between Pamplona and Roncesvalles, making communication with France difficult, isolating the garrisons inside Roncesvalles and Burguete for days at a time, and generally hampering requisitions in north-central Navarre. The sixth battalion, now on its feet in Aragon, began forcing the French garrisons there to remain inside their forts.[42] As a result, a whole range of Aragonese towns previously dominated by the French escaped their tax obligations for the first time. By June Benavarre, Barbastro, Tarrazona, Borja, and Jaca could no longer be taxed, and by the fall the list expanded to include Teruel, Daroca, Alcañíz, and Calatayud.[43]

Mina returned to action in the first week of July, taking half of his force to Vitoria, where he besieged the city and sealed Cafarelli's division inside, while other guerrilla units retrieved another shipment of weapons on the Biscay coast. The French in Vitoria actually possessed a slight superiority in numbers over the guerrillas, and they attempted to do battle in the plains outside the city. But by this time they were no match for the Division even in a regular battle. The French lost 300 killed in a "slaughter" that lasted five hours, before the French commander called his troops back into the city. It was the first time the people of Vitoria had seen a Spanish force defeat the enemy, and it brought the population to the walls for a view of the action.[44]

Mina now placed most of his troops in and around Puente la Reina in order to sever the tie between Pamplona and the Ribera. From Puente they could strike east to the Tafalla road, or west towards Estella, if Abbé attempted to pass that way toward Castile. During the rest of July Mina, who had reopened his wound in the battle outside Vitoria, did not lead the battalions in any actions. The sixth battalion in Aragon and the fourth stationed around Roncesvalles remained active, however. In July the Aragonese destroyed a detachment sent to escort a group of patriot sympathizers to prison in Huesca, and attacked another detachment from Huesca and two from Zaragoza, killing ninety-five of the enemy and capturing sixty, while suffering only twenty-eight casualties. The fourth battalion drove a column trying to requisition sheep in Valcarlos into the city of Roncesvalles, killing fifty-eight and taking eight prisoners. The fifth battalion was active around Vitoria and fought as far afield as Guipúzcoa. In September a new center of insurrection was born when men in Mina's customs service began to undertake their own military operations. In Baztán they killed sixty French and captured eighty-six in two separate ambushes.

The real focus of the insurgency, however, remained in Mina's camp in Puente. From August to December 1812 the French could hardly stir from Pamplona without attracting the attention of the guerrillas in Puente. The fighting drew ever closer to the capital, as the insurgents established control in all of the villages of the Pamplona basin. For the French, even to forage for food and fuel an hour from the city became a perilous undertaking.

On 10 August the first and third battalions besieged the garrison stationed in the fort known as the "Casa Colorada," located almost within gunshot of the city walls, killing forty-nine of the men inside. On 13 August in an action in Astráin Mina recovered seventy sacks of grain, which were redistributed to the populace. Three days later, a French column of 1,400 was forced to return to Pamplona before it could even begin to requisition. And on 19 August occurred what Mina called "Abbé's day of humiliation," when the first, second, third, and fifth battalions smashed a column of 3,200 men on the Tafalla road near Tiebas. Abbé had ordered grain from Tudela brought up to Tafalla so that he could personally escort it into the capital. Not only did he lose this cargo of grain and a shipment of weapons, he abandoned 320 dead on the field of battle. Hundreds more were wounded, including Chacón, the most famous of the turncoats. Chacón died and was buried in Pamplona soon after the battle.[45]

On 29 August the French attempted to cut wood in the Tajonar, a mountain just south of Pamplona. Abbé emptied the capital of his best troops to accomplish the job, but Mina heard of the project and attacked Abbé with three battalions and his cavalry. The guerrillas drove the French, minus both their firewood and the carts they had brought along to transport it, back to Pamplona, after inflicting forty-five casualties. To dramatize the changed balance of power in Navarre, Mina formed his battalions into columns, holding them within sight of the city walls for several hours, to taunt the garrison. In this and the other actions during July, August, and September, the guerrillas killed 1,144 and captured 213.

This pattern remained consistent until the end of November. The guerrillas caught Abbé five times trying to exact contributions in the Pamplona basin. On each occasion Abbé was forced back into the city with heavy losses. In October and November the French lost 887 killed and captured, and hundreds more filled the hospital beds in Pamplona. On the day after a particularly bloody battle on October 11 the hospitals in Pamplona admitted 548 wounded French soldiers. Yet Abbé had no choice but to continue making these sorties, since the garrison had been reduced to living practically from hand to mouth by the blockade. Since the previous December the guerrilla blockade had been growing daily more complete, so that peasants no longer dared even consider bringing supplies into the city. Finally, the only way to get food was to send out columns thousands strong, and even then they were not safe. It was particularly demoralizing, complained Abbé, for these requisition columns to return empty-handed, as they so often did, after battling all day with the guerrillas.[46]

In these months also the sixth battalion increased its hold on Aragon. In a series of ambushes against convoys and columns traveling between the northern garrisons, the Aragonese killed 139 of the enemy and captured 39. At the same time, the fifth battalion operating now in Guipúzcoa and several observation corps along the French border reported killing another 227 French soldiers and capturing 14.

In late November Mina passed into Aragon with elements of the first two battalions and part of the cavalry, raising the number of troops there to some 3,500 men.[47] In a month of operations he destroyed a column from Ayerbe, menaced the garrison in Huesca, and attacked another column outside of Jaca, killing 248 and capturing 72. During the entire year, from the capture of Huesca in January 1812, the guerrillas had killed or captured at least 5,500 French troops, not considering those incapacitated with wounds or illness.

The year 1813 was one of sieges and of operations conducted in combination with regular units under orders from Wellington or one of the other Allied commanders. As the Allied armies advanced, the French withdrew over a period of several months through the territory controlled by the Division of Navarre, making the presence of the guerrillas more important than ever, as they disrupted the retreat, pinned down thousands of troops that would otherwise have entered the fight against Wellington, and mopped up the last pockets of resistance in the Pyrenees. During the last several months of fighting, the altered circumstances forced Mina to abandon the strategies and tactics of the "heroic" phase of the guerrilla war in order to fulfill, none too brilliantly, the broader objectives of the Allied offensive.

The last full year of war in Navarre began with Mina's return from Aragon in January 1813. With five battalions and the cavalry again encamped around Puente la Reina, the insurgents were situated to reimpose a total blockade on Pamplona. Marshal Bessières from San Sebastián assessed the situation in a letter sent to the French minister of war. Supplies in Pamplona were running out and Abbé would soon have to abandon Navarre if he did not receive a reinforcement of at least 20,000 men. The army under Mina had become "so numerous and war-hardened that General Abbé is incapable of facing it, in spite of having under his orders a Division of some of the best of the Emperor's troops." (This is an exaggeration, since a good number of Abbé's men had been conscripted in December 1811.) Abbé's ability to administer the province was "absolutely nil," according to Bessières, and the wisest course of action would be to admit defeat in Navarre and withdraw.[48]

Yet, even after the Russian disaster, when troops of the Army of Spain had to be called back to France, Napoleon was still unwilling to go so far as to abandon Navarre. As a result, the French troops languishing inside Pamplona, though no match for the Division, were soon forced to attempt to break through the blockade in order to keep from freezing and starving. On 28 January Mina caught Abbé (now dubbed the "woodcutter" by the guerrillas) between Pamplona and Tafalla trying to gather fuel and food for the capital, and on 7 February they stopped another expedition in the town of Tiebas. In these actions, the guerrillas inflicted some 1,100 casualties.

The most important event from this period, however, was the acquisition by Mina of siege weapons. The English landed two large cannon at Zumaya on the coast of Guipúzcoa on 1 February. A small detachment of Mina's men spent the next week carrying the precious weapons over the most difficult and remote paths imaginable, while the bulk of the Division spread out in every direction to provide a security net for the operation. On 9 February the cannon were wheeled into place facing the fortifications in Tafalla. After Pamplona, Tafalla was the most important fortified place in Navarre. The French had spent years reinforcing the castle and turning a convent into a fort with fosses and outer walls. The garrison, usually consisting of 400 to 500 troops, was the linchpin of French communications between Pamplona and the rest of Spain. The thousands of lives Abbé had sacrificed in expeditions to Tafalla for supplies and intelligence provided evidence of the place's importance. Now, having just been defeated in the plains south of the city and forced to retreat behind the walls of Pamplona, Abbé could do nothing as the bombardment of Tafalla began.

After a day of shelling, a breach was opened in the outer wall of the compound, and Mina attempted to storm over it. Like Wellington, Mina found that his particular talents and those of his men were not suited to siege operations, and the fosse soon became filled with Navarrese dead. Mina called the action off and sent an embassy to suggest surrender. The French refused at first, since they thought Abbé would be coming to their aid at any moment. On the following day, however, they realized that there would be no rescue this time, so they surrendered. Of the defenders, 330 marched out to lay down their weapons, 52 were hospitalized, and 30 had died in the siege. The guerrillas destroyed the fortifications, including a castle that had been one of the jewels of medieval architecture in Navarre.

Mina quickly took his new weapons and 1,400 men to Sos, which possessed one of the strongest citadels in Aragon. The two twelve-pound cannon and two four-pounders destroyed part of the old town wall, and the guerrillas took Sos by storm. The fortress itself, however, was too strong for this artillery. A mine was blown, but even that had little effect, perhaps because the Division still had no engineers to conduct siege operations. For six days Mina blasted away at the stones of Sos fortress. On the seventh General Paris arrived from Zaragoza with 3,500 infantry and 250 cavalry. Strangely, instead of engaging the guerrillas, who were overmatched and had withdrawn to a height not far away, Paris simply evacuated the garrison. Thus, the purpose of the expedition was achieved even though the siege failed. Out of 160 men in the Sos garrison 32 died. During the evacuation Mina attacked Paris's rear guard, inflicting another 150 casualties.[49] It was now March. A second Aragonese battalion was being formed and another was begun in Álava—the seventh and eighth in the Division—so that Mina's army numbered around 10,000 men. From Aragon, Álava, Guipúzcoa, and Navarre came reports of engagements, not all glorious, but all costly to an occupation that was beginning to show signs of collapsing.

The most courageous action in March involved none of the battalions but rather a small observation team of fifteen men stationed in Vera de Bidasoa. The commander of this unit, Fermín de Leguía, decided he could storm the important coastal fortress of Fuenterrabía, located only a few miles from the French border, with his small following. On 11 March, using a grappling hook improvised from ropes and nails, Leguía and a companion scaled the walls of the fortress, captured the lone sentinel, and let the rest of their party in the front gate. Together they disarmed the remaining troops (most of the garrison slept in houses in town) and began to destroy the castle. The Navarrese spiked three large cannon, tossed 4,100 balls into the sea, and removed what they could of the smaller firearms for their own use before setting fire to the interior of the castle. By the time the flames and explosions woke up the French in the town of Fuenterrabía, it was too late either to catch Leguía or to stop the fire. The destruction of the fortress in Fuenterrabía by fifteen men was one of the most heroic events of the war. Even as Mina was learning to use regular battlefield tactics and to besiege forts with artillery, it remained characteristic of the guerrilla struggle that spontaneous, isolated acts were sometimes the most dramatic. During the first three months of 1813, the guerrillas had killed or captured 2,777 French troops.

Good news reached Spain in January 1813. Napoleon had met disaster in Russia. On 17 March 1813 Joseph abandoned Madrid for the last time. There ensued a long march of enormous and well-defended columns laden with the spoils of war and trailing a mob of afrancesados, the talented human booty whose loss was one of the most enduring wounds inflicted by France on Spain. The columns passed through Burgos and on to Vitoria, where Joseph planned his last stand against the Allies. The guerrilla strongholds in Aragon, Navarre, and the Basque country soon became overrun by thousands of French troops in retreat. General Clausel brought 13,000 infantry and 1,200 cavalry into Navarre, where they joined Abbé's 5,000 troops in pursuit of Mina. The size of these forces would seem to have fulfilled Bessières's requirements for the occupation of Navarre. Yet, even with over 19,000 troops, the French could not occupy the province.

In contrast to the situation after Bailén, when the province had also been inundated with retreating troops, there was no collapse of the resistance in April 1813. In fact, the first action by Clausel's men was an utter disaster. Clausel placed 5,000 soldiers in Lodosa, a large town on the Ebro River. Of these, 1,100 under Colonel Gaudin were dispatched a short distance north to Lerín (the site of the guerrillas' greatest defeat) in order to collect contributions. Mina, who had independently ordered a reunion in Lerín for the same day, found himself perfectly placed to surprise the French detachment.

Mina attacked Gaudin with the second battalion, elements of the sixth, and the cavalry. The troops remaining in Lodosa were neutralized by a cordon established to prevent anyone escaping Lerín to seek assistance. As a result, Mina annihilated Gaudin's column, killing 462 and capturing 635. Only three men, including Gaudin himself, succeeded in escaping on horseback. Even after they reached Lodosa, however, there was no attempt to pursue the Division and rescue the captives. The cowardice of the commanding officer in this engagement, the inability of the rest of Clausel's forces in Lodosa to join the fray, and the fact that 60 percent of a large column was forced to surrender to the guerrillas were signs of the waning military capacity of the French.

Wellington, who was rapidly advancing east through Castile, had asked Mina to occupy Clausel and prevent him from reinforcing Joseph Bonaparte. The Division was still outmanned, however, and could not remain united. To fulfill Wellington's request, Mina directed his battalions to operate separately. The first and second fought in Álava, the third, fourth, fifth, and eighth in Navarre, and the sixth and seventh battalions in Aragon. The French were again able to requisition widely. They even penetrated Roncal with 14,000 men, burning and looting, forcing Mina to evacuate his hospitals, and bringing back another contribution to Pamplona. In all this time, however, Clausel gained no glory in battle. The guerrillas were adept at avoiding Clausel's main force, and were deadly against detachments and stragglers. The Division killed or captured 414 enemy troops in late April and May, and Clausel's total losses in Navarre numbered some 2,500 men.

Clausel had seen enough. Already on 4 May he had written to Joseph complaining that he would need a minimum of 20,000 and perhaps as many as 25,000 troops—aside from those assigned to garrison duty— to defeat Mina. Realizing that in the present conditions he would not receive this level of reinforcement, he suggested, as Bessières had before, that Navarre be evacuated. "I see everything lost in Navarre," wrote Clausel. "[There is] no hope of success. I am going to abandon it."[50] He did not receive his wish until months later, so that he was still in

Navarre when the battle of Vitoria took place on 21 June. Mina had succeeded in occupying 19,000 troops that could have turned the tide against Wellington. Another 35,000 troops in Aragon had been similarly entertained both by the guerrillas of the Division and by those fighting under other commanders.[51]

After Vitoria, the French abandoned Tudela and Zaragoza, leaving behind a token force of 500 to 600 men inside the fort. Zaragoza would have to face another siege. Mina brought his troops up in front of the walls on 4 July, but was then forced to wait almost a month for artillery. Finally, in late July the bombardment began. On 2 August his cannon exploded powder inside the fortress, and the 405 French troops remaining alive surrendered. On 23 August the garrison at Mallén surrendered with the loss of forty-three men. San Sebastián and Pamplona were also besieged, the first surrendering on 17 October and the last on 31 October.

That fall the guerrillas began the sieges of Jaca and Monzón, the two least brilliant actions ever undertaken by the Division. A ninth battalion, the third in Aragon, was formed to help clear the last French troops from Spain. These troops were as successful as ever at punishing the French when they tried to requisition or pasture their animals outside of their compounds, but actually taking the remaining citadels was beyond their capacity.[52] Monzón did not surrender until 15 February 1814, and the Jaca garrison gave up two days later, after withstanding almost six months of blockade and a series of halfhearted assaults. In these sieges and in the other actions Mina was called upon to undertake, the French lost 1,206 killed and captured.

After a number of battles around Baigorry and St. Jean de Pie de Port, the last battle of the war was fought at Bayonne on 14 April. Four days later Wellington and Soult signed an armistice that brought an end to hostilities six years and two months after the attack on the Ciudadela of Pamplona. The war was not quite over, however, for Mina and the guerrillas.

Between 1808 and 1814, the French apparently destroyed the guerrilla movement in Navarre four times, only to see it reborn with greater strength than before. Eguaguirre and Gil were driven from Navarre in the fall of 1808, but were replaced by Javier Mina early in 1809. Javier's corso terrestre dissolved after Dufour captured its leader in March 1810. In turn, Francisco Espoz y Mina replaced Javier in the spring of 1810. Twice in the next two years, at Belorado and at Lerín, Mina's Division of Navarre was practically annihilated, but each time the guerrillas recovered quickly. After December 1812, Mina's guerrillas were strong enough to take over Navarre, Upper Aragon, and parts of the Basque provinces. What were the reasons for the resilience and ultimate success of the guerrilla movement in Navarre?

To explain the guerrilla victory it is not enough to consider the strengths of Mina and his men. It is also necessary to consider the weaknesses and errors of the French government, for the French made many political mistakes that ensured the continued hostility of the Navarrese peasants, without which the guerrillas of Navarre could not have survived.

The French failure in Navarre (and in Spain generally) stemmed in part from the personal inadequacies of French officers and soldiers. The men Napoleon sent to Spain between 1808 and 1814 were not inspired by any revolutionary impulse or ideal but by the promise of booty.[1] Napoleon regaled his servants with fiefs and endowments carved out of conquered lands, and by the time he took Spain, such rewards were an expected part of a systematic neofeudalism that generated its own momentum for further aggression. From the beginning, therefore, intervention in Spain went hand in hand with visions of plunder.[2]

French officials had been groomed to fit this imperial system. The military schools at Saint-Cyr and Fontainebleau trained good officers but not idealists, liberals, or even patriots.[3] Men like Soult and Victor were more concerned with robbery than with war. Their one object was to extract as much for themselves from the territories under their command in as little time as possible.[4] In Marshal Masséna's estimation it was the rapacity of the French generals that ensured the failure of the occupation. When the war was over, Napoleon, seconding Masséna's opinion, expressed regret at not having shot some of his generals, especially Soult, "the most voracious" of them all and a man who shipped some of Spain's most valuable art treasures back to France.[5]

Navarre had no Murillos to steal, but the French governors in Pamplona could still extract fantastic sums from the population, and they were creative when it came to finding ways of tapping the springs of popular hatred. The lower echelon officers employed as garrison commanders were, if anything, worse than the generals. Many had entered the service in the hope of amassing a fortune in foreign lands. These were the men who, implementing the day-to-day business of the occupation of Navarre, "rendered the French name hateful to the foreigner."[6]

Thus, French personnel were inadequate to the task of occupying Navarre. An even greater problem for the occupation, however, was the political program that the French tried to implement, especially in the Navarrese context. The military governors in Pamplona attacked seigneurialism, the church, and privilege in Navarre, just as French reformers did everywhere. In Navarre, however, such reforms alienated most people. Señoríos were unimportant, as seen in an earlier chapter, so attacks on the señorial regime were viewed as arcane. Above all, the French attack on the church and on regional privileges could not but generate opposition in Navarre, where "feudalism" in the form of the foral constitution was valuable to everyone and worth defending and where the population was wedded to the Catholic cult.

Defense of the Church

The French pursued their assault on the church with great consistency and vigor in Navarre. Of course, the looting by soldiers of churches and convents in Navarre was no different in kind from that long practiced

among the soldiery of Europe. One need only recall the excesses of the
Thirty Years' War or the looting of the Palatinate in 1688 by Louis XIV's
troops. What was new was the extent of the French anticlerical fury. The
anti-Catholic disposition of the generation of 1789 made the persecution
of the church seem reasonable and progressive to the French. In a place
like Navarre, however, where ecclesiastics had maintained much of their
power and prestige, such persecution was bound to generate resistance.

Indeed, French anticlericalism dramatically affected the public spirit
in much of Spain. As early as July 1808, Joseph complained to Napoleon that the troops' unbridled attacks on churches and convents were
making Spain ungovernable.[7] In later years, when Madrid was faced with
crushing deficits, Joseph became less fastidious in his dealings with the
church. In June 1809, Joseph shut down many religious orders and required most members of the regular clergy to reestablish residence in
their home parishes, where their movements could be monitored. The
property of religious orders was expropriated and sold at public auction.
Clerics caught preaching against the government or "in any way inciting
the people to disobedience" were taken to Madrid for military trials.[8]

The church in Spain was divided in its response to the French government. Much of the church hierarchy collaborated, and even many priests
and monks obeyed Napoleon when he reminded them that their mission
was wholly spiritual. However, the rigor of French policies against the
church forced many clerics to adopt a posture of active resistance to the
regime. For example, French troops burned or destroyed thirteen Capuchin convents in Andalusia, and by 1814 only a few properties remained
to the order. It is not surprising, therefore, to find that many Capuchin
monks lent assistance to the juntas in southern Spain. They had no other
employment.[9]

Politicians in the Central Junta were happy to accept any assistance
the church could provide, but at first they were unwilling to see the
clergy armed. Indeed, the government circulated instructions insisting
that clerics might resist so long as they stopped "short of spilling blood."
The bishops forbade members of the clergy to use weapons or to take
lives.[10] Despite such discouragement, however, some priests and monks
joined guerrilla bands in 1809. Finally, in December 1809, the Spanish
government decided to recognize this fait accompli and set about regu-
lating the clerical guerrilla movement, or Crusade. It was a sign of how

desperate the government was at the end of 1809 that it directed "all ecclesiastics, even parish priests, to consider taking up arms."[11]

Ironically, just as the government accepted the arming of the clergy, the Crusade began to wane in importance. During 1810 the government continued to receive reports from priests and monks in small formations like the "Exterminating Legion" in Aragon and the "Volunteer Defenders of the Faith and Nation" in Asturias. By the end of the year, however, most of these groups had been destroyed by the French, demobilized, or absorbed by more successful, secular guerrilla parties.[12]

What explains the resistance of some clerics and not others? In Galicia the clergy in the cities collaborated with the French, whereas the rural clergy favored the resistance.[13] This suggests that the fact of belonging to the clergy was not in itself what determined the likelihood of a cleric's resistance. Rather, it was the overall environment within which a particular cleric operated.

In most urban environments, for example, Madrid, Granada, and Málaga, most ecclesiastics actively supported the French regime. In the larger cities, especially in the South, the church had long since attached itself to the interests of the rich and had surrendered popular leadership, such as it was, to other urban elites. Indeed, the clergy in much of Andalusia had already lost its grip over the popular classes, and within a few generations its members were supplanted by the priests of anarchism.[14] The primary relationship of the church hierarchs to the people was often exploitative, since they were themselves members of the landed elite. It is understandable, therefore, that the clergy in such areas feared the French less than they feared the Spanish population. It is notable that the popular fury of crowds in the urban revolutions of 1808–9 vented itself indiscriminately against clerics, all of whom were perceived as part of the same oppressor class with nobles and French sympathizers. In general, therefore, clergy in urban areas, and in southern Spain generally, collaborated with the French more than clergy in rural areas and in the North; and this collaboration had nothing to do with the status of the clergy as such but with the environment in which they operated.

In Navarre, as in the rest of Spain, French troops behaved as if they were charged with the de-Christianization of the province. French soldiers lodged inside convents found they could express their hatred of the church and collect valuable booty at the same time without any fear of reprisal from their superiors. In July 1808, 150 French troops were housed and fed in the Convent of San Francisco in Tafalla, and when they left, all of the sacred images were smashed up, and the valuable silver objects used in the mass were missing.[15] This kind of episode was liable to occur wherever French troops passed in Navarre, since they routinely treated the buildings of the religious orders even before expropriation as if they already belonged to the state for use as barracks. For example, the Carmelite Convent in Sangüesa, used as a hospital and barracks, was destroyed during the war by French troops lodged there.[16]

Religious houses paid heavy taxes and fines to French, Spanish, and insurgent forces, and these alone were enough to ruin many orders in Navarre. For example, the Monastery of Fitero reported that it had paid 129,896 reales to Spanish forces in 1808 and during the last months of the war, and 175,558 reales to the French. In addition, it owed 254,418 reales for the repair of damages to its buildings. As a result of these costs, some convents and monasteries voluntarily sold off portions of their property during and immediately following the war in order to meet debts, and from these alienations some orders never quite recovered.[17]

The confiscations of capellanías, obras pías, and lands belonging to hospitals, initiated under Godoy, continued under the French. The city of Tudela and surrounding municipalities felt the disentailment more than anywhere else, though the impact was also great in and around the cities of Pamplona and Estella. Some rich individuals gobbled up enormous estates, but there were also dozens of smaller landowners who purchased one or two plots taken from the hospitals and lay religious organizations.[18]

The actual sales resulting from the suppression of the religious orders were of comparatively little importance in Navarre. Legislation in 1809 paved the way for precise inventories of the monasteries and convents, and detailed plans were made for their alienation. However, lack of confidence in the French regime's survival was such that only forty-four buildings and 150 acres were actually sold, mostly in Pamplona.[19]

This religious persecution profoundly disrupted the church in Navarre and generated hostility in a province that took pride in its historic devotion to Catholicism. Nevertheless, the Crusade in Navarre attained nothing like the development it did elsewhere. A few monks from Pamplona resident in Seville planned *partidas de cruzada*, but these never materialized. Clerics never formed a guerrilla party in Navarre nor contributed significantly to the corso or Division. The only clergymen in Mina's army were the chaplains. Miguel, the priest of Ujüé, played an independent role in the resistance, but he failed miserably during his brief stint as leader of the guerrillas. Moreover, his example was offset by the collaboration of other prominent Navarrese clerics in the Josephine government. Thus, the most successful guerrilla army in the peninsula, the Division of Navarre, was thoroughly secular. The case of Navarre stands as warning against arguing that it was the clergy that filled the ranks of the guerrilla armies, as some have.[20]

It is another matter, however, to consider the influence disgruntled priests exerted from their pulpits. The clergy in some Ribera towns aided the French in quelling rebellion, as has been seen. In most of Navarre, however, priests and monks supported the guerrillas, at least in theory, and suffered greatly at the hands of the French. While there is no sure way to quantify the ideological support lent by the clergy to the guerrillas, laws passed to prevent priests from speaking against the regime and the large number of priests arrested in Navarre argue for an important clerical role in fomenting resistance. After the regidores and alcaldes, it was the parish priests who suffered most at the hands of the French police. From village after village, especially in the Montaña, priests were among the first to be hauled away to Pamplona or France.[21] One author estimated that as many as 300 priests were either sent into exile or imprisoned during the war.[22]

The "patriotism" of the Navarrese clergy was rooted in its close integration into the rural environment. Observers agreed that clerics in the Montaña were "less aristocratic" than in the rest of Spain. Indeed, most priests were hardly distinguishable from the peasant proprietors among whom they lived. Priests usually had relations in their parishes, they understood the daily struggles of their parishioners, and they "knew how to speak the language" of the people.[23] In small villages, there was no alternative to clerical leadership, since the priest was likely to be one of only two literate individuals, the other being the notary. The priest had more experience with the outside world than any of his flock. He interpreted the actions and words of the government into the language of the people and easily assumed political direction in times of crisis. Although guerrilla-priests like Merino were the exception, the average parish priest was uniquely placed to foment rebellion and to inspire others to take up arms. In the War of Independence, as in the Carlist wars, priests were inspirational leaders willing to sacrifice themselves for their calling and their parishes.[24]

The French were deluded by vocal Spanish anticlericals into thinking that most Spaniards would support the expropriation of the church. However, it was one thing for Spanish *luces* in Madrid to write about such projects, it was another to put them into practice in a place like Navarre. The French found that when they closed convents in Navarre, the people responded by taking defrocked regulars into their homes, hardly the result desired.[25] The anticlerical legislation of Spanish liberals later in the century produced similar results and created the same popular opposition. The clerics of Navarre were the "spiritual chiefs" of the land, and even if they did not become the "political chiefs," as Desdevises thought they did, they nevertheless served to arouse popular sentiment against the French.[26]

Despite all of these considerations, it is doubtful that defense of religion, by itself, motivated the people of Navarre to join the resistance. Nor is it self-evident that the Navarrese needed much spiritual encouragement from their pastors to take up arms. The French had damaged most people in material ways that allowed the resistance in Navarre to dispense with religious justifications. In the language used by the diarists and chroniclers of the war in Navarre, the religious theme came up less than the defense of national and provincial rights and far less than issues of personal freedom and economic survival. The preface to the account given by the third regiment of the Division of Navarre speaks of the "small but loyal" kingdom of Navarre, "constant" and "faithful" to its sovereigns. It parades the "privileges and fueros" as "proof" of Navarre's historical bravery and devotion to its kings. And it dwells on the physical and financial suffering of individuals. But it never mentions the defense of religion.[27] The text left by the second regiment speaks more specifically of loyalty to the person of Ferdinand VII and generally about the defense of the nation, but only mentions religion as an aside.[28] Similarly, the account left by Iribarren, the commander of the Division's cavalry, dwells on the qualities of the Navarrese, but only mentions personal, provincial, and national goals, never religious ones.[29]

The only person who seems to have placed defense of religion high on the list of motives for the resistance was Andrés Martín, but he was a priest and a chaplain in the Division, and even he intoned the crusading spirit in a perfunctory, formulaic way, while he seemed most sincere when writing of the "noble" and "warlike" people of Navarre.[30] Mina explained the motives of his soldiers and supporters in entirely unideological terms. According to Mina the main reason for the French failure to gain adherents in Navarre was "the exorbitant contributions apportioned to the towns and the brute force used to extract them."[31]

Although priests and monks played less of a military role in Navarre than in other provinces and religious ideals did not figure as highly in the Navarrese resistance as they perhaps did for the national politicians or followers of the Crusade, this does not mean that religious motives were absent in Navarre nor that priests and monks did not play a part in the resistance. We know from specific examples that they did. What it means, rather, is that French outrages to religion were not sufficient by themselves to account for the guerrilla movement. Other factors must have been involved. Taking up the leads left to us by Mina and the military chronicles, we must consider the other ways in which the French turned civilians into enemies.

Defense of the Nation and Fueros

Historians traditionally consider nationalism and loyalty to the person of Ferdinand VII, even more than religious sentiment, to be the main inspirations behind the Spanish resistance. The ease with which Napoleon turned Württembergers against Swabians and Bolognese against Romans within the German and Italian "nations," highlighted for contemporaries the degree of national unity with which Spain responded to the French invasion. It became commonplace, especially inside Spain, to point to this contrast as the basis for the Spanish success against Napoleon.

This patriotic view was expressed in the ultraliberal newspaper, the *Semanario Patriótico*, in October 1808. "If the nations France has assaulted in its delirium had truly been nations," wrote the poet and editor Quintana, "they would have easily contained France: the French installed a depraved and corrupt government in Spain, and we devoured it." Napoleon's international crusade could have no appeal, the argument ran, inside a country like Spain with a highly developed sense of national identity.[32]

Certainly, the circumstances of Ferdinand's deposition and the treachery of the occupation were enough to injure the pride and focus the national awareness of Spaniards. That pride and identity had been developed over many centuries. Spain's history of expansion and self-definition against the Moors and the people of America, followed by the traumatic experience of decline and defeat at the hands of the northern powers, make it possible to speak of a well-developed sense of nationalism in Spain even before the Napoleonic invasion. Of course, competing regional loyalties remained as strong as ever, but the national separatism of the Basques and Catalonians and the federalist movement in other regions attained full force only toward the end of the nineteenth century. Thus, even in collaborationist Barcelona, the French experienced nothing like the enthusiastic reception they had in, for example, Milan.

Nevertheless, if a sense of national outrage is to be entertained as an explanation for the resistance, it remains to answer why the Navarrese were more nationalistic than the people of Barcelona, Granada, and other locations where the resistance was weak. The Navarrese themselves claimed that they were by nature the greatest patriots in Spain, but for historians such a position cannot be accepted at face value. It is possible, however, to maintain that special circumstances in Navarre or peculiar actions taken by the French in Navarre generated unusually intense feelings of loyalty to Spain, to the Bourbon monarchy, and, above all, to Navarre itself.

In the first place, Navarre's position on the frontier with France may indeed have lent a particular edge to national sentiments in the province. Peter Sahlins has argued, from his study of Cerdañá, that nationalism is sometimes invented in border regions before it is established in the metropolis.[33] In Navarre, even more than in the Catalonian borderlands, people developed a strong and precocious national identity, both as Navarrese and as Spaniards. Navarre maintained commercial, cultural, and linguistic ties with the French Basque provinces, but there was never any question that the people of Navarre were oriented toward Spain. Thus, in times of national disintegration, Navarre never experienced anything like the popular, separatist revolts in Catalonia in 1640, in Granada in 1648, and throughout Andalusia in 1651. Nor had there been plots like those hatched by the Duke of Medina Sidonia to create a separate kingdom in Andalusia in 1641, or by the Duke of Hijar to take Aragon out of the Spanish union in 1648. In the eighteenth century the separatist movement that found support in the Basque provinces made little headway in Navarre, as indeed Basque separatism in the twentieth century has found little resonance among the Navarrese. Similarly, the federalism of the nineteenth century that as early as 1809 had caused a governmental breakdown in Andalusia passed over Navarre. Even the "rebellion" of the Navarrese in the First Carlist War, far from constituting a threat to the territorial integrity of Spain, had as its expressed purpose the reconquest of Castile for the "legitimate" Spanish monarch and the "true religion." Thus, within the Spanish nation, it is indeed possible to identify Navarre as one of the most fervently loyal provinces.[34]

Navarre remained loyal to Spain partly because Madrid was pledged to uphold Navarre's fueros. The importance of these local privileges in the economic and political life of the province has already been discussed in a previous chapter. Navarre had much to be pleased with in its position inside the Spanish state, so that the defense of that state also implied the defense of the Kingdom of Navarre and of the merindad, valley, and village. Setting out from this point of view, an even stronger argument can be made for the importance of nationalism, broadly understood, as a principal motivating force in the insurgency.

The French armies that occupied northern Navarre in 1794, found, it is true, enthusiastic support among certain sectors of the community in Pamplona. But then the regime of Charles IV and Godoy had proved hostile to Navarrese interests. To deal with mounting deficits in the 1790s the Spanish government had tried to circumvent Navarre's exemptions from taxes and customs duties. It is understandable, therefore, that some people in the city of Pamplona might have perceived little to choose between Revolutionary Paris and autocratic Madrid.

By contrast, after March 1808 most Navarrese viewed Napoleon with suspicion and attached all of their hopes to Ferdinand, a perceived supporter of regional privileges. Where the French had found some collaborators in the 1790s, they found enemies in 1808. Even in Pamplona, Mina could count on more fifth columnists inside the city than the French could count adherents.[35] The untried Ferdinand was deposed so quickly that he had no opportunity to alienate public opinion and disappoint the millenarian expectations attached to his name. There was no question that people preferred the unknown quantity of Ferdinand to the certainty of imperial violence at the hands of the Bonapartes.

Moreover, the comparatively subtle diplomacy of the Directory had been replaced under the empire by brute force. The imperial regime in Navarre had made it clear from the beginning that the region would have no say in its political future and that the slightest disobedience would be met with Mongolian justice. From the time of Bayonne, it had been understood that France would strip Navarre of its traditions of autonomy and privilege. Indeed, Napoleon planned to annex Navarre together with Catalonia, parts of Aragon, and the Basque provinces. Some Spaniards were already aware of these designs. Miguel Azanza, for one, warned Joseph as early as June 1808 that any change in Navarre's foral constitution would be dangerous.[36]

In fact, the French attack on the fueros had already begun even as the Bayonne assembly got under way. The foral government first lost its judicial functions. In the month of June 1808 conflicts between civilians and French soldiers caused General D'Agoult to usurp the prerogatives of the Royal Council and the court in order to try suspects deemed dangerous to the French regime in a military tribunal.[37]

Representative government lasted a few months longer. The Diputación, after a period of indecision, fled Navarre at the approach of the Spanish armies in August 1808. D'Agoult immediately appointed new deputies, but they never sat. Some, like the deputy from Lumbier, emigrated, while others provided personal excuses for failing to respond. The Diputación then ceased to exist until it was revived as an unrepresentative, appointive body by Reille. The Cortes was, of course, never allowed to sit.[38]

The French also curtailed the powers of the viceroy. Joseph protected the viceroys' prerogatives as long as he could in order to have a counterweight to the military governors. Individuals he dismissed, but he protected the institution. The Marqués de Vallesantoro was deported to France for disloyalty in September 1808, but Joseph immediately sent a replacement in Francisco Javier Negrete, who served until April 1809, when the Duke of Mahón succeeded him. Mahón, a French-born military careerist, remained in the post until 1810, when the last vestiges of the viceregal regime were eliminated by Napoleon. On 8 February 1810 the emperor established an autonomous government in Navarre (and in other northern Spanish provinces) preparatory to full annexation. The real power in Navarre was henceforward the military governor. Indeed, this had always been the case, and the measures of 8 February merely formalized an already existing situation. This was the condition of Navarre when the city of Pamplona surrendered to Spanish forces in October 1813.

Through these rough dealings with their traditional institutions, the

Navarrese became aware that their homeland was scheduled for annexation to France. As early as the summer of 1809 the French were forced to deny rumors that Napoleon planned to annex Navarre, a sign of how serious such rumors had become. The stories continued, however, as true stories often do. In October 1810 Napoleon warned Cafarelli in Biscay and Reille in Navarre to keep the plans for annexation secret, but the ultimate purpose of the French could no longer be doubted.[39] In February 1812 Catalonia became a French department. By then it was evident that a similar fate awaited Navarre and that only military difficulties (by 1812 the French barely held on to Pamplona) delayed annexation.

There can be no doubt that people in Navarre perceived separation from Spain as ruinous. Navarrese officials, by and large, resisted efforts to break with Madrid and many were dismissed or transferred to other posts as a result. Officials in Pamplona pleaded with Joseph not to abandon Navarre. The Navarrese, they said, wished to remain within the Spanish monarchy and could be "of the greatest use" to Madrid. The people had on the whole shown "submission, love, and loyalty" to Joseph and should not be punished for the crimes of a few "small armed bands."[40] It was this "unequivocally pro-Spanish attitude of the foral corporations of Navarre" that distinguished them from officials in, for example, Catalonia.[41] That Navarrese chose to sacrifice their careers in order to preserve Navarre's independence was ominous for the French occupation.

Afrancesados in Navarre understood how unpopular they would be if Navarre was annexed to France. They were placed in an awkward position by the February 1810 decrees and by the subsequent annexation scare.[42] Joseph sent Miguel Azanza to Paris for the emperor's wedding, but his presence was also designed to give him, in Joseph's name, a last chance to convince Napoleon that carving Spain up would cause his supporters to jump ship.[43] Both Joseph and Azanza understood that autonomist feelings in Navarre were too strong to be decreed out of existence and that concessions to national pride would have to be made if there was to be any hope of pacification. By contrast, in Catalonia the decrees of February met little armed opposition, and it was for this reason that Napoleon felt safe enough to go ahead with annexation of that province in 1812.

The Navarrese were devoted to their autonomy within the Spanish monarchy out of immediate self-interest as well as out of patriotic sentiment. The economic interests of the Navarrese, particularly of the Montaña, tied them to the preservation of the decentralized Bourbon monarchy. The enormous value to Navarre of a separate customs border, control of taxation, and exemption from various services and contributions has already been discussed. The French, of course, sought to curtail these very privileges. They had the same fiscal reasons for doing so as Godoy, and they achieved similarly poor results.

In October 1809 Joseph abolished the thirty-three internal customs barriers along the borders of Navarre, at the same time promising to enforce penalties against running contraband.[44] This measure promised to undermine an important sector of the economy. It spelled the loss of enormous revenues from customs. In addition, Pamplona's fair in July as well as its weekly market were based in large part on the resale of French merchandise. The economies of Roncal, Salazar, and the other Pyrenean valleys were locked into the export of raw wool to France and the importation and trade in cheap French textiles and other manufactures. Finally, the enormous contraband industry in Navarre was threatened with destruction by the new laws. These factors no doubt lent an edge to the foralism and patriotism of the Navarrese in these zones.

In the Ribera people had always been more ambivalent about the value of the fueros. It had long been argued that the Ribera stood to profit more from access to the Castilian market than from autonomy. Even Ribereños, however, must have reacted with horror at the prospect of becoming, in an age of costly transportation, a southern appendage of highly developed France. It did not help the Ribera to have the fueros abolished if it remained cut off from nearby Castilian markets.

Everyone could agree also on the advantages of Navarre's limited military obligations toward Madrid. While in theory, Navarre under French rule was subject to conscription equally with other military districts, the French recruited very few soldiers in Navarre and never took the step of impressing men who might have been guerrilla or rebel sympathizers. The repeated rumors of French conscription, however, demonstrated the sensitivity of the Navarrese on this subject.

Every French effort to reform society in Navarre created more enemies than friends. The seizure of church land, for example, brought no advantages in a province where members of the clergy, far from monopolizing land and wealth, were perceived as good neighbors. Similarly, the abolition of señoríos created no groundswell of support for the French.

Above all, the abolition of "feudalism," which included Navarre's foral rights and privileges, caused chagrin in a people who had thrived for centuries in the interstice left by the weak absolutism emanating from Madrid. Perhaps more than all of these factors, however, it was France's naked exploitation of Navarre to feed the occupation that created a climate favorable for guerrilla warfare.

The Plunder of Navarre

Tax exemptions were probably Navarre's most valuable foral privilege, but of course such exemptions ended as soon as French troops occupied the province. The French requisitions of food, labor, animals, and transport that began in the spring of 1808 generated immediate unrest. In the years that followed, requisitions and taxes grew and threatened to ruin the economy. Sometimes the connection between French fiscal pressure and resistance was obvious. The revolt of Roncal was triggered by an attempt to requisition sheep, and in towns like Ujüé the French had to abandon attempts even to register the granaries, much less collect grain, due to the opposition encountered. Indeed, it is possible—leaving aside any considerations of offended religious, nationalist, or provincial feeling—to explain the fervor of the resistance in Navarre as a response, at least in part, to unsupportable French exactions. So to complete the picture of French political failure in Navarre, it is necessary to look more closely at the effect of taxes and requisitions.

Thanks to the excellent work by Joseba de la Torre, we know that the French regime collected over 152 million reales in taxes and requisitions during the period 1808 to 1814.[45] This figure represented over 40 percent of Navarre's normal five-year agricultural and industrial output.[46] And times were not normal. The effects on productivity of five years of executions, sackings, burnings, losses of livestock, and other depredations, though impossible to measure, must have been great. In a province accustomed to receiving more inputs from Madrid than it sent out, such a burden, impossible to maintain over the long haul in any case, appeared criminal.

It is no surprise, therefore, to find peasants flocking to Mina's standards in the winter of 1811 when he began to operate again after the disaster at Lerín. For one thing Mina could provide protection from French tax collectors and requisition parties, especially after December 1811. Thus, less than 29 percent of the "Territorial Contribution" of

1811–12 was ever collected by the French, a figure that fell to 10 percent for the contribution of 1812–13.[47]

It is not possible to arrive at any global figure for the value of requisitions collected by Mina's Division and by the other guerrilla parties in Navarre. However, partial data, compiled by Joseba de la Torre, do make it possible to compare the weight of French and guerrilla exactions in certain locations.[48] The evidence leads to several important conclusions. First, in the 116 towns and villages for which accurate data are available, the French collected more than seven times as much as the guerrillas. Moreover, only 7 percent of the value of guerrilla requisitions was collected by force, without receipts, while 93 percent of the value of French requisitions was carried out by force.

A second conclusion is that the guerrillas had almost no presence in the Ebro valley, which contributed only 430,000 reales worth of goods to the guerrillas, while supplying the French with some 9 million reales worth. In fact, the guerrillas were never on good terms with Tudela, which was considered pro-French. Mina sacked it in 1809. Durán (the Aragonese guerrilla) sacked it again in 1812. Mina even held three Tudelan officials hostage in 1812 to punish the city for paying French taxes.[49] In contrast, the guerrillas collected some 3 million reales in specie in the Montaña. The value of French exactions in the Montaña came to 17 million reales.

Third, the importance of Estella to the insurgents stands out. Eight percent of the Division's resources originated in the city of Estella. The French also milked Estella for over 7 million reales in specie.

Fourth, the French requisitioned most heavily in areas close to Pamplona or to some other large city, garrison, or major road. For example, Villava, a small town in 1808 and today practically a suburb of Pamplona, contributed 57,000 reales to the French and only 4,376 reales to the guerrillas. The upper Arga and Erro valleys, on the road between Pamplona and Roncesvalles, contributed more to the French than to the guerrillas, and the small village of Iriberri, off the Pamplona-Irurzún road, gave more per capita to French requisition parties than almost any other locale for which records exist.[50]

Fifth, the guerrillas were generally more successful collecting rations and supplies in small villages, while the French dominated larger towns. Even Sangüesa, an insurgent town of some importance for most of the war, contributed twenty-four times as much to the French as to the

Division.[51] The guerrillas drove out the garrison and tried on more than one occasion to defend the city, but its size made it worthwhile for the French to send in large columns periodically to extort contributions and taxes. Only in small and remote villages did the Division truly have the upper hand in terms of its ability to tax the population. Zugarramurdi gave six times as many rations to the guerrillas as to the French and had no money requisitioned. Sada, in the mountains west of Sangüesa, and the valleys of Aézcoa, Ulzama, and Atez also gave much more to the guerrillas than to the French.[52] Evidently, the "congenial sea" that supplied Mina's troops lay primarily in remoter regions of the merindades of Pamplona, Estella, and Sangüesa. In such areas the dispersion of the population made it impossible for the French to requisition effectively, allowing the guerrillas to establish themselves in the vacuum.

Some areas contributed heavily to both sides. The valley of Echauri, for much of the war the home base of the fourth battalion and a favorite refuge for the insurgents, held receipts for nearly 836,000 reales contributed to the French.[53] Yet, during 1810 and from late 1811 on, the guerrillas succeeded in isolating Echauri from Pamplona, and Mina received 587,000 reales in rations from Echauri. Over the course of the war Echauri gave the French 466 reales per capita and the guerrillas 327 reales. Considering the region's proximity to Pamplona, this is a small disparity, indicating the success of the insurgency in the area.[54]

Finally, there was no simple equation between the level of misery created by French exactions and the enthusiasm of the population for the insurgency. For example, no one from hard-hit Iriberri volunteered to serve with the Division, and heavy requisitions in Corella and Tudela did not lead to any special resistance there.[55] On the contrary, the constant French presence in such places made it difficult for young men to join the insurgency. In contrast, the communities that contributed most men to the guerrilla war—like Echauri, Lumbier, Roncal, and Ujüé—escaped the inroads of French requisition parties at least part of the time and certainly after late 1811, by which time Mina had acquired the strength to protect what was his.

The answer to any particular area's enthusiasm is clearly a product of a more complex set of factors, of which the economic impact of the French occupation was just one. French pressure and violence elicited different responses—including enrollment in the guerrilla army—depending on the internal structure of the community affected. The next section of this chapter analyzes the way two communities, the village of Echauri in the Montaña and the city of Corella in the Ribera, reacted to the fiscal demands of the French government.

The Differential Response of Echauri and Corella

Under the Bourbons the Diputación had been empowered to raise money. The actual job of assessing and collecting taxes, though, was decentralized. The Treasury in Pamplona assigned an amount owed by each merindad, then the merindades determined the contribution owed by each municipality, but it was up to the communities to draw money from a combination of municipal assets and taxes. These arrangements left the real power of taxing in the hands of ancient corporate structures: the merindad and commune. The French regime did not have the time or the power to alter this system completely. It sought to fill municipal offices with its own creatures, but the threat of guerrilla reprisals made this difficult. Except in the larger cities, therefore, the old community councils still had the task of dividing the tax burden among the people as they saw fit.

Money could be raised through proportional taxes, head taxes, taxes on consumption, loans from individuals or the parish, or the alienation of community assets. It all depended on what interests were represented in the community council. As described in chapter 2, the structure of these councils differed widely between the Montaña and the Ribera. It is now time to see how these councils raised taxes in actual practice.

Echauri, like most communities in the Montaña, at first sought to meet French demands by tapping its normal revenues, which were sizable.[56] But these were not ordinary times, and by September 1808 Echauri was already taking special measures. One way of raising money was to alter the system by which public services were rented. Instead of one-year arrangements, concessions could be leased for two or three years, resulting in immediate windfalls to the community. Echauri also diverted to the French the proceeds from a portion of public land normally used to pay the tithe to the parish priest. The woods in the Sierra de Andía were logged to raise money, and portions of the enormous but relatively infertile community lands known as the *baldíos* were leased to individuals. They could be expected to produce a few normal harvests before losing their vitality, but, in the meantime, the community could at least collect a few years' rent.[57]

All of these operations taken together still created only a paltry breathing space. Soon Echauri had to turn to loans to raise required money. The community raised a forced loan of 20,000 reales from its parish church.[58] Echauri also borrowed money and grain from neighboring villages and wealthy landowners. It took many years to recover from these debts. As late as 1828 Echauri still owed 8,500 reales from the war.[59]

The impact of all of these forced loans and taxes was less devastating to individuals than might be supposed. Only some fifty privately held acres changed hands during the war. Moreover, there were no special winners or losers in this minor land shuffle, so that it is safe to say that the war years did not alter landholding patterns in Echauri.[60] Individuals preserved their private fortunes in Echauri because the government found ways to buffer residents, especially the poor, from contributions. First, the valley began to assess taxes proportional to income, something that was not a normal practice. This made it less likely that the poor would have to sell off their land to meet obligations, and indeed the biggest landowners had to sell more property than they were able to buy in the war years.[61]

Echauri, like municipalities throughout Navarre, also had large corporate holdings that could be used to pay taxes. Normally, municipal and communal property was untouchable. In the entire decade from 1797 to 1807 Echauri sold only two plots of municipal land, each under one-eighth of an acre, to two landowners. This was a pattern common to most communities in the Montaña.[62] Then, from 1807 to 1822 Echauri sold 381 acres of communal and corporate property. Still, this equaled only 6 percent of the privately held land in the valley. Moreover, Echauri saw to it that the land was sold in small plots at prices affordable by dozens of people. Indeed, the records show that eighty individuals made 116 purchases from sixty-eight different sellers. Thus, even the pressure of war did not cause any significant concentration of landownership.[63] The open council of Echauri could not sell assets to the richest residents or to outsiders, and it could not get away with regressive or heavy personal taxes. When faced with outside aggression, Echauri, because of the relatively democratic nature of its local government, sought collective solutions to its problems.

In contrast, the city fathers of Corella sought to protect their own interests and to shift the weight of the occupation onto the poor. Judging from the number of land sales, the war seems to have caused no more disruption to private fortunes in Corella than it did in Echauri.[64] While global figures on the amount of land changing hands in Corella are lacking due to poorer record-keeping by the notaries, the examples of land sales that do exist suggest that big landowners released small parcels, probably the minimum required to cover their tax obligations. There seems to have been no great change in landholding patterns.

This is not surprising, since wealthy landowners made up the municipal government in Corella, and they would do anything to protect their fortunes. There was no chance that they would tax wealth, as occurred in Echauri. On the contrary, the city fathers' first resort was to an excise tax on the most common items of consumption, a procedure Echauri never employed. Nor was it likely that the city council would tax rents or income, against the wishes of the men who elected it. Instead, Corella's officials taxed all households regardless of income.[65]

Corella, like other municipal corporations in the larger cities, also chose to dip early and frequently into the reserve of community properties, selling them at auction to whomever could afford to buy. As early as July 1808 the city decided it was justified in alienating its assets, "however privileged they may be," in order to pay the French. In 1810 the city began systematically to sell off its properties, both those long since assigned to municipal use and those leased out of the commons.[66]

Dealing with the debt crisis in this manner was profoundly inegalitarian. Like taxes on items of consumption, it made the landless poor and smallholders pay the bill. In most of Navarre, common lands were still generally used in common.[67] As a result, small owners and landless laborers, who used the commons for firewood and fodder, stood to lose most from the sale of common lands, while the same men who were eagerly snatching up the seized church lands were glad to see communal properties on the block. Popular displeasure with the sales could be delayed for several years, until the full impact of the loss of commons and the services that could no longer be provided by the city government began to be felt. Besides, the powerless proletariat in Corella was not capable yet of threatening the social order.

The men who framed the plan for the alienation of municipal property drafted by Corella in 1810 said they were acting in the interests of the community as a whole. It is not just that they wanted to raise quick money to pay the French, nor were they simply after community lands for private gain. In the fashion of the political economists, they also claimed that their new possessions would lead to a more prosperous commercial agriculture, and that this would ultimately enrich the entire community.[68] This physiocratic idyll was not put to the test immediately, because the sale of the commons was cut short by the ouster of the French a few years later. Still, it is significant that the project was attempted. Rich Corellans had a vested interest in French success, for they knew that only under a French government could they proceed with the spoliation of the community's assets. Is it any wonder that Corella remained loyal to the French or at least passive during the war?

Corella's plan was more fully realized in other cities. Wherever the communal and municipal lands were alienated, the result was poverty, depopulation, and social violence, as exemplified in the case of Olite. Beginning in the War of Independence, Olite's town fathers sold off practically all of the city's lands to pay off war debts. A few big landowners, who promptly removed themselves from the city and became absentee lords, came to control the local economy, and as a result, Olite lost population during the nineteenth century. It was only after a long and bitter struggle that the community recovered some of its assets.[69]

Communities like Echauri possessed both the means to resist the French and a social configuration conducive to solidarity against the enemy. Municipal councils that governed communities in the Montaña represented their populations. There was little scope for popular displeasure with a local government in which all heads of households had a role. Indeed, one of the regidores of Echauri worked for Mina and was ultimately executed for it by the French. Communities like that in the valley of Echauri produced the largest number of guerrillas, as will be shown, supplied the food, clothes, and other requirements of the Division, and became the home bases for Mina's regiments. They were able to do so because solid community institutions acted systematically to shelter individuals from the French regime.

In contrast, the city of Corella, with its closed municipal government, collaborated openly with the French. The notables of Corella eagerly participated in the plunder of the nationalized church and municipal lands, and they hoped for nothing so much as the survival of a regime favorable to their material interests.[70] The enormous fiscal demands of the government in Pamplona served to divide rather than unite Corella, as the city corporation passed the cost of the occupation on to laboring folk through taxes on food and basic necessities. The result was that the people were crushed under the combined weight of the occupation and the collaboration of local elites. Resistance in such circumstances, always difficult anyway in an urban setting, became nearly impossible. Taking up arms in Corella had to be, in effect, a personal choice, bordering on social banditry, rather than a community affair, underwritten by municipal authorities and local elites.

Who Were the Guerrillas?

There is a great deal of evidence to suggest that the guerrillas were men from the Montaña. Most of the battles were fought in the Montaña. In times of trouble, the guerrillas sought safety in the Pyrenees or in the mountains of Sangüesa and Estella. And the data on requisitions and taxes indicates that the French controlled the cities of the Ribera and the communities lying on major arteries, while the guerrillas controlled the rural spaces of the Montaña, where the French could penetrate only for brief, punitive raids, without ever establishing credible government.

There are several additional sources for testing this hypothesis. First, the narratives left by the guerrillas together with some French proclamations and letters revealed the identity and background of a certain number of volunteers. Second, the French police generated some sketchy data on volunteers and their families. The third and most important source of information about the guerrillas is the set of records left by communities about their involvement in the war.[71] Considered together, this evidence strongly supports the notion that the guerrillas were mainly from the Montaña.

When the war ended, the Diputación in Pamplona solicited each community for responses to the following questions. Who joined the guerrillas? Who died at the hands of the French? Who was imprisoned? According to the available data, 3,477 men from all Navarre volunteered to fight either with Eguaguirre, Javier Mina, Francisco Espoz y Mina, or one of the other bands. Clearly, in six years of war, the number of guerrillas from Navarre was much higher. In fact, since only 40 percent of the communities surveyed by the Diputación actually responded, the data are incomplete. Nevertheless, by handling the data carefully, we can attempt to create a profile of the volunteers.

Two observations about the way the records are skewed must be mentioned. First, the records do not tell us anything about the Alavese,

Aragonese, or Guipúzcoans who fought under Mina. There were five "foreign" battalions—Basques and Aragonese—in the Division at war's end. These battalions formed about half of the final strength of the Division, though some became active only at the very end of the war. Thus, the records do tell us a great deal about the core battalions: the first, second, third, and fourth, composed of veteran Navarrese troops.

Second, and more significant, the data are not complete even for Navarre. In Pamplona, 60 percent of the municipalities responded, accounting for an equal proportion of the population. In Estella the analogous figures were 46 percent and 62 percent. Sangüesa and Tudela trailed behind, with 22 percent of the communes (44 percent of the population) reporting in Sangüesa, and 30 percent of the communes (42 percent of the population) reporting in Tudela. Olite supplied the least information of all, since only 19 percent of the municipalities (accounting for 31 percent of the population) completed the surveys.

It is important to consider some of the reasons for these partial returns. Although only 40 percent of the communes in Navarre responded, they represented 52 percent of the total population. This indicates that the data are systematically skewed toward larger communities, which tended to be more faithful in completing and returning the forms.

Some communities probably failed to comply with the survey because there was nothing to report or because a full account would have shown that the community had failed to contribute significantly to the resistance. This may explain the lack of data for Corella, Tafalla, Vera, and a number of other large towns that were almost constantly subjected to French control. Conversely, the epic accounts left by Estella, Ujüé, Roncal, and some of the other towns most involved in the war were certainly inspired by local pride.

At the same time, however, the valleys of Burunda and Ergoyena, among other areas that we know from the narrative sources to have been heavily committed to the guerrillas, also failed to report, leaving us with a serious underestimate for the merindad of Pamplona. Even more serious, the valley of Ibargoiti, including Monreal and Mina's own village of Idocín, together with the entire eastern half of the Pamplona basin, including Otano and Badostáin, did not leave any records. These lacunae are certainly troubling, since we know that the area was at the heart of the insurgency. This region gave birth to Javier, Mina, the Gorriz brothers, and Andrés Martín, among others in the Division. The totals for the merindad of Sangüesa would be much higher if a complete set of data for the area was available.

It may be that some communities failed to respond to the questions of the Diputación out of fear. The Restoration government did not look kindly on the guerrillas, especially on those who had shown themselves too devoted to the Constitution of 1812. This might explain the lack of information about Ibargoiti, since it is likely that many of the volunteers from Mina's home followed their leader in his attempt to overthrow the Restoration and restore constitutional government in 1814. Unable to follow him into exile, these volunteers may have wished to remain anonymous. If this occurred, it would help explain the lack of information on areas we know to have been guerrilla strongholds.

With these distortions in mind, it is still possible to glean a few conclusions from the data. In the merindad of Pamplona, 3 percent of the surveyed population fought with Mina. The highest percentages of involvement occurred in villages just west and north of the city of Pamplona, in the region of Echauri and Juslapeña. The merindad of Estella also contributed 3 percent of the population surveyed to the insurgency, with one village, Guirguillano, reporting that 11 percent of its residents fought in the war. Fully 4 percent of the surveyed population in the merindad of Sangüesa joined the insurgency, and this is without any data for Monreal or Ibargoiti, Mina's home. The data for Olite are particularly unsound, but approximately 4 percent of the surveyed population in that merindad also joined the Division, including 7 percent of the population in Ujüé. In Tudela, 3 percent of the surveyed population fought, though most of them came from the city of Tudela only at the very end of the war.

Overall, the data once again highlight the importance of the Montaña as a supplier of volunteers to the guerrilla army. The merindad of Pamplona supplied over a third of the volunteers, Sangüesa one-fourth. Moreover, over two-thirds of the volunteers reported from Estella originated in the northern sections of the merindad and must be counted as men of the Montaña as well. All together, something like three-fourths of the volunteers came from the Montaña. It is possible to identify three areas that supplied the bulk of the volunteers. In first place is the band of territory running from northern Estella to the Pamplona basin. In second place are the districts of eastern Sangüesa, along with the easternmost portions of Olite, including Ujüé. Missing data for the eastern reaches of the Pamplona basin, including Idocín, Monreal, Otano, and other important insurgent centers conceal the importance of this region to the resistance. If complete data were available, it would probably show one solid band of guerrilla territory encompassing the entire region of small villages that stretches across north-central Navarre, with islands of French control in the cities of Pamplona and Tafalla. A third important source of volunteers was the city of Tudela, though it is certain that the insurgents from this region were most active either early in the war—prior to the fall of Zaragoza—or later, after May 1812. In addition there were important outposts of resistance in Roncesvalles, Viana, and other places.

The information available on the number of civilians killed and imprisoned adds to the picture of massive involvement in the Montaña. The areas of greatest police repression corresponded almost exactly with the areas that contributed the largest numbers of volunteers. Over 50 percent of those killed or imprisoned by the French police in Navarre were from the merindad of Pamplona, and the western half of the Pamplona basin contributed the bulk of these victims. Sangüesa supplied 7 percent and Estella 21 percent of the civilians killed and arrested by the French. Only 9 percent of the victims of the French police came from the merindad of Olite, and only 3.5 percent were from Tudela.

Thus, the vast majority of the victims of the French police, as well as the volunteers identified in the survey of 1817, came from the land of the caserío and village in north-central Navarre. By itself, this suggests that it was the independent labrador of the Montaña who formed the basis of the resistance. Separate data taken by the French in 1812 reinforce this impression. Mendiry gathered information for four villages in the valley of Echauri. These included Arraiza, Echarri, Echauri, and Ubani. All four reported only fifteen volunteers with the Division of Navarre, an obvious underestimate.[72] Of these, twelve had been born within the villages reporting and the other three were all born within the valley. These were not outsiders or people on the margins of society. Their average age was twenty-nine, so that we can assume they were not hot-headed youths working as hired hands while waiting for their inheritance. More decisively, fourteen were listed as independent landowners and one was named a *hacendado* (big landowner). This excludes the possibility, in Echauri at least, that the guerrillas were landless peasants. Unfortunately, these statistics exist only for a few locations and are not collected together within the archives. To assemble information for a number of different areas would be useful, but the data that could be obtained would still be partial, since villages and towns clearly reported only a few of those who had joined the insurgents. Nevertheless, these bits of information are one more clue as to the identity of the insurgents. Most came from the Montaña. Most were probably small landowners, young but not necessarily dependent, and not newcomers or outsiders.

Hints left by contemporaries offer one final source for analyzing the background of the Navarrese volunteers. Mina identified his followers as "respectable" farmers, and he contrasted his men with the "undisciplined" men from the Ribera and from outside Navarre who fought with the likes of Echeverría and Tris.[73] On the other end of the spectrum, Mina noted the complete absence of titled or wealthy men among his followers.[74] His closest collaborators were the owners of small farms, who were neither poor nor rich. Félix Sarasa, the "closed minded" and illiterate Basque farmer/merchant from Artica ran the customs. The Cruchagas were a family of hidalgos from Roncal who brought the men of that valley into the resistance. Mina himself was from a family of well-to-do farmers. His brother was vicar in the hospital in Pamplona (until his death in Portugal on a mission for the Division), and his youngest sister was married to the administrator of the house of charity in the city. Javier's family had possessed the wherewithal to send their son to a seminary.

To complete the picture of who fought with Mina as much as possible it is necessary to consider those men from outside Navarre who fought in the Division. In 1811 and 1812 hundreds of Catalonians joined Mina, and the Aragonese and Basques in the Division numbered in the thousands.[75] There were also volunteers from farther afield. One important source of volunteers was the prison convoys that passed through the region on their way to France. In the spring of 1811 the 600-man garrison of Tortosa captured by Suchet made it as far as Burdeos before the prisoners overpowered their escort of 300 men. The refugees made their way back across the Pyrenees and some eventually joined up with Mina's forces.[76]

The Division also attracted a number of deserters from the imperial ranks. Germans and Italians were particularly susceptible. Germans in the garrison of Pamplona deserted in 1809–10 in groups of ten to fifteen with all their baggage and arms. The guerrillas generally placed such deserters among the front ranks to ensure that they fought, and according to Andrés Martín they acquitted themselves well. Mina placed Charles Hohenstein in charge of the German volunteers. In a formal letter, Baron Hohenstein called upon Germans to desert the French side "to take up service with the Spanish. Many of your comrades are already in my company," he wrote. "Here you will find a better life. You will receive a salary of ten sols, and bread, wine, and meat in abundance."[77]

Italian troops were also attracted by the high pay and generous rations offered by the guerrillas.[78] During August and September 1812, while passing through Navarre, half of the third battalion of the Sixth Italian Regiment deserted to Mina, adding over 200 troops to the Division.[79]

By the time the Division was disbanded at the end of the war it comprised four Navarrese infantry battalions, two regiments of Navarrese cavalry, and two companies of light cavalry attached to the first battalion. In addition, there were two Alavese and three Aragonese infantry battalions. The total number of troops fighting under Mina came to 11,000 men, not including the hundreds of men working in the customs service and in the munitions and uniform factories. The Navarrese contingents remained the core of the Division throughout its life, however. They were men of the Montaña, likely to be landowners with both the resources and material motives to resist the occupation. They lived in small villages and towns, which the French could not steadily occupy, and they loved their clergy and fueros, both attacked by the French government. They were the basis of the most successful guerrilla movement in Spain, and a most important strand in the "fatal knot" that destroyed the French Empire.

❦ *Epilogue*

SOON AFTER THE Allied victory at Vitoria, Mina's guerrillas fell apart. The towns and villages that had nurtured the Division now had to supply exorbitant contributions to English, Portuguese, and Spanish regulars as well as to the guerrillas. As a result, the province became as impossibly overburdened as it had been during the worst times under the French. Enthusiasm for the war turned in the winter of 1813–14 to despair. Then, when the coming of peace and the return of Ferdinand VII to the throne did not result in the immediate demobilization of the troops stationed in Navarre, despair turned to sullen resistance and open rebellion against the guerrillas.

These problems were the more acute for Mina because he found himself challenged in recently reoccupied areas like the Ebro valley by men who had done nothing to liberate the country and who yet claimed the right to reassume their customary positions at the summit of Navarrese society. The loyalty that the men of the Division had come to expect from the villages and towns had turned to hostility, and it was channeled and led by the old array of elites who had done so much to allow the French to install themselves in Navarre in the first place.[1] During the war years, the towns had often received rough treatment from the guerrillas, and in the postwar period they sought to pay back the armed peasants of the Division for their wartime insubordination. This conflict was quickly resolved in favor of the towns. The restored municipal and provincial authorities were able to erase all memory of the guerrillas and to reimpose their own vision of society as an ordered, hierarchical organism.

Adding to Mina's problems, the troops themselves had begun to lose heart. For seven months they had fought less than brilliantly in sieges in Aragon and southern France. They were not accustomed to such long absences from home nor to continuous mobilization in the long periods between actual battle. In the guerrilla war it had been possible to return home, or at least to disperse in safe cantonments, between engagements. This was not the case in the offensive operations the guerrillas were called upon to undertake in 1813–14, and the boredom and economic hardship of regular military life must have seemed a cruel reward for their years of service.

Moreover, the bureaucracy for raising contributions was no longer operating effectively, since it was expected to compete with the requisitioning apparatuses of the English and Spanish armies. Mina pleaded with the Allied military government in Pamplona to help him raise money and supplies, but to no avail. At the same time, the system of frontier customhouses collapsed, eliminating Mina's main source of hard cash.[2]

As the troops became desperate for food, clothing, and pay, they grew unruly. By the summer of 1814, anonymous broadsheets began to appear urging the guerrillas to return to their homes. Thousands of men followed these suggestions, and the Division began to disintegrate. Meanwhile, Mina was in Madrid begging the restored government of Ferdinand VII to recognize his corps as a regular division, as the revolutionary government of Cádiz had done. Mina obtained an audience with the king but ultimately failed in his mission. Ferdinand's reaction to the peasant "king" of Navarre was to haughtily dismiss him. In late July, Mina hurried back on his own initiative to try to end the desertions.[3]

During July the reinstalled Diputación and the military governor in Pamplona, Antonio Roselló, instigated another conflict with the Division. A royal order of 25 June 1814 required that offices and governing bodies not extant in 1808 should cease in their functions. Based on this order, the Diputación sought to reacquire all of its prerogatives, even against the still functioning administrative bodies set up by Mina. The first area of conflict was over the administration of justice.

As the guerrillas had extended their influence in 1812, the French courts had ceased to function in most of Navarre. Mina had therefore created a special Tribunal to take over judicial responsibilities. The primary task of the Tribunal had been to enforce the blockade of Pamplona, but it had also taken over all of the other duties normally carried out by the royal courts in peacetime. In July 1814, despite the royal order of 25 June and the complaints of the Diputación, the Tribunal continued to operate. This particularly dismayed the towns formerly dominated by the French, where the justice administered by the Division tended to be both cruel and swift. The Diputación began to receive complaints against the Tribunal and decided to order Mina to dismantle it. In justification of its continued activity, the Tribunal sent a long letter to the Diputación and Roselló on 28 July. All the towns and villages "including the city of Tudela," added the author of the letter, "have recognized this Tribunal as supreme and legitimate." Almost everyone with a seat in the Cortes, as well as most alcaldes had come to the Tribunal to settle disputes since 1812. Surely, thought the judges, these facts justified the court's continued existence.[4]

As the Diputación was quick to point out, however, these circumstances justified nothing. Only the king in Cortes could legitimately establish a new judicial body. And on 2 August 1814, Ferdinand had issued a direct order disbanding the Tribunal. Thus, the Diputación felt justified in rejecting the "long-winded" and "weak" excuses of the Tribunal, and it once again ordered its dissolution. The correspondence makes clear that both the deputies and the men appointed by Mina knew quite well that at stake was the question of who or which bodies could claim sovereignty in Navarre.

Despite the hostility of both the king and the provincial authorities, the Tribunal continued to operate in August on direct orders from Mina. Among its other "crimes," the Tribunal sought to punish municipal officials who neglected to deliver requisitions to the Division and to collect debts left over from the war.[5] These activities resulted in a flood of letters demanding that the Tribunal be outlawed. On 18 August the Diputación wrote a furious letter to Mina. "With what right" did his court function? asked the deputies. "Under the rights granted by yourself. And how and from whom did you obtain this attribute of sovereignty?"[6] The issue had been placed squarely in front of Mina, and he found himself unable to answer the Diputación. In the face of opposition from Madrid, Pamplona, and dozens of municipalities, Mina finally ordered the dissolution of the Tribunal on 22 August.

The next dispute involved the right of the Division to collect contributions in Navarre and ultimately to remain in existence. The government in Pamplona had already denied its responsibility to help the guerrillas obtain supplies. Now, on orders from Madrid, it required that the civilians mobilized in irregular formations during the war be dispatched to their homes.[7] Mina chose to interpret this order as not applying to himself and his men, since the wartime government had recognized the Division of Navarre as a regular formation. This was open defiance of the government, which specifically denied the Division regular status. Mina dispatched officials to reenlist his dispersed troops, not only in Navarre but in Álava, Guipúzcoa, and Aragon. Officials there suddenly found their territories "invaded" by a force from Navarre, which began forcibly to impress young men. The foral government of Álava wrote to the Navarrese Diputación complaining that "Marshal Mina, who must be aware of these sovereign decisions [the king's order demobilizing guerrillas], is bent on evading them and breaking them through armed force." He was insisting that the men of his Division "were not included under the rubric of partisans or guerrillas but were reputed to be regiments of the line and light infantry." This showed that "Marshal Mina still maintains his spirit of domination from the war."[8]

With feeling in the province, and now even in neighboring provinces, turning against Mina, more and more towns denied requisitions to the Division's agents. With the Tribunal disbanded, draconian justice was meted out to such recalcitrant municipal officials as if they were "collaborators."[9] In August and September from Milagro, Villafranca, Andosilla, and Mendigorría—Ribera towns that had escaped guerrilla control during most of the war and that had received rough treatment by Mina after the war—complaints poured in about the extortions carried out by the Division.[10] Things were quickly coming to a head.

In September a royal decree sought to defuse the situation by ordering Mina to evacuate his troops into Aragon. But the corresponding instructions from Pamplona to Mina's superiors never reached their destination. The Diputación's courier was waylaid by Mina's men outside of Olite on the night of 25 September. That night Mina decided to strike against Pamplona.[11] A large portion of the Division had been reassembled, and the majority was placed in Puente la Reina. From Puente Mina marched north with the first battalion and elements of the fourth. This time, however, not all of his troops were willing to follow him. The soldiers given the task of carrying the ladders that were to be used to scale the city walls were the first to realize what their objective was. Officials in these units began to call on their men to desert. Mina sought to defuse their rebellion by appealing directly to the destitute troops, bypassing their unwilling company commanders. He explained that his efforts to obtain recompense for them had failed with the viceroy and the minister of war. They would have to take by force what was their due. "Take heart, boys," Mina announced, "we're going to get rich." [12]

This argument was insufficient, however, to reanimate most of the volunteers. At around six o'clock on the morning of 26 September, most of the men returned to Puente. At nine o'clock a courier reached Pamplona from Puente to tip off the viceroy, the Conde de Ezpeleta, of Mina's plans. Shortly afterward, Mina and his remaining followers attempted to enter Puente in order to try once again to gain the confidence of the rebellious troops. Only when the men fired upon him from the windows did Mina realize that the game was up. He fled to France, which, ironically, was now willing to shelter him. In the days that followed, the goods belonging to the Division were seized by the government.

Mina's lieutenants either fell into the hands of the police, fled across the border, or proclaimed themselves for Ferdinand VII. On 3 October Cruchaga submitted with the cavalry and Barrena with the second and sixth battalions. In Aragon, the third battalion submitted a few days later.[13] The history of Mina's rebellion helps to illustrate an important point about the guerrillas who became Liberals under the Restoration. There is nothing inherently Liberal about any of the demands made by Mina and his officials, either with regard to the Tribunal, the right of the guerrillas to continue requisitioning, or the status of the Division as a regular corps. In the history of the guerrilla struggle, the men of Navarre had not demonstrated a knowledge of any ideological program, unless the "Idea" of 1810 can be considered an ideology. Yet, the claims made by Mina in 1814 struck at the heart of the monarchy. Mina and the other guerrillas had performed a military role of transcendent importance to the very existence of the Spanish state, and they perceived compensation in the form of pay and honors as their just reward. In the case of the dispute over the Tribunal, this compensation was even to include political privileges. Perhaps, under the influence of years of Liberal propaganda, Mina's men thought they had a right to political power.

Such an attitude went against everything for which Ferdinand VII stood. His government was based on the absolute sovereignty of the king, constrained only by those customary institutions and laws that had existed before the War of Independence. The mobilized, armed peasants of Navarre, with a court and a system for collecting contributions, were a threat every bit as serious as the Liberal politicians who were being purged with such cruelty during this very period. The guerrillas were therefore spurned as a danger to the closed society Ferdinand was attempting to constitute. Most of the guerrillas were happy to return to their prewar occupations, especially since the regular pay, booty, and rations of wartime were not forthcoming in peace. For Mina this was not an option. Having tasted absolute power, he could not return to a life as a simple layador working on his mother's (later his sister's) estate. As a result, he fell by default into the Liberal camp. During the next twenty years, his services to the Liberal cause meshed with his struggle to regain the status he had briefly enjoyed during the War of Independence. And the acceptance of much of the Liberal program during the reign of Queen Cristina in the 1830s spelled his own triumph and the rehabilitation of the guerrillas' reputation.

Guerrillas played a major role in the defeat of Napoleon in Spain. The contribution of the guerrillas of Navarre by itself had an enormous impact on the course of the war. For those who measure military success by a body count, a simple total of the French troops killed or captured by the Navarrese is impressive enough. The French lost hundreds of men to the first guerrillas, especially to Renovales and the Roncalese. These last, by themselves, inflicted over 1,000 casualties in the summer of 1809. The corso terrestre under Javier Mina accounted for at least 358 killed or captured. And under Mina the guerrillas killed or captured at least 16,745 of the enemy, and the total number of French losses including those wounded during six years of fighting could not have been less than 50,000.[14] This figure is about three-fourths of the number of casualties produced by Wellington in all of his battles. Clearly, if the object of war is to inflict as many casualties as possible on the enemy, then the guerrillas of Navarre played a key role.

Casualties in battle, though, do not begin to tell the whole story of the insurgents' contribution. The primary purpose of the guerrillas was not to inflict casualties. Nor was it to perform auxiliary tasks for regular units, however indispensable such services may have been in particular situations. The function of the guerrillas was to occupy French troops in duties far from the main battlefields. The guerrillas did not necessarily seek to achieve this objective by presenting themselves for combat. Instead, they denied the French access to the resources of the countryside and forced most of the occupation troops to struggle for mere survival. In guerrilla country, the French were kept busy wresting rations and fodder from a sullen and hostile population. It was the objective of the guerrillas to protect these civilians, to channel their hostility, and to engage their services, as spies, couriers, and volunteers.

The people of Navarre had ample reason for hating the French government. The French taxed and requisitioned in a way that ensured popular hostility. In addition, France threatened to destroy the church and the foral government, institutions that were both generally popular and, in the latter case, of economic benefit to the majority of the population. Guarding villages from French columns sent to gather supplies was an important part of the guerrillas' strategy. As part of this strategy, the insurgents had to discipline individuals and towns that were discovered collaborating, thereby ensuring the belligerency of most of the population. In performing this task, the guerrillas functioned as much like a police force and a judiciary as an army.

The success of the guerrillas in Navarre was not the result of a unanimous patriotic or religious impulse. During the first year of the war, Navarre was one of the quietest provinces in Spain as most provincial and municipal officials chose to collaborate with the French. It was only during the summer of 1809, after the old elites had been eliminated from the scene and the predatory nature of the French government had become evident, that the insurgency became really widespread in Navarre.

There was nothing inevitable, however, about the outcome of the struggle. Under the corso and the Division of Navarre, the guerrilla movement passed through several cycles of dissolution and reconstruction. During the first phase of Mina's campaign, lasting almost two years from his rise to power in the spring of 1810 to December 1811, the guerrillas suffered two crushing defeats at Belorado and at Lerín and were frequently on the defensive, chased at intervals by 10,000 to 20,000 enemy troops. At the worst times, the guerrillas hid in the mountains north and east of Pamplona or in the high plateaus west of Estella. As French armies approached to encircle the guerrilla positions, Mina's men broke out by secret paths, crossed the plains of central Navarre in forced marches, and hid again in the mountains on the other side of the province.

This pattern repeated itself throughout this supremely difficult period. The most dangerous moments, from the middle of August to early December 1810 and the months of February to late March and June to October 1811 were spent in flight and hiding. This phase was punctuated by brief and limited offensive operations, when the guerrillas united to hit specific targets, as with the first ambush at Arlabán. Most of the time, however, they remained dispersed in order to give the French as many elusive targets as possible.

Broken into companies, the guerrillas melted easily into the surrounding population. This allowed them to requisition without overburdening the people in any one area. As a last resort, even the companies were dissolved, each individual returning to his village to await more favorable times. Most of the guerrilla bands in Spain that had made the transition to disciplined armies lost the ability to disappear among the civilian population. They gradually became dependent upon support from the government, or, as was the case with the Empecinado, became appendages of the regular army and ceased to operate as guerrilla forces.[15] It was one of the great strengths of Mina's army that it achieved the highest degree of discipline, ultimately including recognition as a regular division, and still preserved its early independence, flexibility, and close ties to the villages that sustained it. This achievement allowed Mina's forces to recover from blows so severe that they would have spelled the end of guerrilla parties organized differently.

The insurgency could not always disperse in time to avoid unfavorable battles. When French columns succeeded in catching and engaging the body of the guerrilla army in open terrain, the results were disastrous: Tarrazona, Belorado, Lerín. They nevertheless survived these slaughters and even seemed to emerge the better for the bloodletting, as new recruitment drives quickly replaced lost personnel and swelled the ranks of the insurgents. The ability of the guerrillas to recover rapidly from setbacks is one of the most significant phenomena of this defensive phase of the war.

In the second phase of the war, from December 1811 to the battle of Vitoria in June 1813, the guerrillas could usually match or surpass the enemy in numbers, and Mina went on the offensive. Although there were still difficult moments, by the middle of 1812 the French had become hostages within the fortified cities of Pamplona, Tudela, and a few frontier forts, barely able to venture out for supplies, cutting down trees in the municipal parks for firewood, and burning sticks of furniture when the trees were gone. The insurgents succeeded in isolating the French from the countryside, thereby undermining the basis of the occupation at its source, destroying the resolve of the French, and hastening the end of the war.

The final phase of the war began with the irruption into the province of Spanish and English armies in July 1813. After this date, the guerrillas had to learn to operate as adjuncts in regular offensive operations, mostly outside of Navarre. The guerrillas played important but uncharacteristic roles in a series of sieges at Zaragoza, Jaca, and other forts, and they played a small part in the campaign in southwestern France, before being disbanded by the thankless Restoration government.

A complex set of structural and contingent factors determined the success of the Navarrese insurgency. First, the geopolitical position of Navarre made it the nexus for communications between France and the peninsula. This gave the insurgents obvious targets and an early strategy: to attack supply columns, prisoner convoys, and stragglers. In the Montaña, the geography provided the ideal setting for irregular warfare, attenuating the numerical, material, and technological superiority of the French. But there were other mountainous regions in Spain that were also of geostrategic importance where guerrillas did not achieve the kind of success they did in Navarre. The difference in Navarre was the human geography and social structure of the Navarrese Montaña. This was its decisive edge in guerrilla warfare.

Among such factors favoring the guerrillas, the dispersion of the population in hundreds of small villages and towns figured strongly. This dispersion limited the ability of the French to dominate the population with garrisons. Moreover, to tax the population in the Montaña, the French had to maintain their presence in hundreds of villages. And because of the democratic nature of local government in the Montaña, the French were unable to dominate municipalities by controlling a few pliant elites.

The widespread ownership of land in the Montaña was another key. In the first place, it was the precondition for the democratic town council. Second, the tools, animals, and products of Navarre's agricultural economy were distributed among thousands of proprietors. This made tax collection a war in itself and gave the peasants all the motive they needed to take up arms.

It was also important that peasants constituted the leadership as well as the rank and file of the guerrilla movement in Navarre. The strategy of defending villages from French extortion came naturally to such men. And it was this strategy that undermined the occupation at its base. Likewise, only a popular army could have collected the requisitions and custom duties that were the lifeblood of the resistance, and only a popular Tribunal could have enforced compliance with the blockade of Pamplona that ultimately brought Abbé's troops to their knees.

Napoleon's "open wound" in Spain had been inflicted through a combination of English, Portuguese, and Spanish efforts. But it was the insurgents, and among them especially the Division of Navarre, who ensured that the wound did not heal over. Combat against the insurgent population of Navarre was an extremely bloody and demoralizing affair. Forcing much of the population to adopt a belligerent attitude, especially with the declaration of the blockade of Pamplona in December 1811, the guerrillas raised the violence in Navarre to a level that brutalized the French occupier. In Spain, as in other colonial encounters, the occupation troops forced to attack or despoil hostile civilians eased their consciences by convincing themselves that they were at war with a racially and morally inferior opponent. The enemy was rendered subhuman in the French propaganda, authorizing individuals to perpetrate barbarities they would never consider normally. Military rules were forgotten in a war of extermination, and sound military judgment was sacrificed. Thus, unchecked French violence fed the hatred of the population, securing a never-ending source of insurgents.

The guerrilla war in Navarre destroyed French morale in a number of other ways as well. Those assigned garrison duty in Navarre lived in constant hunger, fear, and frustration. Fantín des Odoards, garrison commander at Puente del Arzobispo, expressed the predicament faced by all garrisons stationed in guerrilla country. According to Odoards, "only the same hunger that drives the wolf from the woods" could convince his men to venture out in search of supplies. When an isolated garrison finally received the help needed to track down and overwhelm its antagonists, the guerrillas were able to resume a faceless existence, melting into the local population. Among such people, there was for the French "neither winter quarters nor any secure haven" and "rest [was] possible only for the dead or the victorious."[16] As a result of these factors, the level of French casualties from disease, exhaustion, and sheer depression was extremely high in Navarre.

The use of terror against the enemy is normally considered an integral part of guerrilla tactics. In fact, however, it belonged as much to the tactical repertoire of the counterinsurgency forces as it did to the guerrillas. The insurgents were always anxious to obtain the enemy's recognition as legitimate military personnel in order to secure the right of quarter. Thus, for example, they were always more likely than the French to provide medical treatment for enemy wounded and take prisoners for later exchange. Only for a few months after December 1811 did Mina systematically execute captured combatants, until he had convinced Abbé to grant consideration to captured guerrillas. The guerrillas did, however, use terror against collaborators. The "chacones" who fought for the French were summarily executed, and even civilians forced to supply services or information to the French faced draconian justice. From this point of view, the guerrilla war was really a civil war fought within the War of Independence.

Among the innovations introduced into the French army under Napoleon was his elevation of the notion that "war must feed war" to the dignity of a sacred maxim. The principle that an army must live off the territory through which it passed meshed perfectly with another of Napoleon's military innovations: the mobile corps, each a complete fighting force with infantry, cavalry, and artillery, which were supposed to move independently of a commissariat and spearhead Napoleon's offensives. Reinforcing this system, Napoleon had directed that imperial troops be trained to march at a pace never approached by any of his enemies—until the guerrillas of Navarre taught his infantry the true meaning of a forced march. These rather simple organizational changes had underpinned many of Napoleon's most brilliant victories in Europe. In Navarre, however, they proved inappropriate. It was not the case in Navarre, as it was in some Spanish provinces, that French armies had difficulty raising supplies because the local economy was too poor. On the contrary, Navarre produced huge yearly surpluses of grain and other agricultural products, enough, in fact, to supply thousands of insurgents for five years. Thus, the sense of Colbert's adage that large armies starve in Spain and small armies are swallowed up must be modified to describe the French predicament in Navarre. There was no shortage of food and other supplies, but the guerrillas prevented the French from obtaining them. The Division of Navarre won the battle over the harvests, the most characteristic aspect of guerrilla warfare and the greatest blow to the French regime.

❧ Notes

Abbreviations

AAT   Archives de l'Armée de Terre, Paris
AGN   Archivo General de Navarra, Pamplona, Navarre
AHN   Archivo Histórico Nacional, Madrid
AMC   Archivo Municipal de Corella, Navarre
APE   Archivo Parroquial de Echauri, Navarre
APN   Archivos de Protocolos Notariales, Pamplona and Tudela, Navarre
BN   Biblioteca Nacional, Madrid

Introduction

1. This figure compares with some 400,000 casualties in the Russian campaign. About one-third of the 300,000 French casualties in the peninsula were caused by the English. For casualty figures, see Goodspeed, *The British Campaigns in the Peninsula*, and Gates, *The Spanish Ulcer*.

2. There were 406,348 French troops in Spain in 1811 according to Marshal Masséna, and France had maintained these levels since mid-1810. AHN, Estado, legajo 3003. They faced some 40,000 English troops, supplemented by about 23,000 Portuguese. Even after Napoleon withdrew forces for the invasion of Russia, he still had 260,000 men in Spain. Gates, *The Spanish Ulcer*, appendix 2.

3. The importance of the guerrillas in the defeat of France, though well understood by Napoleon, is not always appreciated today. For political reasons, English and French combatants unjustly dismissed the guerrillas as ineffectual brigands, while the Spanish exaggerated their value. For a recent contribution to this debate, see Esdaile, "Spanish Guerrillas: Heroes or Villains?"

4. One could easily cite other instances in which guerrillas drew French forces away from the "main theater" of fighting. At the decisive battle of Vitoria in June 1813 many of Napoleon's troops in Spain were unavailable, still trying to stop the in-

surgents in Navarre, Aragon, and Catalonia. Wellington's army at Vitoria consisted of 57,826 English, 13,604 Portuguese, and 48,149 Spanish troops facing an army of 68,551 French under Joseph. There were, however, over 60,000 other French troops under Marshal Suchet to the east and in garrison duty in Biscay, Navarre, Aragon, and Catalonia. If these had not been pinned down, the outcome at Vitoria might have been different. Gates, *The Spanish Ulcer*, pp. 138–44, 518–19, 521–22; Toreno, *Historia del levantamiento*, 2:190; Oman, *The History of the Peninsular War*, 3:484; Alexander, *Rod of Iron*, pp. 220–21.

5.   *La Centinela de la Patria*, 3 July 1810.

6.   General Cartaojal, AHN, Estado, legajo 42, no. 2. For example, guerrilla intelligence changed the course of the siege of Ciudad Rodrigo in 1812. See Llopis, *Un héroe inédito*.

7.   Of his campaign in Galicia, Marshal Soult wrote: "I was fighting the entire population; all the inhabitants, men, women, children, old folks and priests, were in arms, the villages abandoned, the defiles guarded." Soult, *Mémoires*, p. 68.

8.   In 1812 Czar Alexander wrote: "If the emperor Napoleon makes war on us, he could perhaps defeat us, but this will not result in peace. He defeated the Spaniards on numerous occasions, but he did not conquer them." Ibañez de Ibero, *Episódios*, p. 31. In the multinational Hapsburg state, a war of national liberation against France was not possible, yet, when the French entered Vienna in 1809 the fosses around the city were littered with German translations of a famous Spanish nationalist tract jettisoned by prudent readers. Las Cases, *Mémorial*, 1:820–21. The tract in question was Cevallos's *Exposición*.

9.   English historians have resisted crediting guerrillas with any part of Napoleon's defeat for fear that it would detract from Wellington's glory. This is clearest in two of the English classics on the war: Napier, *History of the War in the Peninsula*, 1:iv; 2:127–29, 331, 349; 3:269; and Oman, *The History of the Peninsular War*, 2:1, 3:461. However, even some recent histories suffer from this old polemic. In 1986, David Gates in *The Spanish Ulcer* could still write that the guerrillas "infested" Spain, and Charles Esdaile could suggest in 1988 that the guerrillas were a military liability to the Allies. Esdaile, *The Spanish Army*, pp. 125, 141–43, 163, and "Spanish Guerrillas: Heroes or Villains?" French historians have tended to view the guerrillas as bandits in the pay of the English, since to do otherwise would require a recognition that Napoleon's project in Spain was illegitimate and unpopular. See, for example, Foy, *Histoire de la guerre*, pp. 181–82; Geoffroy de Grandmaison, *L'Espagne et Napoléon*, 1:88, 90–96; and Thiry, *La Guerre d'Espagne*, p. 328.

10.   The Liberal historian Toreno wrote that "women and children, youths and old men unanimously and simultaneously demanded a quick, noble, and terrible revenge" for Napoleon's treachery. Toreno, *Historia del levantamiento*, 1:98. The conservative historian Gómez de Arteche believed in a "unanimous will to resist" based on the "conservatism of the Iberian race." Gómez de Arteche, *La Guerra de la Independencia*, 1:9–20. And the Marxist historian Ramos Oliveira thought that "the Spanish nation rose en masse against the invader." Ramos Oliveira, *Politics, Economics, and Men of Modern Spain*, p. 22.

Chapter 1

1. At the time of the French invasion, with a corridor to the sea at Irún, the Kingdom of Navarre would have been slightly larger than the present-day province.

2. The average gradient in northern Navarre is about 15–20 percent, whereas the average in the South is about 5 percent. *Atlas de Navarra*, p. 64. General Reille, one of the many French commanders given the unhappy task of trying to contain the Navarrese insurgency, remarked on the difficulty presented by the topography of the Montaña. Any contact with Pamplona, he wrote, had to pass through "extremely difficult gorges" that gave all sorts of opportunities to the Spanish "brigands." Charles Honoré Reille to the Prince of Neuchâtel, 12 October 1810. AAT, C8, 268.

3. In the Ribera, on the other hand, occupation troops breathed more easily. Emmanuel Martin, *La gendarmerie française*, p. 207.

4. According to the census of 1786, the merindad of Pamplona supported a population density of thirteen people per square mile and that of Estella ten people per square mile. The Ribera merindades, more vulnerable to dearth and disease, had a population density of seven people per square mile, a figure in line with that of the Spanish average. AGN, Estadística, legajos 6, 16, 20, 25, 31, 49, census of 1786–87 (hereafter AGN, census of 1786–87).

5. The war with the Directory devastated parts of the Montaña, and this is evident in the census of 1796–97. AGN, Estadística, legajos 7–8, 16–17, 20, 25–28, 31, 49, census of 1796–97 (hereafter AGN, census of 1796–97).

6. Indeed, population was declining in parts of the Montaña and remained stagnant during the nineteenth century. In addition to the censuses already cited, see AGN, Estadística, legajos 11, 20, 28, 31, 33, and 49 for data from 1637, 1646, 1810–11, and 1816–17; for 1678, see Romero de Solis, *La población española*, p. 130. The period from the late 1600s to the mid-1700s has been called "the hour of the Navarrese" in commemoration of Navarre's impressive contributions during the century, made possible by its relatively early recovery from the seventeenth-century crisis. Caro Baroja, *La hora navarra*.

7. This migration pattern resulted in a sexual imbalance between the Montaña, with a surplus of women, and the Ribera, which was overpopulated with men. In addition to the censuses, see García Sanz, *La respuesta*, pp. 63–68.

8. In Corella, for example, aside from 900 acres planted in vine and olive, there were over 2,333 acres under irrigation, and only 595 acres in dry farming in 1817. The rest of the land was too dry to be cultivated. AGN, Estadística, legajo 43, car. 7.

9. Caro Baroja, *Vecindad, familia, y técnica*, pp. 59–112, contains a discussion of the caserío.

10. Fantin des Odoards, *Journal*, p. 187.

11. One of the French commanders in Navarre, Charles Honoré Reille, recognized that it was the dense yet dispersed population of the mountains, not the mountains themselves, that made the Montaña difficult to control. Reille to the Prince of Neuchâtel, 12 October 1810. AAT, C8, 268.

12. AGN, census of 1796–97. The second estate formed 5 percent of the Spanish popu-

lation in general, a high figure by contemporary standards. More significant than the total number of nobles, however, was their distribution within Spain. Seven provinces along the northern littoral, among them Navarre, accounted for 84 percent of the nobility. Unless otherwise indicated, population data for Navarre are from the local returns of the censuses of 1786–87 and 1796–97 in the AGN. Statistics for Spain as a whole are from the published national censuses of those years.

13. Julio Caro Baroja compared the Basque hidalgos with the English gentry because of their willingness to engage in trade and industry, but this is about as far as the comparison goes. Cited in Whyte and Whyte, *Making Mondragón*, p. 12.

14. Foy, *Histoire de la guerre de la péninsule*, 2:277.

15. On the collaboration, see Artola, *Los afrancesados*, and Juretschke, *Los afrancesados*.

16. Indeed, as the Cortes of Cádiz prepared to abolish feudalism in 1811, secular lords still controlled more territory than the crown and the church combined. Anes, *El antiguo régimen*, p. 58. There were many benefits to a señor aside from the rents he collected. Señoríos sometimes included the right to appoint officials in the towns and villages within the señor's jurisdiction, thereby granting the señor a measure of control over town business, public opinion, and the commons and other properties of the municipalities. Within their domains, señores also collected money, just as independent municipal governments did, by renting out essential services. The butcher, fishmonger, baker, miller, tavernkeeper, and others paid yearly fees for the right to do business within a señorío. Sometimes señores collected all or part of the tithe, and some types of señoríos allowed their owners to collect royal taxes and to monopolize the use of forests and fishing rights.

17. For example, the señorío of Elio, estate of the Marqués de Vessolla, was of little importance next to the other villages in the valley of Echauri. Elio amounted to fewer than 66 acres and supported a population of only 15 people. Elio was dwarfed by the nine other villages in the valley, which supported a population of 1,780 cultivating 6,091 privately owned acres. The señorío was leased out at low prices and was not commercially developed. The four leaseholders who worked Elio were themselves substantial landowners in the valley of Echauri. They paid rent to Vessolla equal to just 6 percent of the value of the harvest that could be obtained from the property. This lack of commercial rents in an area close to Pamplona indicates that the Montaña was many years away from an agricultural revolution. Only in Vizcaya, where there were no señoríos, and in Guipúzcoa, where 4 percent of all settlements belonged to señores, did the weight of the señorial regime press more lightly. Data are from the censuses and surveys in AGN and from APN, Pamplona, Velaz.

18. Artola, *Los orígenes*, pp. 61–64.

19. García Sanz, *La respuesta*, pp. 76, 114.

20. Rents could also be low on señorial lands in the Ribera. The Marqués de Santa Cara, the biggest landowner in the region of Corella, renewed fifty leases in 1811 at prices originally set in the early eighteenth century or late seventeenth century, with one dating from as early as 1636. APN, Tudela, Laquidáin. The same was true throughout Navarre. In Echauri the average price of leased arable land was set at between 2 percent and 6 percent of the value of the harvest. APN, Pamplona, Velaz. It was also

true of the other Basque provinces. In Álava, for example, rents were said to amount to an average of about 2 percent of the annual income from the harvest. Desdevises du Dezert, *L'Espagne de l'Ancien Régime*, 1:261.

21. Señorial rents were low in much of rural Spain, but especially in the North, even in Galicia, where señoríos were common. Pardo de Andrade, *Los guerrilleros gallegos*, p. 40. In such areas, French land reform schemes promised to hurt, rather than help, the small renter. Land to be seized by the state from entails and sold on the market was likely to rise in price. The new owners, to recover the high purchase price, were likely, in turn, to raise rents. Moreover, the expectation of such reforms was that new owners would put capital into agriculture and farm at least some of the land directly, removing a portion of arable from the rental market and creating additional upward pressure on rents. These dynamics were not mysterious to farming communities and are sufficient explanation for their opposition to agrarian reform.

22. García Sanz, *La respuesta*, pp. 76–77, 114.

23. "Interrogatorio político," AMC, legajo 81, no. 3. Plot size was calculated on the basis of leases recorded between 1806 and 1816 in the city of Corella, APN, Tudela, Guesca y Alfaro, Laquidáin, Resa.

24. "Rolde de los propietarios," AMC, legajo 85, no. 32.

25. APN, Pamplona, Velaz, folder dated 22 March 1810.

26. In Naples, for example, the mutual fear and loathing of the local nobility and the populace had been manipulated by Joseph Bonaparte in order to secure his rule there. Bigarré, *Mémoires*, pp. 201–6.

27. Thus, as will be seen, social divisions had condemned the defense of Tudela in June 1808 to failure, as the city junta abandoned resistance at the first sign of enemy troops. (See chapter 4 for a discussion of these events.) The French exploited the division between the rich and the poor in Tudela to secure the nearly total pacification of the city during the war.

28. Espoz y Mina, *Memorias*, p. 9.

29. Anes, *El antiguo régimen*, p. 65. Net agricultural production is what remained after the subtraction of seed and other production costs. In some branches of agriculture more than one tithe was collected. Sheep breeders, for example, paid tithes on the animals slaughtered, the wool, the milk, and the cheese. Anes provided a calculation showing that tithes would also have absorbed half the net product obtained from a planting of wheat. Little of the tithe, which in theory was collected by priests acting as the local fiscal agents of the church, actually remained in the hands of clerics. Of the total of 648 million reales collected in 1797, the royal coffers absorbed 24 million in the form of the *excusado* (a contribution to the government exempting the church from other taxes). Two-thirds of what remained went to laymen with the right to collect tithes within their señoríos, leaving the church about 200 million reales. Desdevises du Dezert, *L'Espagne de l'Ancien Régime*, 1:48–55.

30. Monasteries controlled 1,123 jurisdictions, the secular clergy 1,560. Half of the villages and towns in Galicia and La Mancha were church señoríos.

31. Desdevises du Dezert, *L'Espagne de l'Ancien Régime*, 1:55. According to Herr, *Rural Change*, p. 23, the church owned 15–20 percent of the arable land in Castile. As

much as one-fourth of all the arable land in Catalonia and over half of the arable land in Galicia belonged to the church. Mercader Riba, *Barcelona durante la ocupación francesa*, p. 31.

32. The census of 1796–97 broke down "other secular" clergy into 44 canons, 29 prebendaries, 950 benefice holders, 63 clerics ordained by major and 242 by minor orders, 467 sacristans and acolytes, 19 servants, and 169 hermits. AGN, census of 1796–97.

33. AGN, Estadística, legajo 49, car. 19.

34. Mutiloa Poza, *La desamortización*, pp. 155–56.

35. AGN, Estadística, legajo 20.

36. These figures exclude Pamplona, a city that was and still remains a great ecclesiastical center. At the time of the French invasion, nine convents for men and two for women housed many of the 534 members of the regular clergy living in the capital. The visitor to Pamplona in 1808 could not have missed the presence of ecclesiastics in the city, where they formed over 7 percent of the population and owned 217 buildings. AGN, census of 1786–87; Mutiloa Poza, *La desamortización*, pp. 615–18.

37. Thus, in the nineteenth century there was a strong anticlerical sentiment among workers in the Ribera, while the Montaña remained "fanatical" for the church.

38. García Sanz, *La respuesta*, pp. 74, 115; "Interrogatorio político," AMC, legajo 81, no. 3; Mutiloa Poza, *La desamortización*, pp. 615–18.

39. "Rolde de los propietarios," AMC, legajo 85, no. 32.

40. There is a discussion of the movement to disentail church lands in the Ribera in García Sanz, *La respuesta*, p. 92.

41. Mutiloa Poza, *La desamortización*, pp. 155–56. In a few cities in the Montaña, like Estella, Pamplona, and Sangüesa, the domination of the clergy was also marked. This domination did not extend to the countryside, however, where most people lived in the Montaña.

42. García Sanz, *La respuesta*, p. 115.

43. APN, Pamplona, Velaz, legajo 89, nos. 27–34. During the war with France, when villages were forced to lay hands on every asset to meet French exactions, Echauri sold these lands and agreed to pay the priest (against his strenuous protest) fifty reales a year compensation, a kind of "civil constitution" of the clergy from below.

44. Mutiloa Poza, *La desamortización*, pp. 124–27; Anes, *El antiguo régimen*, p. 66. Censo rents remained fixed or actually declined during the period immediately preceding the War of Independence. For example, the prior of Iarte renewed one lease in 1789 at the same price charged in 1549. On average, censo lands rented for between 3 percent and 10 percent of the annual harvest. Most ecclesiastical lords rented out a large part of their domains in the form of censos. The Convent of Nuestra Señora del Carmen in Corella directly worked eighteen acres, mostly olive groves and vineyards for its own supplies of oil and wine. It rented out twenty-one acres under censo enfíteutico. AMC, legajo 81; APN, Tudela, Guesca y Alfaro, Laquidáin, Renault.

45. The Convent of Our Lady of Carmen in Corella had twenty-seven pieces of arable whose rental prices were recorded in 1809, the year of the convent's dissolution by the French. The average price for one of these properties came to 12 percent of the harvest, with the most expensive plot fetching 35 percent. "Inventario de los bienes

del Convento," AMC, legajo 81. The Cathedral Chapter of Corella during these years rented its arable for an average price of 8 percent of the average harvest. APN, Tudela, Guesca y Alfaro. This was all clearly high-quality land and a prize for the money-starved French occupation, which attempted to seize and sell it.

46. "Ventas hechas en virtud de Reales Cedulas," APN, Tudela, Guesca y Alfaro. Capellanías and obras pías included a great deal of urban property and investments in government bonds as well.

47. The analysis of the holdings of five large capellanías in Corella sold in 1807 shows an average rent of 14 percent on fifty-four properties. AMC, legajo 81. The amount of land in obras pías and capellanías was calculated from the record of their dismantling from 1806 to 1815 in APN, Tudela, Guesca y Alfaro, Renault, Laquidáin.

48. The amount of such property sold by the state from 1805 to 1808 came to about 30 percent of all church lands in Navarre, a figure twice as high as that for Castile. Mutiloa Poza, *La desamortización*, p. 263. See also Herr, *Rural Change*, p. 128. In Corella, for example, over 100 acres of arable church property, plus numerous vineyards, houses, and corrals, all from obras pías and capellanías, were sold during the three years preceding the French invasion.

49. French seizures were actually smaller than those that had been carried out under Godoy. In Corella the French government seized and sold 142 acres of church land, the equivalent of 4 percent of the arable. AMC, legajo 81. In both cases, the buyers of church land tended to be local notables who owned depreciated government bonds known as *vales reales* and who were allowed to redeem their worthless paper for land. Mutiloa Poza, *La desamortización*, p. 263.

50. Gómez Chaparro, *La desamortización civil*, p. 11.

51. In the northern merindades even the regular clergy remained relatively popular. Unlike monks in most of Spain, those in the Montaña had fewer aristocratic connections and represented more of a cross-section of society. Desdevises du Dezert, *L'Espagne de l'Ancien Régime*, 1:56–60.

52. Blaze, *Mémoire*, p. 3.

53. Desdevises du Dezert, *L'Espagne de l'Ancien Régime*, 1:46.

54. "Relación de las ocurrencias en la ciudad de Tudela." AGN, Guerra, legajo 19, car. 38.

55. According to the breakdown in the census returns for 1786, 32 percent of the active population in the merindad of Tudela were artisans, compared with 19 percent in the merindad of Pamplona. These figures were both skewed upward considerably, because the census failed to count domestic servants, who accounted for 9 percent of the total work force in Navarre. This means the number of "total active" people was too low, so the percentage of people in any occupational category was inflated. The point, however, is that nearly twice as many people, proportional to the active population minus domestic servants, were artisans in Tudela than in Pamplona.

56. Clearly, many peasants who were primarily farmers must have found additional work in industry without it showing up in census figures. In fact, in Echarri-Aranaz one source reported that women and children were expected to spin wool and hemp, and that men, after working their lands, went to earn extra money in nearby iron mines.

García Sanz, *La respuesta*, pp. 122, 136. Similarly, in the village of Echarri, the census turned up only one master weaver who had no employees, but a police report showed he employed three youths at night. (These three had caused a disturbance one night after work, thus the record of their existence.) APN, Pamplona, Velaz, legajo 88, no. 33. Yet, the point remains that industry did not provide full-time employment to any sizable number of people in the Montaña.

57. These were the complaints of commercial interests in the Ribera. Rodríguez Garraiza, *Tensiones de Navarra*, pp. 71–73.

58. It is of interest that the only industry in which labor was not performed by guild members, the manufacture of licorice, was also the only industry to export its product in any quantity. The licorice industry in Tudela employed forty-five men and twelve women, all unorganized laborers. García Sanz, *La respuesta*, pp. 143–46.

59. The breakdown of labradores into proprietors and leaseholders comes from AGN, census of 1796–97. Only neighboring areas of Aragon had such a preponderance of proprietors over leaseholders as Navarre did. And only the other Basque provinces and Galicia had lower percentages of day laborers, though they had much higher numbers of renters.

60. In Estella the figure was 17 percent, but this is because the southern part of Estella lies within the Ribera.

61. For example, the Conde de Guendul_in, who lived in Puente la Reina, owned in Echauri seventeen acres divided among twenty-one plots, which he let for an average of 2.5 percent of the value of the harvest. APN, Pamplona, Velaz, legajos 88, 91.

62. The average price in Echauri for land sold in carta de gracia was 580 reales an acre during the period 1798–1818, the equivalent of 145 days of wages for a carpenter. APN, Pamplona, Velaz.

63. Ibid. New sales in carta de gracia outnumbered recoveries by 36 percent in Echauri in the period 1798 to 1818. Pure sales far outnumbered both.

64. Ibid. The price of land for pure sale was actually slightly lower than the price of land sold in carta de gracia. This is explained by the generally poorer location and quality of the plots put up for pure sale, at least in Echauri. People avoided absolutely alienating their best and their oldest ancestral lands.

65. "Interrogatorio político," AMC, legajo 81, no. 3. Plot size was calculated on the basis of leases recorded between 1806 and 1816 in the city of Corella; APN, Tudela, Guesca y Alfaro, Laquidáin, Resa.

66. "Interrogatorio político," AMC, legajo 81, no. 3.

Chapter 2

1. Provincewide data and comparisons with Spanish figures are based on the *Censo de frutos y manufacturas*.

2. Of Navarre's manufactures, aguardiente accounted for 44 percent, linen cloth for 25 percent, and woolens for 12 percent. Most of this production was consumed within Navarre. Navarre contained small reserves of iron ore, and mining accounted for 15

percent of industrial production, but the ore was exported to the Basque provinces and France. Contemporary estimates showed that Navarre sold 733 tons of wool a year to France for 2 million reales and each year bought back cloth valued at 10.8 million reales. Although most of this cloth was in turn transsshipped to Castile and Aragon, the profits went to traders and smugglers, not to manufacturers who could have initiated the economic transformation of rural industry in Navarre. Rodríguez Garraiza, *Tensiones de Navarra*, p. 111.

3. Artisanal production and commerce resulted in 52 reales of income per person in Corella, 35 reales in Tudela, and 1 real in the valley of Echauri. Similarly, the professions (e.g., teachers, doctors, lawyers, barbers) produced 8 reales of income per person in Corella, 6 reales in Tudela, and less than 1 real in Echauri. Wage labor resulted in 69 reales of income per capita in Corella, 25 reales in Tudela, and 9 reales in Echauri. Comparisons between the Ribera and the Montaña in this chapter are based on the following sources, except where indicated: "Estado general de los productos territoriales, comerciales, é industriales del Reyno de Navarra (1811)," AGN, Estadística, legajo 49, car. 19; "Estadística de la riqueza territorial y frutos de la merindad de Tudela (1810)," AGN, Estadística, legajo 43, car. 3; "Estado que manifiesta los granos, frutos, y ganados que hubo en toda la merindad de Pamplona en el año de 1807," AGN, Estadística, legajo 33, car. 1; "Estado de la riqueza territorial, comercial, é industrial del valle de Echauri," AGN, Estadística, legajo 33, car. 22; "Estadística de la riqueza de la Ciudad de Tudela (1817)," AGN, Estadística, legajo 43, car. 6; "Estado que manifiesta la riqueza de la Ciudad de Corella (1817)," AGN, Estadística, legajo 43, car. 7.

4. These examples indicate how weak the market was in Navarre. Had the market been well developed, the law of comparative advantage would have dictated that the Montaña cease producing wine and oil and buy the cheaper, higher-quality wines and oils of the Ribera. In fact, there is some indication that wines produced in the Ribera exerted pressure on producers in the Montaña. Montaña communities fixed the price of wine and prohibited the use of "foreign" wines from the Ribera until all local supplies had been consumed. These laws enforcing a "moral economy" would not have been necessary had there been no flow northward of the superior Ribera wines. For an example of this practice of price fixing, see APN, Pamplona, Velaz, legajo 84, no. 31.

5. The great harvests of maize and chestnuts, used mainly as fodder crops, were one sign of the importance of livestock in the Montaña.

6. The most important areas of wool production were in Sangüesa and Estella, but Pamplona produced 20 percent of all the wool in Navarre, and the city of Tudela, by itself, had almost 41,000 head of sheep, 5 percent of the total in the province.

7. AMC, legajo 85, no. 29.

8. APN, Pamplona, Velaz, legajo 33, no. 6.

9. García Sanz, *La respuesta*, p. 97.

10. Blum, *The End of the Old Order*, pp. 144–45.

11. Laborde, *Itinéraire descriptif*, 2:92.

12. Some contemporaries considered the Basques the hardest-working people in Spain. Bourgoing, *Nouveau voyage*, 3:218–19; Desdevises du Dezert, *L'Espagne de l'Ancien Régime*, 1:xxx, 260; see also Barahona, *Vizcaya on the Eve of Carlism*, pp. 2–13.

13. For a good description of the laya and its use, see Louis-Lande, *Basques et Navarrais*, p. 7.

14. See the discussion of Basque "matriarchy" and of the laya in Caro Baroja, *Los pueblos de España* and *Vecindad, familia, y técnica*.

15. APN, Pamplona, Velaz. In the case of the marriage of Mina's propertied sister, it was her husband—evidently not the eldest in his family—who brought a cash dowry to the marriage. "Contratos matrimoniales de Miguel Ramón de Irure y Vicenta Espoz," 8 July 1800, APN, Pamplona, Peralta, legajo 50, no. 90.

16. García Sanz, *La respuesta*, pp. 122, 136.

17. "Contratos matrimoniales de Miguel Ramón de Irure y Vicenta Espoz," 8 July 1800, APN, Pamplona, Peralta, legajo 50, no. 90.

18. What Navarre did export rarely went to Castile. Over 62 percent of Navarre's trade was with the Basque provinces, 37 percent with France, and less than 1 percent with Castile and Aragon. Rodríguez Garraiza, *Tensiones de Navarra*, p. 177. The network of roads in Navarre indicates an orientation toward internal trade and trade with France, for the Navarrese had the best roads in all Spain, but at the borders of Castile and Aragon they became miserable tracks, a reflection of Navarre's basic economic isolation from the rest of Spain. Canga Argüelles, *Diccionario*, "Caminos."

19. In a normal year, one-third of the cereal harvest could have been exported, but, instead, it was consumed by the peasants who produced it. These were the conclusions of the Diputación of Navarre in the informe written in 1778 to the Sociedad Vascongada de Amigos del País, cited in Rodríguez Garraiza, *Tensiones de Navarra*, p. 101.

20. APN, Pamplona, Velaz. I have changed the Spanish measurements, expressed in fanegas, into Navarrese robos. A fanega was equal to 19.65 kilograms, a robo to 22 kilograms, a relationship of 1 to 1.1. Thus I converted the price of a fanega of wheat in Spain, reported at 44 reales in 1799, into a price of 48 reales per robo.

21. APN, Pamplona, Velaz, legajo 85.

22. Based on seventy sales recorded between 1798 and 1817 in APN, Pamplona, Velaz, and in APN, Tudela, Guesca y Alfaro.

23. APN, Pamplona, Velaz, legajo 84.

24. APN, Pamplona, Velaz, legajos 78, 84.

25. Laborde, writing in 1808, marveled at the enterprising peasants of Navarre. Laborde, *Itinéraire descriptif*, 2:92.

26. Desdevises du Dezert, *L'Espagne de l'Ancien Régime*, 1:xxx, 260–68.

27. Madoz, *Diccionario geográfico*, 12:112.

28. The following discussion of the institutions and attributes of the government of Navarre is drawn from Huici Goñi, *Las Cortes de Navarra*; Mina Apat, *Fueros y revolución*; and discussions with Demetrio Lloperena of the Universidad del País Vasco.

29. Navarre had among the best roads and public services in all Spain. The good administration of Navarrese communities contrasted sharply with the "negligence and aban-

donment under which the people of Castile lived." Desdevises du Dezert, *L'Espagne de l'Ancien Régime*, 1:20.

30. Even in wartime, the occupation government received 3 million reales a year from customs, and it expected that it could raise 6 million reales in peace. "Estado de la totalidad de rentas fijas del Govierno del Reino de Navarra," AGN, Estadística, legajo 49, car. 19.

31. Desdevises du Dezert, *L'Espagne de l'Ancien Régime*, 1:24. The lure of illicit trade was so strong that even war could not disrupt it. In 1793 the Spanish government, at war with France, could not prevent the Navarrese from trading with the enemy. APN, Tudela, Guesca y Alfaro. Nor could the Napoleonic regime in Navarre suppress illegal trade with France. The guerrillas even obtained lead and sulfur from across the frontier. Pérez Goyena, *Ensayo de bibliografía*, pp. 226, 251. On the guerrillas' wartime purchases through French merchants, see Espoz y Mina, *Memorias*, pp. 204–5.

32. Rodríguez Garraiza, *Tensiones de Navarra*, pp. 73, 93–94. Madoz, *Diccionario geográfico*, 12:70.

33. Madoz, *Diccionario geográfico*, 12:69.

34. Ibid., 12:68. Second to Navarre in both the importance of smuggling and the availability of weapons was Málaga, also a mountainous "border" region (whose border was the thinly patrolled Mediterranean coastline). Not coincidentally, Málaga was one of the few areas in the far south to produce an effective guerrilla force. Logroño too was a center of smuggling, as goods brought through Navarre generally entered Castile through Logroño.

35. Espoz y Mina, *Memorias*, pp. 15–16.

36. In the period 1803–5 dearth and high prices in Castile tempted many Navarrese producers to contravene the law on exporting grains. When the culpable grain merchants were detected, the situation became a national problem, requiring a royal decree forcing the government of Navarre to pardon the guilty parties and to allow commerce in grain during times of shortage. Nevertheless, it took two years for the Navarrese to admit the authority of the king in the matter and comply with the decree. Pérez Goyena, *Ensayo de bibliografía*, pp. 138–39.

37. APN, Tudela, Guesca y Alfaro.

38. See, for example, the informe of the Marqués de San Adrián, one of the biggest and most dissatisfied landowners in the Ebro valley. Rodríguez Garraiza, *Tensiones de Navarra*, pp. 109–11.

39. Informe of Ramón Giraldo y Arquellada, in Rodríguez Garraiza, *Tensiones de Navarra*, p. 41.

40. Escoiquiz, *Idea sencilla*, p. 25.

41. The later career of Navarre during the Carlist wars, when the defense of foralism formed the bedrock of support for a movement espousing religious and dynastic goals, must also be taken as a sign of the strength of regional sentiment. See Olcina, *El Carlismo*.

42. APN, Pamplona, Velaz, legajos 81–84.

43. APN, Pamplona, Velaz, legajo 89, nos. 10, 51.

44. Anes, *El antiguo régimen*, pp. 321–23. Under the system of insaculación, only men over twenty-five years of age with 1,650 reales of annual rent were eligible for the position of *alcalde*, or mayor, and to be a *regidor* candidates had to have 660 reales of rent. Eligible names were placed in a hat and drawn at random.

45. The Bourbons' object in pushing for these changes was to gain control over the enormous properties still in the possession of communities. In the nineteenth century, this government offensive against municipal autonomy would be crowned by the seizure of municipal and communal lands throughout Spain. In Navarre, however, these confiscations were resisted. As a result, half of the land in Navarre is owned by communities even today. Gómez Chaparro, *La desamortización civil*.

46. Evidence for all of these practices abounds in the notarial archives for Echauri and Ibargoiti. APN, Pamplona, Velaz and Peralta.

47. APN, Pamplona, Velaz.

48. APN, Tudela, Guesca y Alfaro, Laquidáin, Renault.

49. In some towns in the Pyrenees all land was considered communal and had to be divided annually or biannually by lot among all households.

50. Corella rented 253 separate properties in its commons in 1819, usually for a sum of wheat. These sums were so small, though, that the total income came to only about 2,000 reales. The value of the commons was usually low in the Ribera, because the dry climate made most such lands little more than desert wastes. "Razón de los sugetos que han renovado Censos perpetuos," AMC, 28 June 1819.

51. This procedure was followed in Monreal, the valley of Elorz, and the valley of Ibargoiti, the home of Mina. APN, Pamplona, Peralta, legajo 54, nos. 54, 57, 90.

52. APN, Pamplona, Velaz, legajo 87, no. 88.

53. The village of Echauri had 1,400 reales of its own. The treasuries of the other villages would have been smaller, but what they contributed from this source is unknown.

54. APN, Pamplona, Velaz, legajo 87, no. 55.

55. "Interrogatorio político," AMC, legajo 81, no. 3.

56. APN, Pamplona, Velaz, legajo 79, no. 21.

57. Pérez Goyena, *Ensayo de bibliografía*, pp. 138–39.

58. APN, Tudela, Guesca y Alfaro.

59. "Interrogatorio político," AMC, legajo 81, no. 3.

Chapter 3

1. The seizure of Pamplona is reconstructed from D'Armagnac's correspondence between 4 and 19 February 1808, AAT, C8, 4. Some interesting details from the Navarrese side may be found in the work by the priest Andrés Martín, *Historia de los sucesos militares*, but it is in some important respects evidently inaccurate and therefore suspect, as is the only French work to discuss the taking of the Ciudadela, Grasset's *La Guerre d'Espagne*.

2. Etcheverry to Moncey, 10 February 1808, AAT, C8, 4.

3. D'Armagnac to Clarke, 10 February 1808, AAT, C8, 4.

4. French sources say the house belonged to the "Comtesse d'Ayance," apparently a relative of the French general Harispe. Etcheverry to Moncey, 10 February 1808, AAT, C8, 4.
5. Andrés Martín, *Historia de los sucesos militares*, p. 5.
6. Dupont to Clarke, 24 February 1808, AAT, C8, 4. The French position was rendered more difficult by the Spanish habit of carrying daggers hidden beneath long capes, their identity concealed by a high collar and broad brimmed hat. This fashion created special problems of public order for the French, just as it always had for the Bourbons.
7. D'Agoult to the Prince of Neuchâtel, 30 March 1808, AAT, C8, 5. This is another piece of evidence showing that the Spanish uprising was far from an unpremeditated, popular explosion, as it is often represented.
8. Napoleon had more pliable agents issue pleasing reports on the "perfect tranquility" of the city. Napoleon to Clarke, 5 March 1808, AAT, C8, 4.
9. Napoleon to Clarke, 20 February 1808, Clarke to D'Armagnac, 21 February 1808, and Buchet, "Note sur l'Espagne," 17 March 1808, AAT, C8, 4.
10. Decree of 16 March 1808, AMC, legajo 85.
11. Rodríguez Garraiza, *Tensiones de Navarra*, p. 211.
12. As an indication of the depth of the crisis, the population of Barcelona, the Spanish city most closely tied to the international economy, declined by some 12 percent between 1798 and 1808. Mercader Riba, *Barcelona durante la ocupación francesa*, pp. 43–46.
13. Herr, "Good, Evil, and Spain's Rising against Napoleon." It might be better to say that pro-English sentiment had formed around Ferdinand's wife, María Antonia, who, as a Neapolitan, had obvious reasons for favoring an alliance with England. Ferdinand himself seemed to have no deeply felt political convictions, beyond a belief in his own divine right to rule Spain. Upon the death of María Antonia, Ferdinand showed his flexibility when he sought to find a new wife from among the Bonaparte clan.
14. These secret sections of the treaty were published in 1812 in Spain. Presle, "Mémoire Historique," AAT, MR, 1777. Napoleon revealed his intentions in a letter of 31 October 1807 to his brother Joseph, at the time king of Naples: "My brother, I do not know whether you have established the code Napoleon in your kingdom. I wish it to become the civil law of your states, dating from the first of January next. Germany has adopted it; and Spain will do so soon." Napoleon Bonaparte, *The Confidential Correspondence*.
15. Napoleon secured Godoy's signature on the treaty by promising him a personal fief in Portugal. The details of the treaty were publicized by Pedro Cevallos. Cevallos, *Exposición*.
16. Roy, *Les Français en Espagne*, p. 6.
17. Llorente, *Memoria*, 1:16–20.
18. General Bessières, commanding the Corps of the Western Pyrenees, had so many stragglers killed after 20 March that he had to prohibit men from trying to join their

units by themselves. Instead, they were to wait in Irún until a large enough detachment could be formed to travel into the mountains of Biscay and Navarre. Order of 10 April 1808, AAT, C8, 5.

19. Letter from Ferdinand to his brother Antonio, 28 April 1808, AAT, C8, 5.

20. Cevallos, *Exposición*, p. 30; Escoiquiz, *Idea sencilla*, p. 58.

21. This account of events in Madrid is drawn from different sources. On the French side, see the reports and correspondence of Murat and Grouchy, AAT, C8, 5, 6, and 381. On the Spanish side, see Pérez de Guzmán, *El 2 de Mayo de 1808*; Alcázar, "El Madrid del Dos de Mayo"; Corona, "Precedentes ideológicos de la Guerra de la Independencia"; and Alía y Plana, "El primer lunes de Mayo de 1808 en Madrid."

22. Gómez de Arteche, *La Guerra de la Independencia*, 1:322–35.

23. Experts disagree on the total number of casualties on 2 May. Pérez Guzmán, *El 2 de Mayo de 1808*, identified 409 Spanish killed, whereas Alcázar, "El Madrid del Dos de Mayo," thought 500 Spanish died. Neither estimate includes 1,000 peasants the French claim to have killed afterward. Gómez de Arteche, *La Guerra de la Independencia*, 1:356, thought the number might be around 1,200.

24. One recent Spanish estimate is that 80 civilians and 1 soldier were executed. Alía y Plana, "El primer lunes de Mayo de 1808 en Madrid," p. 135. Murat claimed to have executed 100 civilians. Murat to Dupont, 3 May 1808, AHN, Estado, legajo 13, no. 4.

25. Roy, *Les Français en Espagne*, p. 62. Spanish estimates of the numbers of French casualties are inflated. The figures most frequently cited are 1,600 French killed and some 500 wounded. One account printed in Valencia in 1808 claimed 5,000 French losses and only 30 Spanish dead in a struggle the author likened to that of "Hebrews against Phoenicians." These numbers, which even contemporary readers must have realized were absurd, serve nevertheless to indicate the feeling of invulnerability combined with religious zeal that Spanish partisans exhibited from the first. "Suplemento al diario de Valencia," 6 June 1808, BN, manuscript no. 18683/23.

26. Grouchy, "Etat des officiers et soldats tués ou blessés," AAT, C8, 6.

27. Azanza and O'Fárrill, *Memoria*, p. 173.

28. Article 144 of the Bayonne constitution preserved the fueros of Álava, Guipúzcoa, Navarre, and Biscay, but promised, ominously, to bring them into line with the "interests of the nation" at the meeting of the first national Cortes. The meaning of this article was not lost on the Navarrese. Conard, *La constitución de Bayonne*; Priego López, *Guerra de la Independencia*, 2:140–53.

29. AHN, Estado, legajo 28, no. 34.

30. García Prado, *Historia del alzamiento*.

31. Rico, *Memorias históricas*, p. 97. Rico reported that a mob led by a crazed canon, Baltazar Calvo, murdered 330 people for their French origins or sympathies. See also Priego López, *Guerra de la Independencia*, 2:42. Some details are confirmed in reports by French spies, AAT, C8, 6.

32. Valencina, *Los capuchinos de Andalucía*, pp. 38–76. Gómez de Arteche, *La Guerra de la Independencia*, 2:11–12.

33. A summary of these events may be found in Toreno, *Historia del levantamiento*, 1:56–81.

34. Junta Suprema Central, "Proclama a la nación española" (1808), AHN, Estado, legajo 13.

35. Rico, *Memorias históricas*, p. 82; Llorente, *Memoria*, p. 122.

36. *El Robespierre español*, no. 1, 30 March 1811.

37. The junta of Murcia crushed a social revolution in order to foster solidarity against the French, and went so far as to order the death penalty in August 1808 for anyone guilty of insulting monks, priests, officials, and other people who had not exhibited sufficient patriotism. AHN, Estado, legajo 42, no. 140.

38. Pardo de Andrade, *Los guerrilleros gallegos*, pp. 80–81.

39. Anonymous letter from a Spaniard in El Ferrol, 1 June 1808, AAT, C8, 7.

40. General Joaquín Blake to the Junta of Galicia, 28 July 1808, AHN, Estado, legajo 42, no. 23.

41. For a recent example, see Roux, *Napoléon et le guêpier espagnole*, p. 135.

42. Letter of D'Agoult, 10 June 1808, AAT, C8, 7.

43. Thouvenot to Neuchâtel, 12 June 1808, AAT, C8, 7; Grouchy to Murat, 5 June 1808, AAT, C8, 7.

44. D'Agoult's report of 15 June 1808, AAT, C8, 7.

45. Bessières to Neuchâtel, 2 June 1808, AAT, C8, 7.

46. Juretschke, *Los afrancesados*, p. 174.

47. Priego López, *Guerra de la Independencia*, 3:15.

48. Ayerbe, *Memorias*, pp. 101–2; AHN, Estado, legajo 81, A.

49. AHN, Estado, legajo 81, A.

50. AHN, Estado, legajo 28, nos. 15, 23, 35; legajo 42, nos. 97, 102.

51. Rocca, *Memoirs*.

52. AHN, Estado, legajo 13, nos. 3, 11. Most of these proclamations may also be found in Quintana's *Semanario Patriótico*, published in Cádiz during the war.

53. In June Captain Roy needed a pass signed by the insurgents to authorize his movement in the company of a Spanish friend from Aranjuez to Madrid. Roy, *Les Français en Espagne*, p. 79.

54. Situation reports of Grouchy, AAT, C8, 381. To muster a favorable crowd for Joseph's triumphal entry into the city on 19 July, the French had to pay a band of beggars and ply them with liquor. Rocca, *Memoirs*, p. 47.

55. Valencina, *Los capuchinos de Andalucía*, p. 52.

56. Dupont to Belliard, 7 June 1808, AAT, C8, 7.

57. For example, Pedro Cevallos abandoned Joseph on 28 July, and by September his patriotic *Exposición* was ready for the publisher.

58. Situation report of Grouchy for 24 July 1808, AAT, C8, 381.

59. AHN, Estado, legajo 28, no. 34.

Chapter 4

1. Captain de Choisy, report of 2 April 1808, AAT, C8, 3.
2. The French commander, General D'Agoult, wrote on 8 May 1808 that a "general stupor reigned" in the city. AAT, C8, 6. The general's situation reports from April on attest to the "continued tranquility" of the capital, aside from a brief period of unrest occasioned by the festival of San Fermín. AAT, C8, 381.
3. Decree of the Diputación, 31 May 1808, AAT, C8, 7. Government officials agreed with Miguel Azanza, Joseph Bonaparte's chief collaborator and a Navarrese, that the "capricious, indolent, and unjust" government of the Bourbons should be replaced by a Bonaparte monarchy, which was expected to rejuvenate Spain. AGN, Guerra, legajo 15, car. 5. The deputies and the viceroy were present in Irún for Joseph's triumphal entry into Spain on 9 July, and they were among the first of many Spanish officials to take the oath of allegiance in the presence of the new king.
4. "Relación histórica de los sucesos más notables ocurridos en Estella durante la Guerra de la Independencia," AGN, Guerra, legajo 21, car. 21. There is also information on Estella in AGN, Guerra, legajo 14, cars. 50, 55.
5. AGN, Guerra, legajos 14, 15.
6. AGN, Guerra, legajo 15, car. 9.
7. AGN, Guerra, legajos 14 and 15, cars. 1, 11–13.
8. AGN, Guerra, legajo 21, car. 21; legajo 14, cars. 50, 55.
9. A group of students at the university, perhaps including a young Navarro named Javier Mina, had burned Godoy's portrait after Aranjuez and had acclaimed Ferdinand the new king. For events in Zaragoza I used the account of Alcaide Ibieca, *Historia de los dos sitios*, supplemented by notices and letters written by French spies and Spanish observers at the time and preserved in the AAT, C8, 6 and 7. The role of the students at the seminary is attested to by all sources. Iribarren, *Espoz y Mina, el guerrillero*, p. 67, said that the leader of the students was Javier Mina.
10. See Herr, "Good, Evil, and Spain's Rising against Napoleon."
11. There are several versions of this miracle. The details vary slightly, but all versions attest to its great impact on Zaragoza. Prefect J. P. Chazal to Neuchâtel, 1 June 1808, and a summary of news from Spain dated 8 June 1808, AAT, C8, 7. See also Belliard's report on Catalonia, 20 May 1808, AAT, C8, 6.
12. The history of Tudela in this period was reconstructed primarily from the "Relación de las ocurrencias en la ciudad de Tudela durante la Guerra de la Independencia," AGN, Guerra, legajo 19, car. 38; "La defensa de la Ciudad de Tudela," AGN, Guerra, legajo 19, car. 32; Forcada Torres, *Tudela durante la Guerra de la Independencia*; and the letters and reports of General Lefèbvre-Desnöettes, 8–9 June 1808, AAT, C8, 7.
13. AGN, Guerra, legajo 15, cars. 6, 15. Young men from the surrounding countryside had fled to Tudela to escape a rumored French impressment, adding to the climate of unrest in the city. Three hundred men from Estella also went to Tudela when it became apparent that the French were bypassing their town. AGN, Guerra, legajo 15, car. 9.

14. In a letter to the Diputación, Félix Bergado, the administrator of city funds, explained the ruinous sack of Tudela as retribution for the acts of "a hundred barbarians" who had foolishly decided to resist at all cost. AGN, Guerra, legajo 15, car. 16. After 1814, citizens like Bergado who were eager to exonerate themselves from charges of treason claimed that around 1,000 people from Tudela and neighboring towns joined in a resistance backed fully by the authorities. There may have been 1,000 Navarrese insurgents joining the 2,000 Zaragozans, but Bergado's original statement that the insurgents had acted on their own without the help of the authorities was more truthful. An order issued by Napoleon on 11 June provides an interesting glimpse at the way the French also sacrificed the truth. According to Napoleon, Lefèbvre had lost only 2 wounded at Tudela, while of the 12,000 (!) insurgents who had fought, 1,000 (!) were killed. AAT, C8, 7.

15. On 3 August 1808 General Berthier explained to Savary that if Navarre were to rise in the way Asturias or Valencia had, it would condemn French troops still in Madrid and Burgos to annihilation. Napoleon Bonaparte, *The Confidential Correspondence*.

16. Alexander, *Rod of Iron*, p. 36.

17. In early June the priest of Valcarlos, Andrés Galduroz, led a small band in the remote mountains along the French border. This seems to have been the first guerrilla operation in Navarre. Olóriz, *Navarra en la Guerra*, p. 19.

18. AGN, Guerra, legajo 15, car. 20.

19. AGN, Guerra, legajo 21, car. 21.

20. For example, when Eguaguirre came to Ujüé (long after Gil's activities there), he ordered all single males and widowers to report for enlistment within three days. When he got no response, he threatened to shoot men eligible for conscription as traitors. Fortunately, Eguaguirre did not make good on his threat, and his order was ignored by Ujüé. AGN, Guerra, legajo 15, car. 34. The peasants in Echarri-Aranaz also ignored Eguaguirre's threats, hiding their arms for later use. AGN, Guerra, legajo 15, car. 29.

21. For example, Puente la Reina asked that French troops be sent in to protect the town from Eguaguirre. The authorities in Pamplona could not commit French forces, but they recommended that city officials hide arms and supplies and prepare to resist the guerrillas on their own. AGN, Guerra, legajo 15, cars. 21, 23, 30, 39.

22. Montoro Sagasti, *La propiedad privada*. The author discusses the weakness of Olite in the face of the French occupation as a result of an unrepresentative and unpopular municipal government. According to the account written in Ujüé, which probably exaggerated matters, the city folk of Tafalla and Olite were enthusiastic collaborators. AGN, Guerra, legajo 21, car. 22.

23. AGN, Guerra, legajo 15, car. 19.

24. AGN, Guerra, legajo 15, car. 33.

25. AGN, Guerra, legajo 16, car. 33.

26. AGN, Guerra, legajo 15, car. 48.

27. AGN, Guerra, legajo 15, car. 43.

28. AGN, Guerra, legajo 16, cars. 2, 36. The Diputación's harangues were, whether the deputies wished it or not, revolutionary documents: legally, only a new Cortes could

declare war, proclaim a monarch, and raise taxes. The restrictions imposed by the Diputación from May to July can be found in the AMC, legajo 85.

29. In addition, a handful of Eguaguirre's dwindling troops wrote to the Diputación complaining of their commander's methods and offering their services in the planned battalions. AGN, Guerra, legajo 16, cars. 8, 12, 13.

30. Situation reports of French armies in October 1808, AAT, C8, 377.

31. AGN, Guerra, legajo 15, car. 47, legajo 16, cars. 40–41; and AGN, Estadística, legajo 49, car. 34. An indication of the government's isolation was that almost two-thirds of its small war chest came from just nine individuals, residents in Tudela and other cities of the Ribera, and the remainder came from a few religious institutions in the Ebro region, above all from the bishop of Tudela and the monasteries of Fitero and Tulebras.

32. The French recognized that the only real threat in Navarre lay in its villages. Navarrese peasants had taken potshots at French stragglers from the beginning, even wounding D'Agoult's nephew in an ambush, and French commanders had warned of a general rising in the countryside. See D'Agoult's reports for 13 May and 7 June 1808. AAT, C8, 5, 7. Guns were habitually present in the region, since hunting and contraband were major economic activities, and in 1808 two new sources of arms became available. The Aragonese provided some weapons. And a windfall of new muskets flooded into Navarre when drafted Portuguese troops passing through the province on the way to assignations in France sought asylum among the peasants of Navarre and handed over their weapons in exchange. Order of General Bessières, 13 May 1808, AAT, C8, 5. General Verdier (in Vitoria) warned the Prince of Neuchâtel of a possible uprising in a letter of 8 May 1808, AAT, C8, 5. These were all warning signs of the coming conflagration.

Chapter 5

1. The English lost 7,000 men during the retreat, not just to the French but also to the Spanish. The English cut a wide swath of desolation through Galicia on their retreat, and English stragglers suffered the consequences, as many were lynched by the enraged peasants, who showed that they knew how to protect themselves against allies as well as foes. Napoleon Bonaparte, *The Confidential Correspondence*, letter of 7 January; Martínez Salazar, *De la Guerra de la Independencia en Galicia*, p. 122.

2. Goodspeed, *The British Campaigns*, p. 72.

3. Martínez Salazar, *De la Guerra de la Independencia en Galicia*, p. 26.

4. Ibid., pp. 26–36; Priego López, *Guerra de la Independencia*, 4:136; and Gómez de Arteche, *La Guerra de la Independencia*, 6:92–102.

5. *Semanario Patriótico*, 27 July 1809.

6. Captured letter of 25 June 1809 in *Semanario Patriótico*, 27 July 1809. Perhaps it was Soult's early disillusionment with the war that made him such a rapacious adventurer in his later Andalusian command, when he emptied churches and residences of their riches and works of art as fast as he could arrange transport to France.

7. Cádiz always retained a strong prejudice against the guerrillas. From time to time,

when the government felt strong enough militarily, it readopted this negative attitude. AHN, Estado, legajo 13, no. 4.

8. AHN, Estado, legajo 13, no. 1. The hyperbolic rhetoric of the Central Junta reflected a real phenomenon. The cruelty of the French in Spain, captured in Goya's spectral images of the *Desastres de la guerra*, forced people to redefine their notions of what was allowed in warfare. Marshal Soult's infamous declaration of 9 May 1810, defining resistance to French rule as banditry and condemning all Spanish captives to summary execution, merely codified French practices that had been in place from the start. See Toreno, *Historia del levantamiento*, 3:265–66.

9. Alexander, *Rod of Iron*, pp. 28–31.

10. "Partidas mandadas por guerrilleros," AHN, Estado, legajo 41, E.

11. "Expedientes personales de los generales," AHN, Estado, legajo 42, no. 152.

12. AHN, Estado, legajo 42, no. 220. Gómez de Arteche, *La Guerra de la Independencia*, 1:7–8.

13. "Partidas mandadas por eclesiásticos," AHN, Estado, legajo 41, C.

14. See Esdaile's argument in "Spanish Guerrillas: Heroes or Villains?"

15. "Partidas mandadas por guerrilleros," AHN, legajo 41, E. See also Ontañon, *El Cura Merino*, and Gómez de Arteche, "Juan Martín el Empecinado."

16. The military history of this period, unless otherwise noted, is reconstructed from the "Resumen histórico del segundo regimiento," AGN, Guerra, legajo 21, car. 20; and the "Relación de las operaciones militares del tercer regimiento," AGN, Guerra, legajo 17, car. 51.

17. "Relación de Estella," AGN, Guerra, legajo 21, car. 21.

18. "Relación de Ujüé," AGN, Guerra, legajo 21, car. 22.

19. Miranda Rubio, *La Guerra de la Independencia en Navarra*, p. 84; Olóriz, *Navarra en la Guerra de la Independencia*, pp. 34–41. Roncal had always seemed like a separate republic. The maintenance of a particular Basque dialect throughout the valley, the communal ownership of the land, and the existence of important trans-Pyrenean ties, had always made Roncal unusual.

20. Javier Mina's father was a man of some local standing, judging from his political prominence (he was the deputy for Otano in valleywide meetings) and his wealth. In 1802 the elder Mina agreed to take over the considerable debt of María Theresa de Ilundáin, Espoz y Mina's mother; in 1807 he purchased an obra pía confiscated and sold by the state; and during the war, the elder Mina was able to lend grain to various individuals and communities. Indeed, Javier's father appears to have been a war profiteer. APN, Pamplona, Peralta, legajo 51, nos. 11, 143; legajo 54, nos. 53, 54, 63.

21. Iribarren, *Espoz y Mina, el guerrillero*, p. 67.

22. The second siege of Zaragoza lasted three months. When the city fell on 20 February, the French found 54,000 dead, more from typhus than from bullets, out of a population of 40,000, augmented by 10,000 armed peasants and a 34,000 man garrison. The French suffered 10,000 dead, 6,000 of these lost to the fever. Oman, *The History of the Peninsular War*, 2:139; Gates, *The Spanish Ulcer*, pp. 124–28.

23. Espoz y Mina, *Memorias*, p. 20.

24. Ibid., p. 21.

25. "Relación de Ujüé," AGN, Guerra, legajo 21, car. 22.

26. Andrés Martín, *Historia de los sucesos militares*, p. 36. Martín's work also contains information on these early battles of the Corso not available elsewhere.

27. Olóriz, *Navarra en la Guerra de la Independencia*, p. 20.

28. Correspondence between the Diputación and the generals Blake and Areizaga, AGN, Guerra, legajo 17, cars. 3, 4. Petition of the Navarrese delegates to the Central Junta, AHN, Estado, legajo 41, no. 78.

29. In August 1809 the Diputación made one last effort (before its members dispersed in hiding) to gain the support of a Spanish general (Blake) against the pretensions of the guerrillas. By this time, Javier was active in Navarre under a license from General Areizaga in Lérida. It was significant that Blake, after informing the deputies that they were wasting his time, referred them to Areizaga. Olóriz, *Navarra en la Guerra de la Independencia*, p. 14.

30. Andrés Martín, *Historia de los sucesos militares*, pp. 48–49.

31. Areizaga had been a retired colonel living in Goizueta (northwestern Navarre) at the time of the French invasion, and Javier established contact with him in the fall of 1808.

32. In the summer of 1809 there were garrisons at Alsasua, Burguete, Caparroso, Espinal, Huarte, Huarte-Araquil, Irurzún, Lecumberri, Lumbier, Monreal, Orbaiceta, Pamplona, Sangüesa, Tafalla, Tudela, Urroz, Valtierra, and Zubiri. Other garrisons added later or in some cases replacing these were at Aoiz, Argüedas, Arriba, Biscarret, Bocal, Elizondo, Estella, Fuenterrabía, Irati, Irún, Lodosa, Los Arcos, Mendigorría, Olcoz, Peralta, Puente la Reina, Roncesvalles, Santestebán, Tiebas, Urdax, and Villafranca. AAT, C8, 377, 387.

33. The circulars are printed in Olóriz, *Navarra en la Guerra de la Independencia*, pp. 28–32.

34. Correspondence of Reynier, AAT, C8, 252.

35. "Relación de Ujüé," AGN, Guerra, legajo 21, car. 22.

36. These figures are not inclusive. French casualties in three engagements are listed merely as "some" or "unknown number" killed and wounded. In addition, there were no doubt other skirmishes of which the writer of the regimental diary was unaware. These missing numbers are probably balanced, however, by the tendency to exaggerate enemy losses, which the insurgents could not possibly have known with any precision, since they were forced to retreat rapidly after most engagements due to the approach of French relief columns. Finally, it was the tendency on both sides to minimize one's own losses. Casualties among the guerrillas were no doubt higher than admitted by the chronicler of the second regiment and those for the French lower. Unfortunately, French figures that might be used to check or correct those supplied by the guerrillas are not available until the spring of 1810, after the destruction of the corso. AAT, C8, 387. The first complete report is given by Dufour on 1 April 1810.

37. Correspondence of January and February 1810, AAT, C8, 252.

38. There are two works on French taxes and other exactions in Navarre. Torre, *Los*

campesinos navarros, supersedes Miranda Rubio, *La Guerra de la Independencia en Navarra*. The amount of the tax may be appreciated by comparing it with the extraordinary 6,821,000 reales in taxes sought by Godoy in 1799. At the time, Godoy's tax had seemed so high and generated such resistance that it could never be fully collected.

39. Mina later recognized Dufour's merits as an opponent. Espoz y Mina, *Memorias*, p. 13.

40. The offer was in the form of a proclamation, an extant copy of which was issued by the municipal government of Tudela, announcing that the French had put up reward money (the amount is not given) for the capture of "a certain Javier Mina, of Jewish origin." Popular anti-Semitism was always an easy card to play. The resistance also took advantage of it to brand Napoleon the "protector of the Jews," because of the laws passed granting Jews civil equality. AGN, Guerra, legajo 19, car. 38.

41. Iribarren, *Espoz y Mina, el guerrillero*, p. 85. Napoleon once claimed that with two generals like Suchet he could have held on to Spain. Suchet's success was partly the result of his savagery. When he mopped up the patriot stronghold of Lérida in April 1810, he sacked and burned the town, levied a punitive fine of over a million pesetas, and shot twenty-six residents on suspicion of sympathy with the guerrillas. During the next four years the pattern established by Suchet was followed exactically as 204 more people were executed in Lérida. Gras y de Esteva, "Notas sobre la dominación francesa en Lérida," p. 90. For Napoleon's views on Suchet, see Gómez de Arteche, *La Guerra de la Independencia*, 6:20.

42. Pérez Goyena, *Ensayo de bibliografía*, p. 185. Some said that Dufour had Javier sign a letter telling his followers to lay down their arms in exchange for his life and amnesty. The only evidence that such a letter was actually composed and signed appears in a sensational exposé written by one of the guerrillas' most violent enemies. See Saint-Yon, *Les deux Mina*. The other, circumstantial evidence, is that Javier was, in fact, spared and imprisoned in France, a most generous proceeding considering the usual practice of exemplary cruelty against captured insurgents. Such clemency appears inexplicable unless one assumes that Javier collaborated to save his skin. Nevertheless, there can be no firm conclusion in this matter until such a letter is discovered.

43. Dufour might have foreseen the failure of amnesty from the experience of his predecessor. The previous October D'Agoult had offered amnesty and a doubloon for any guerrilla who surrendered his arms within twenty days. Pérez Goyena, *Ensayo de bibliografía*, p. 169. On that occasion the Navarrese had answered with a bold stroke, the invasion and sack of Tudela.

44. Among these efforts, in the summer of 1809, Joseph had required all government officials to be reconfirmed in their offices after taking an oath of allegiance. This requirement could not be enforced in Navarre. *Gaceta de Madrid*, 20 August 1809.

45. These included four regiments in Andalusia, four in La Mancha, one in Soria, and one in Murcia. Gómez de Arteche, *La Guerra de la Independencia*, 10:69–71. Such regiments, however, proved to be untrustworthy. One regiment from León deserted en masse in 1809 with all of its arms and baggage, and this made Joseph cautious about using his Spanish troops. Napoleon Bonaparte, *The Confidential Correspon-*

dence, Napoleon to Joseph, 21 February 1809. Indeed, the fear of mass desertion touched even the "Joseph Bonaparte Regiment," an elite force, which was supposed to be sent to France in 1810 for later action in northern Europe. The project was abandoned because Joseph feared that sending the regiment through Navarre would be tantamount to a free gift of personnel and equipment to Mina. Letter of 28 May 1810 from Juan Kindelán to Gonzalo O'Fárrill. AHN, Estado, legajo 3003.

46. AHN, Estado, legajo 42, no. 259. Recruits from Catalonia became especially active in counterinsurgency efforts against Mina. The French placed these Catalonian turncoats in the first ranks to take advantage of their reputation for ruthless abandon in battle, a reputation stimulated, no doubt, by the knowledge that they would be killed if captured in battle by the guerrillas. The Catalonians usually fought better than the best French troops and became known in Navarre as the "butchers of the French army." Adjutant I., *Souvenirs de la Guerre*, p. 108; Mercader Riba, *Barcelona durante la ocupación francesa*, pp. 190, 219. In general, the number of Spaniards fighting with French units or in counterguerrillas decreased during the course of the war. For example, after 1810 Suchet could form no new regiments in Aragon, and even the Catalonians began to enlist with Mina rather than with the French by the end of the year. Alexander, *Rod of Iron*, pp. xviii, 98, dates the decline of enthusiasm for Suchet in Aragon to early 1810, but this seems too early. Ironically, the French seem to have made little effort to organize their own antiinsurgency units. In December 1809 a French officer stationed in Tudela volunteered to raise and command a "counterguerrilla." His band of fifty intrepid volunteers slipped out of the city in the early morning and were not seen again in Tudela until July 1810. By that time they had passed through several provinces and engaged the guerrillas seventy-seven times, inflicting enormous casualties on the enemy, according to the commander. Adjutant I., *Souvenirs de la Guerre*, p. 18. Yet, this type of initiative was extraordinary, although competent guerrilla fighters, like General Hugo in Castile, did emerge during the war.

47. "Relación de Estella," AGN, Guerra, legajo 21, car. 21. The garrison commander of Estella gave up on his mission in the city during the last half of 1810. A permanent garrison could never be reestablished in Estella.

48. Pérez Goyena, *Ensayo de bibliografía*, p. 167.

49. These decrees were printed in the *Gaceta de Madrid*, 22 and 23 July 1809.

50. Pérez Goyena, *Ensayo de bibliografía*, pp. 182–83. The March 1810 decree included the following clause with respect to the clergy: "The principal obligation of ministers of God is to preach His message to the people, teaching them and admonishing them to maintain the peace and render unto Caesar that which belongs to Caesar: those who do otherwise will be arrested and transported to France." The afrancesado Consejo de Navarra had earlier announced to the clergy a ban on sermons dealing with news or current issues of any kind and under any circumstance.

51. Ibid., p. 166.

52. Desboeufs, *Souvenirs du Capitaine Desboeufs*, p. 143.

53. Pérez Goyena, *Ensayo de bibliografía*, pp. 172–73.

54. Ibid., pp. 160–61.

55. For a brief time in the fall of 1809, Javier Mina had been able to obtain quarter for his troops and to arrange for the exchange of prisoners. Such exchanges, however, served merely to legitimize the guerrillas and to encourage young men to take up arms with the corso. The humane treatment of prisoners was not sustained for long by either side. Espoz y Mina, *Memorias*, p. 24.

56. These scenes are described by Adjutant I., *Souvenirs de la Guerre*, pp. 1–12. This anonymous author was one of those in charge of escorting the monks from their prison to the place of execution.

57. Ibid., p. 184.

58. Emmanuel Martin, *La gendarmerie française*, p. 213.

59. Suchet, *Memoirs*, 1:82, 233, 325. In January 1810 Reynier also distributed arms to villagers who requested protection from the guerrillas. Although he expressed reservations about the practice, the fact that he went ahead with it is evidence that peasants were still not entirely under the domination of the guerrillas. AAT, C8, 252.

60. *Gaceta de Madrid*, 27 December 1809. Carrasco and nine of his men were immediately hanged.

61. Ibid.

62. Alexander, *Rod of Iron*, p. 27.

63. Suchet, *Memoirs*, 1:331.

64. Desboeufs, *Souvenirs du Capitaine Desboeufs*, pp. 165–66.

65. By April four squadrons of gendarmes had been distributed among the capital and eleven other towns. Emmanuel Martin, *La gendarmerie française*, p. 50. Suchet had over 11,000 men garrisoning the area in the spring of 1810. Alexander, *Rod of Iron*, p. 33.

66. Adjutant I., *Souvenirs de la Guerre*, pp. 34–39. The villages of San Gregorio and Santa Cruz de Campezo were burned at this time.

67. Miranda Rubio, *La Guerra de la Independencia en Navarra*, pp. 167–68.

68. Espoz y Mina, *Memorias*, p. 11. Even Javier's discipline was none too rigorous, as witnessed by the transformation of the Tudela venture of November 1809 into an orgy of robbery.

69. Estella had its church silver stolen and its arms requisitioned. In Betelu the house of a criollo was sacked, and in Urdax a French ironmaster's home was looted. Such actions produced a torrent of complaints to the afrancesado government in Pamplona. Iribarren, *Espoz y Mina, el guerrillero*, pp. 102–4.

70. Andrés Martín, *Historia de los sucesos militares*, p. 62.

71. Espoz y Mina, *Memorias*, pp. 15–16.

72. Ibid., p. 14.

73. AGN, legajo 21, car. 21.

74. AHN, Estado, legajo 42, no. 38.

75. *Semanario Patriótico*, 9 May 1811.

76. Espoz y Mina, *Memorias*, p. 15.

77. Ibid., p. 14; Iribarren, *Espoz y Mina, el guerrillero*, p. 104.

78. Ayerbe, *Memorias*, pp. 220–50. These details are taken from testimony offered after the war by Ayerbe's guide, the third man in the party, whom the assassins allowed to

escape. The evidence is appended to Ayerbe's memoirs. In one version of the Ayerbe murder, written by Antoní Puigblanch, Espoz y Mina was said to have ordered the execution in order to eliminate a rival. Puigblanch, *Opúsculos*, pp. xxxv–xli. Puigblanch's version does not correspond, however, with evidence from official testimony nor with the subsequent actions of Mina, who carried out his own investigation of the rumored murders. Above all, the Puigblanch story does not accord with the logic of the situation, in which Mina had many more serious rivals for the leadership of Navarre.

79. Adjutant I., *Souvenirs de la Guerre*, pp. 109–20.

Chapter 6

1. Another attempt in April 1810, by Francisco Glaría, a cleric from the valley of Roncal, to recreate a unified command in Navarre failed. Glaría applied for and received approval of his status as leader of the guerrillas of Navarre from a junta that still operated secretly in Lérida. However, in what must be considered a transcendental accident, Glaría was killed in battle before he learned of his approval. His death opened the way for Espoz y Mina. "Relación del tercer regimiento," AGN, Guerra, legajo 17, car. 51.

2. Espoz y Mina, *Memorias*, p. 14; Andrés Martín, *Historia de los sucesos militares*, 1:61. Mina was cousin to Juan Martín de Mina, Javier's father, making his relationship to Javier Mina less close than is normally realized. APN, Pamplona, Peralta, legajo 50, no. 90.

3. Espoz y Mina, *Memorias*, p. 15. These events occurred on 10–11 April.

4. In April 1812 Mina's bravado saved him at one of the most dangerous moments in his career. In Robres, in Aragon, a detachment of French cavalry, tipped off by a traitor, surprised Mina while he was alone in his lodgings. As the French tried to force their way through the front door, Mina emerged holding a staff and, while buffeting his nearest enemies into submission, shouted: "Lancers, to the rear! Cavalry sergeant, take the first squadron to the left!" The French thought themselves the victims of a doublecross and withdrew just long enough for their intended victim to escape on horseback. Andrés Martín, *Historia de los sucesos militares*, 2:53–54.

5. Espoz y Mina, *Memorias*, pp. 17–18; "Relación del tercer regimiento," AGN, Guerra, legajo 17, car. 51. Even this junta had no legitimate authority in Navarre, which was under the jurisdiction of the newly installed Regency in Cádiz.

6. "Resumen del segundo regimiento," AGN, Guerra, legajo 21, car. 20. In the mountain village of Zuriáin, in one of his last independent actions in April, Cruchaga killed or captured all 104 men in a column traveling between the French border and Pamplona. Many of the captives were badly injured and, despite the summary executions meted out by the French to captured insurgents, Cruchaga allowed the injured French soldiers to be returned to Pamplona for medical attention. This incident was taken by Mina as a sign of Cruchaga's humanity.

7. As a military "expert" on Spain, Saint-Yon was asked to assess the characteristics of all of Spain's chief military men. His view of Mina was colored by the beating

Saint-Yon and the French took in Navarre during the war, but it is interesting nonetheless. Mina was "cruel to the point of brutality," according to Saint-Yon, and had no friends. "Gross, ungrateful, false, and a habitual liar," Mina had an overinflated military reputation, so Saint-Yon said. AAT, MR, 1349, 10.

8. APN, Pamplona, Peralta, legajo 50, no. 90.
9. Ibid.; Espoz y Mina, *Memorias*, p. 7.
10. AGN, Estadística, legajo 25, car. 2; legajo 26, car. 2.
11. Espoz y Mina, *Memorias*, p. 9.
12. Ibid., p. 21.
13. Condesa de Espoz y Mina, *Memorias íntimas*, p. 363; Iribarren, *Espoz y Mina, el guerrillero*, p. 34.
14. Olóriz, *Navarra en la Guerra de la Independencia*, p. 51; Iribarren, *Espoz y Mina, el guerrillero*, p. 35.
15. *Galería militar*, p. 168.
16. APN, Pamplona, Peralta, legajo 55, no. 91.
17. The chief of Mina's custom services handled immense sums of money constantly but was poorer after the war than before; Mina's treasurer died in 1814 with only three gold pieces to his name. Espoz y Mina, *Memorias*, p. 21. Mina also lived modestly, even during his moments of triumph under Liberal governments after the war. Condesa de Espoz y Mina, *Memorias íntimas*, p. 363.
18. Espoz y Mina, *Memorias*, pp. 367, 423–44.
19. Ibid., p. 22.
20. "Resumen del segundo regimiento," AGN, Guerra, legajo 21, car. 20.
21. AAT, C8, 387. The report for 1 June 1810 is missing, so the French figures should be even higher. The higher numbers in the French records could be accounted for by additional losses to guerrilla bands other than Mina's.
22. The largest number of troops assembled by Javier was 1,200 infantry and 40 cavalry in December 1809 according to the "Resumen del segundo regimiento." AGN, Guerra, legajo 21, car. 20. The same source, however, counted only 200 cavalry and 800 infantry under Javier at a slightly later date.
23. "Resumen del segundo regimiento," AGN, Guerra, legajo 21, car. 20; Espoz y Mina, *Memorias*, pp. 22–23.
24. "Resumen del segundo regimiento," AGN, Guerra, legajo 21, car. 20.
25. "Relación del tercer regimiento," AGN, Guerra, legajo 17, car. 51.
26. "Relación de Estella," AGN, Guerra, legajo 21, car. 21.
27. Espoz y Mina, *Memorias*, p. 26.
28. Ibid., p. 37.
29. "Relación de Estella," AGN, Guerra, legajo 21, car. 21.
30. Espoz y Mina, *Memorias*, pp. 28–29.
31. Ibid. These details exist only in the account given by Mina.
32. Puigblanch, *Opúsculos*, p. xli.
33. Napoleon to Berthier, 9 April 1810, Napoleon Bonaparte, *The Confidential Correspondence*.
34. Napoleon to Berthier, 29 May 1810, ibid.

35. Napoleon to Berthier, 10 July 1810, ibid.; and Andrés Martín, *Historia de los sucesos militares*, 1:59.
36. Reille to Neuchâtel, 30 July 1810, AAT, C8, 268.
37. "Resumen del segundo regimiento," AGN, Guerra, legajo 21, car. 20. Reille's report of the battle dated 1 August 1810 listed eight killed and seventy wounded, but said nothing about the Navarrese renegades captured. AAT, C8, 268. The truth probably lies somewhere in between these two partisan accounts. The Navarrese source indicated that the guerrillas wounded 400 enemy troops. This demonstrates how the guerrillas exaggerated enemy losses, particularly the numbers of wounded. Combatants have always "rounded off" or changed body counts, but the Navarrese estimates have to be treated with particular skepticism, since the guerrillas almost never maintained the field (until 1812) even in victory, and the French were usually able to retreat in orderly fashion with their wounded. That battle figures were dispatched to officials hundreds of miles away in Valencia or Cádiz with no means of verification is another good reason to discount the figures given by the guerrillas. In most cases, I have discarded Navarrese figures for French wounded. Usually this results in a close correspondence between the French and Spanish estimates for casualties, and it is probably as near to precision as we will ever get.
38. Espoz y Mina, *Memorias*, pp. 29, 34.
39. "Resumen del segundo regimiento," AGN, Guerra, legajo 21, car. 20.
40. AAT, C8, 387 and 268.
41. This number is probably conservative. First, it excludes several engagements for which there are no figures. In addition, bands aside from the corso were still operating in Navarre during this period, and, disorganized as they were, they would have had some effect. Finally, I have discarded guerrilla figures for enemy wounded, which in some instances reached the absurd ratio of ten times the number killed. I have chosen to cite the most conservative numbers possible throughout in order to nullify the tendency of the Spanish chroniclers to exaggerate their victories and minimize their defeats. French sources are a corrective, though there is no reason to believe them wholly accurate either. In the period from 1 April to 30 September, French forces in Navarre lost 1,077 killed, captured, wounded, or deserted according to the French reports and correspondence, but for the period from mid-July to October Reille also reported a doubling of the number of troops confined to hospital.
42. "Relación del tercer regimiento," AGN, Guerra, legajo 17, car. 51.
43. Situation report of 15 September 1810, AAT, C8, 387.
44. These and the following movements of the guerrillas are constructed using the "Resumen del segundo regimiento," AGN, Guerra, legajo 21, car. 20; "Relación del tercer regimiento," AGN, Guerra, legajo 17, car. 51.
45. Reille to Neuchâtel, 4 September 1810, AAT, C8, 268.
46. Espoz y Mina, *Memorias*, p. 35.
47. In addition to the regimental diaries, see Andrés Martín, *Historia de los sucesos militares*, 1:94–95; Espoz y Mina, *Memorias*, p. 36; and Reille's account in AAT, C8, 268.
48. "Resumen del segundo regimiento," AGN, Guerra, legajo 21, car. 20. The second

battalion alone lost 200 men killed. Martín gives a number for all three battalions of 350 killed with 80 shot afterward. Mina said he lost 400 and that the number executed was 70. Espoz y Mina, *Memorias*, p. 37. In all of these engagements of October and November, the French forces under Reille lost only 60 men killed and imprisoned. AAT, C8, 387, reports for October and November.

Chapter 7

1. Andrés Martín, *Historia de los sucesos militares*, 1:105.
2. Olóriz, *Navarra en la Guerra de la Independencia*, p. 60.
3. Reille informed the French ambassador at the Court of Joseph Bonaparte that his reestablishment of the Diputación had no purpose outside of the need to set his finances in order. Iribarren, *Espoz y Mina, el guerrillero*, p. 149.
4. Miranda Rubio, *La Guerra de la Independencia en Navarra*, pp. 171–73.
5. The Diputación presented its final recommendations for regularizing tax collection procedures on 26 September 1810, while Mina was in the South. AGN, Guerra, legajo 17, car. 8.
6. Letter of 13 October 1810, AAT, C8, 268.
7. Olóriz, *Navarra en la Guerra de la Independencia*, p. 78.
8. Martín called Mendiry the "fetid abortion of the Lower Pyrenees." Andrés Martín, *Historia de los sucesos militares*, 2:69. Decades later Navarrese parents still intoned his name as a bogeyman to frighten their children, saying "the Mendiry" was going to get them.
9. "Relación auténtica que contiene las personas que fueron aprisionados en Navarra por la policía francesa durante la guerra," AGN, Guerra, legajo 21, car. 19.
10. AGN, Guerra, legajos 18–21.
11. AGN, Guerra, legajo 21, car. 1.
12. AGN, Guerra, legajo 20, car. 53.
13. AGN, Guerra, legajos 18, 19, 20, 21.
14. AGN, Guerra, legajo 21, car. 9.
15. AGN, Guerra, legajo 19, car. 26.
16. AGN, Guerra, legajo 19, car. 25.
17. AGN, Guerra, legajo 21, car. 11.
18. AGN, Guerra, legajo 20, car. 53.
19. AGN, Guerra, legajo 21, car. 1.
20. AGN, Guerra, legajo 21, car. 5.
21. AGN, Guerra, legajo 21, car. 15.
22. AGN, Guerra, legajo 18, car. 19.
23. "Relación del tercer regimiento," AGN, Guerra, legajo 17, car. 51.
24. "Resumen del segundo regimiento," AGN, Guerra, legajo 21, car. 20; Andrés Martín, *Historia de los sucesos militares*, 1:105, spoke of sixty men under Mina on 17 November.
25. "Relación del tercer regimiento," AGN, Guerra, legajo 17, car. 51.
26. Ibid.; Andrés Martín, *Historia de los sucesos militares*, 1:105.

27. Espoz y Mina, *Memorias*, p. 41.
28. Iribarren, *Espoz y Mina, el guerrillero*, pp. 197–98. Significantly, the execution of Belza does not figure in Mina's memoirs, where he usually tried to justify all of his more unsavory acts and duties. It may be that he hoped the world would fail to notice the Belza affair.
29. Espoz y Mina, *Memorias*, p. 41.
30. Dated 1 January 1811, AAT, C8, 387; Emmanuel Martin, *La gendarmerie française*, p. 225; Andrés Martín, *Historia de los sucesos militares*, 1:106, 109; "Resumen del segundo regimiento," AGN, Guerra, legajo 21, car. 20; Espoz y Mina, *Memorias*, p. 42.
31. Espoz y Mina, *Memorias*, p. 43; AGN, Guerra, legajo 21, car. 6.
32. Reille's report of 15 January 1811, AAT, C8, 387.
33. Andrés Martín, *Historia de los sucesos militares*, 1:111; "Relación del tercer regimiento," AGN, Guerra, legajo 17, car. 51. Espoz y Mina, *Memorias*, p. 46. One individual, found hiding in a bread oven, was forced to remain inside while the oven was lit, baking the poor devil alive.
34. Alexander, *Rod of Iron*, p. 51.
35. Letter of 1 March 1811, AAT, C8, 268.
36. "Resumen del segundo regimiento," AGN, Guerra, legajo 21, car. 20; "Relación del tercer regimiento," AGN, Guerra, legajo 17, car. 51; letters of 21, 28 March 1811, AAT, C8, 268.
37. Letters of 4, 5, 18 April 1811, AAT, C8, 268.
38. Alexander, *Rod of Iron*, p. 97.
39. Report of 1 June 1811, AAT, C8, 378. The French report of this action by Cafarelli is incomplete, since the general reports only the casualties (130) among the Thirty-second Fusiliers. Cafarelli gave a brief account of the battle. The most interesting fact to emerge in his report is that the English prisoners, instead of taking advantage of the attack to escape, shamelessly retrieved French guns and fired upon the guerrillas. For casualty estimates I relied on Andrés Martín, *Historia de los sucesos militares*, 1:128–32, whose figures are much lower than those given in the other sources. Mina and the battalion diaries place the French losses at 800 killed and 600 captured. Casualties among the Navarrese are known only for the second and third battalions, which lost 13 killed and 49 wounded.
40. Espoz y Mina, *Memorias*, pp. 52–53.
41. *Gaceta de la Mancha*, 13 April 1811.
42. Espoz y Mina, *Memorias*, p. 57.
43. "Relación del tercer regimiento," AGN, Guerra, legajo 17, car. 51.
44. Napoleon to Berthier, 10 June 1811 and 31 July 1811, Napoleon Bonaparte, *The Confidential Correspondence*, pp. 185–87.
45. Espoz y Mina, *Memorias*, pp. 59, 67.
46. Andrés Martín, *Historia de los sucesos militares*, 2:9.
47. "Relación del tercer regimiento," AGN, Guerra, legajo 17, car. 51; "Resumen del segundo regimiento," AGN, Guerra, legajo 21, car. 20; Espoz y Mina, *Memorias*, p. 62.

48. Reille to Neuchâtel, 11 July 1811, AAT, C8, 268.
49. Andrés Martín, *Historia de los sucesos militares*, 2:91–92.
50. Espoz y Mina, *Memorias*, p. 63; Iribarren, *Espoz y Mina, el guerrillero*, pp. 289–92.
51. Spanish casualties are known only for the second battalion, which had sixteen killed and seventy wounded. But the second battalion arrived late and saw action only at the very end. Division casualties were therefore probably nearly as high as those suffered by the French. "Resumen del segundo regimiento," AGN, Guerra, legajo 21, car. 20. Reille admitted only seventy French casualties. Letter of 26 July 1811, AAT, C8, 268.
52. Andrés Martín, *Historia de los sucesos militares*, 2:18. Reille placed Navarrese losses at 300 killed and 204 captured. Report of 1 August 1811, AAT, C8, 268.
53. Espoz y Mina, *Memorias*, pp. 69–71; Olóriz, *Navarra en la Guerra de la Independencia*, pp. 129–43. Mina feared for the envoys' lives, since his men wanted to try them as traitors. Mina formed a special guard that was instructed to arrange for their escape.
54. "Resumen del segundo regimiento," AGN, Guerra, legajo 21, car. 20.
55. Jouffroy, "Operations de l'Armée d'Aragon," AAT, MR, 770.
56. Thouvenot found a copy of the order and reported its contents in a letter of 6 October 1811, AAT, C8, 206.
57. The accounts in Espoz y Mina, *Memorias*, p. 79, and in the "Resumen del segundo regimiento," AGN, Guerra, legajo 21, car. 20, present slightly more exaggerated numbers. I have used those provided by Jouffroy, a French officer stationed in Aragon, in his account of operations, AAT, MR, 770.
58. "Relación del tercer regimiento," AGN, Guerra, legajo 17, car. 51.
59. Andrés Martín, *Historia de los sucesos militares*, 2:27; "Resumen del segundo regimiento," AGN, Guerra, legajo 21, car 20.
60. Report of 15 December 1811, AAT, C8, 387.
61. Alexander, *Rod of Iron*, pp. 135–37.
62. Ibid., pp. 126–27. For example, in March 1811 Mina had been able to escape encirclement in Baztán by seeking refuge inside France! There, in the region of Alduides, he found a sympathetic reception. Reille's letter of 8 March 1811, AAT, C8, 387.
63. A tally of the very incomplete records kept by Reille, Soulier, Cafarelli, and Jouffroy of their battles with Mina resulted in a figure of 2,565 casualties, and this leaves out figures for many engagements.

Chapter 8

1. "Manifiesto de las acciones del Mariscal de Campo Don Francisco Espoz y Mina," AGN, Guerra, legajo 17, car. 53. The Spanish commonly displayed the severed hands of convicted thieves, but at least they executed them first.
2. Ibid.; Espoz y Mina, *Memorias*, p. 111; and Andrés Martín, *Historia de los sucesos militares*, 2:52.
3. This was the surprise at Robres (related in an earlier chapter) when Mina bluffed his way to freedom. Tris must have known that Mina had returned to Aragon in April

expressly in order to relieve him of command. This accounts for the betrayal. Mina had Tris and his assistant, several regidores from surrounding communities, a local priest, and a "spy" from Zaragoza shot for their part in the conspiracy.

4. Report of Cafarelli, 15 January 1812, AAT, C8, 378; Andrés Martín, *Historia de los sucesos militares*, 2:29; "Resumen del segundo regimiento," AGN, Guerra, legajo 21, car. 20, claims that the garrison was made up of 300 men, as does Espoz y Mina, *Memorias*, p. 87.

5. The battle is recounted in the "Resumen del segundo regimiento," AGN, Guerra, legajo 21, car. 20; "Relación del tercer regimiento," AGN, Guerra, legajo 17, car 51; Andrés Martín, *Historia de los sucesos militares*, 2:34; and Espoz y Mina, *Memorias*, pp. 88–89. General Abbé gave few details of this battle, but he did record 264 casualties and 110 wounded evacuated to France in the month of January. These numbers do not include Cafarelli's casualties, and Cafarelli gave no information at all in his reports. If his losses were like Abbé's, 600 casualties seems plausible. AAT, C8, 387 and 378.

6. Report of Abbé, 1 February 1812, AAT, C8, 387.

7. The decree was written by the ex-Capuchin, Uriz, who served as scribe to Mina. The decree was actually twenty-three articles long and included other measures, like the imposition of the death penalty for anyone who murmured against the decree. Espoz y Mina, *Memorias*, p. 86.

8. Evidence for these executions, detentions, and deportations is from Reille's correspondence in AAT, C8, 268, 269. Reille left such a detailed account of his reign of terror because he was constantly forced to answer charges that he was too lenient!

9. AAT, C8, 268, 269.

10. Ibid.; Iribarren, *Espoz y Mina, el guerrillero*, pp. 355–57.

11. Iribarren, *Espoz y Mina, el guerrillero*, p. 360.

12. Espoz y Mina, *Memorias*, p. 100.

13. Mina also lobbied to have his authority over Rioja and Guipúzcoa recognized, to no avail. Ibid., pp. 92–98.

14. "Resumen del segundo regimiento," AGN, Guerra, legajo 21, car. 20. "Factories" like those depicted by Goya in his *Fábrica de pólvora* and *Fábrica de balas* sketches had to be moved constantly in order to avoid detection. See also Espoz y Mina, *Memorias*, p. 123.

15. Letter from General Thouvenot to Berthier, 29 April 1810, AHN, Estado, legajo 3003, no. 42.

16. On 29 July 1811 Mina had picked up 6,000 rifles from the English in Santona. *Gaceta de la Mancha*, 10 August 1811.

17. "Resumen del segundo regimiento," AGN, Guerra, legajo 21, car 20.

18. Espoz y Mina, *Memorias*, p. 69.

19. Ibid., p. 20.

20. "Estado de la totalidad de rentas fijas del Govierno del Reino de Navarra," AGN, Estadística, legajo 49, car. 34.

21. "Resumen del segundo regimiento," AGN, Guerra, legajo 21, car. 20; Espoz y Mina, *Memorias*, pp. 99–100; Andrés Martín, *Historia de los sucesos militares*, 2:35.

22. Andrés Martín, *Historia de los sucesos militares*, 2:37. The loss of Soulier's correspondence was confirmed in the report by his superior, Cafarelli, whose initial report on the battle based on partial information also lends credence to the figure of 600 casualties. Cafarelli recorded the loss of 400 men, but his next report noted another 180 killed and 4 deserters, men lost perhaps during the retreat to Sos.

23. "Resumen del segundo regimiento," AGN, Guerra, legajo 21, car. 20; "Relación del tercer regimiento," AGN, Guerra, legajo 17, car. 51; Alexander, *Rod of Iron*, pp. 147–48.

24. An idea of French losses can be obtained by considering that of 2,800 replacement troops for Suchet that were detoured in Navarre during March, only 1,100 remained active in April when they finally reported to their units. Alexander, *Rod of Iron*, p. 162. On the other hand, the situation reports from Pamplona showed only 84 casualties in March, so Abbé's men saw little action. Abbé's reports of 15 March and 1 April 1812, AAT, C8, 387.

25. Espoz y Mina, *Memorias*, p. 86.

26. Ibid., p. 100.

27. Iribarren, *Espoz y Mina, el guerrillero*, pp. 367–74, discusses some of the evidence for these penalties. The punishment of removing ears was common in Navarre, as indeed it was in other areas. (In the Vendée the victorious republicans created macabre trophies by stringing together ears taken from the unfortunate rebels.) In Navarre, this castigation was applied for a wide range of offenses, even for prostitution. Mina became known as *corteorejas*, because he employed this penalty so frequently.

28. Pérez Goyena, *Ensayo de bibliografía*.

29. "Relación de Estella," AGN, Guerra, legajo 21, car. 21.

30. May 1812 was not a good month for Tudela. The day after Yanguas's capture, General Duran and his guerrilla party from Aragon sacked the city during a brief absence by the Tudela garrison. Olóriz, *Navarra en la Guerra de la Independencia*, pp. 349–52.

31. Iribarren, *Espoz y Mina, el guerrillero*, p. 303. Yanguas's abduction was not an isolated case. The guerrillas kidnapped other collaborating officials as well. Alexander, *Rod of Iron*, p. 51.

32. Puigblanch, *Opúsculos*, p. xxxv. This story is related by one of Mina's great enemies, but it is not out of character for Mina or his men.

33. Iribarren, *Espoz y Mina, el guerrillero*, p. 304.

34. "Relación de Estella," AGN, Guerra, legajo 21, car. 21.

35. Because the second and third regiments were not on hand, information about the second surprise at Arlabán must be taken from Andrés Martín, *Historia de los sucesos militares*, 2:49; Espoz y Mina, *Memorias*, p. 105, and Thouvenot's letters of 10 and 13 April 1812, AAT, C8, 206.

36. "Relación del tercer regimiento," AGN, Guerra, legajo 17, car. 51.

37. Ibid.

38. Like Javier Mina, Juan José Cruchaga was educated in Zaragoza, according to records relating to a petition by his father for recognition of his son's noble status. APN, Pamplona, Ros, legajo 121, car. 114.

39. There is an obvious parallel in Mina's succession to the command of Javier Mina and

his adoption of his nephew's name. Like Mina, the younger Cruchaga turned out to be a worthy heir.

40. "Resumen del segundo regimiento," AGN, Guerra, legajo 21, car. 20; Espoz y Mina, *Memorias*, p. 117.

41. "Relación del tercer regimiento," AGN, Guerra, legajo 17, car. 51.

42. The garrison in Huesca that surrendered in January 1812 had by then been replaced. Marc Desboeufs, the new commander in Huesca, recalled his feelings of isolation. The guerrillas ruled the town, while he and his men remained locked inside the fortress, which, however, the Aragonese could not take due to a lack of artillery. The French had to sneak out at night wearing espadrilles to muffle their footfalls so they could steal supplies. Desboeufs, *Souvenirs du Capitaine Desboeufs*, p. 184.

43. Alexander, *Rod of Iron*, p. 193.

44. In July the Division acquired its own printing press, allowing each battalion to leave detailed accounts of its activities. These records were published under the title *Colección de los trimestres de la División de Navarra*, and are located in the AGN, Guerra, legajo 17, car. 53. The "trimesters" almost always agree with the accounts of the second and third battalions, and Andrés Martín used them in constructing his history. Since, moreover, they include dispatches from the first, fourth, Alavese, and Aragonese battalions, they are the best narrative source for the last year and a half of the war and will be used in preference to the other sources henceforth, except when there are discrepancies.

45. Beginning in 1812, the situation reports filed by General Abbé in AAT, C8, 387, become more detailed. They can be used, therefore, to supplement the Trimesters. Abbé reported 405 casualties, fewer than the guerrillas claimed, but it was a major defeat from any perspective.

46. Abbé's logs from August onward are filled with stories of requisition parties being ambushed, losing their carts and horses, and returning with nothing for their troubles. AAT, C8, 387.

47. Alexander, *Rod of Iron*, p. 197.

48. Olóriz, *Navarra en la Guerra de la Independencia*, pp. 367–69. This is one of the pieces of captured correspondence printed by Olóriz in his appendices.

49. Alexander, *Rod of Iron*, pp. 211–12.

50. Clausel to Joseph Bonaparte, 4 May 1813. The letter was captured by the guerrillas and printed in the *Trimesters*, AGN, Guerra, legajo 17, car. 53.

51. Alexander, *Rod of Iron*, pp. 220–21.

52. "Operaciones militares del séptimo regimiento," AGN, Guerra, legajo 17, car. 5.

Chapter 9

1. Mitchell, "Tocqueville's Mirage or Reality?" The language of liberty and fraternity survived only in official pronouncements, but what had once been a reflection of genuine Jacobin convictions was now a thin veneer intended to serve selfish desires.

2. Bergeron, *France under Napoleon*, pp. 52–79.

3. Foy, *Histoire de la guerre de la péninsule*, 1:77–78.

4. Letter of 10 August 1810 from Masséna to King Joseph, AHN, Estado, legajo 3003. Masséna's personal ties to Joseph and the fact that he was himself an anachronism from the French Revolution may account for his own relatively blameless conduct.

5. Rodríguez-Solís, *Los guerrilleros de 1808*, 2:44.

6. Foy, *Histoire de la guerre de la péninsule*, 1:129.

7. Joseph complained to his brother that Culaincourt's pillage of the churches in Cuenca and the subsequent public sale of Cuenca's church plate in Madrid had destroyed any chance he might have had to pacify his new kingdom. "Every sensible person in the government and in the army," wrote Joseph, "says that a defeat would have been less injurious." Napoleon's insensitive response to his brother was to praise Culaincourt for doing what "was perfectly right at Cuenca." Napoleon Bonaparte, *The Confidential Correspondence*, letters of 22 and 31 July 1808. In Córdoba, just before the battle of Bailén, Dupont's men exercised a special fury against monks and nuns, and converted the city's convents into stables and brothels for the troops. French atrocities against religion brought condemnation from the most unexpected quarters. Even Morocco pleaded with the Spanish to do everything in their power to destroy the "atheist" French hordes. Valencina, *Los capuchinos de Andalucía*, pp. 27, 232–45.

8. AHN, Estado, legajo 3003. AGN, Guerra, legajo 17, car. 1.

9. In Seville, two convents became centers for the manufacture of cartridges until the city fell in 1810. During May–June 1809, the Capuchin convent in Seville produced 500,000 cartridges as well as many uniforms. The monks also worked on the fortifications of the city. Valencina, *Los capuchinos*, pp. 78, 96.

10. Ibid., pp. 88–90. The government did solicit suggestions from the clergy on how best to mobilize the resources of the church against France. Dozens of clerics forwarded proposals to the Central Junta. Juan Ferrer, a Catalonian priest, condemned the church and government for discouraging priests and monks from taking up arms. By encouraging clerics to fight in guerrilla parties, argued Ferrer, the guerrilla movement would be reformed and strengthened from within. Another Catalonian priest, Juan Constans, offered to raise 3,000 men, if the junta would approve the use of arms by priests and monks and provide financial support. "Plan sobre el modo de formar un Exército de Cruzados en la Provincia de Cataluña," AHN, Estado, legajo 41, C, 22 June 1809. "Plan de Juan Pablo Constans, Canónigo de la Colegial Iglesia de Pons de Cataluña," AHN, Estado, legajo 41, C, 24 September 1809.

11. AHN, Estado, legajo 41, A, no. 5.

12. AHN, Estado, legajo. 41, C–D, nos. 24–75.

13. Martínez Salazar, *De la Guerra de la Independencia en Galicia*, p. 13.

14. In Madrid, there was nothing remarkable in the anticlerical feelings of the people both before and during the War of Independence. Mesonero y Romanos, *Memorias de un setentón*, p. 139.

15. AGN, Guerra, legajo 15, car. 17.

16. Mutiloa Poza, *La desamortización*, p. 269.

17. Ibid., pp. 270–71, 286.

18. Ibid., pp. 264–67.

19. Ibid., p. 294.

20. For example, Aymes, *La Guerre d'Independence Espagnole*.

21. AGN, Guerra, legajos 18–21. In the accounts given by local communities, the names of those arrested or executed are not usually given, but a large number of communities did say that their priests were taken away.

22. Olóriz, *Navarra en la Guerra de la Independencia*, p. 190.

23. Desdevises du Dezert, *L'Espagne de l'Ancien Régime*, 1:xv.

24. For example, the long-lived priest of Echauri during both the War of Independence and the first Carlist War, was finally murdered after a lifetime spent at the spiritual center of a village that was almost constantly at war during his lifetime. In August 1837 Cristino soldiers assassinated him. APE, libro de difuntos, no. 5.

25. Members of closed houses in Estella neither had to leave the city nor accept government-paid secular posts, such was the generosity of the townspeople. AGN, Guerra, legajo 21, car. 21.

26. Desdevises du Dezert, *L'Espagne de l'Ancien Régime*, 1:xv.

27. "Relación del tercer regimiento," AGN, Guerra, legajo 17, car. 51. The first few pages contain what little there was of theory and justification.

28. "Resumen del segundo regimiento," AGN, Guerra, legajo 21, car. 20.

29. "Manifiesto de las acciones del Mariscal de Campo Don Francisco Espoz y Mina," AGN, Guerra, legajo 17, car. 53.

30. Andrés Martín, *Historia de los sucesos militares*, 1:20.

31. Espoz y Mina, *Memorias*, p. 68.

32. *Semanario Patriótico*, 27 October 1808.

33. Sahlins, *Boundaries*.

34. In the 1970s the Navarrese resisted pressures to join the autonomous region today identified as the Basque provinces based in large part on their aversion to Basque separatism. The Navarrese and the people of the Basque provinces have followed separate trajectories in times of national crisis, as in the War of Independence, when Mina and the Navarrese first stirred up the resistance in Álava, Guipúzcoa, and Vizcaya, and in the Civil War of 1936–39. See Sánchez-Albornoz, *Orígenes y destino de Navarra*, for a discussion of the relationship between Navarre and the Basque country.

35. Mina even forgave the members of the afrancesado Diputación, saying that they were forced into their collaboration and that they actually performed services that were as valuable to the people of Navarre as they were to the occupier. Espoz y Mina, *Memorias*, p. 39.

36. Azanza and O'Fárrill, *Memoria*, pp. 176–77, 279–84.

37. Miranda Rubio, *La Guerra de la Independencia en Navarra*, p. 141.

38. Ibid., pp. 142–43.

39. Napoleon wrote to Berthier on 12 October 1810 asking him to "let him [Cafarelli] know confidentially that I intend to annex Biscay to France; that it is not to be mentioned, but that it must influence his conduct. Impart the same secret to General Reille with respect to Navarre." Napoleon Bonaparte, *The Confidential Correspondence*.

40. "La Ciudad de Pamplona al Rey Jose," dated 26 May 1810, AHN, legajo 3003, no. 1.

41. Mercader Riba, *José Bonaparte, Rey de España*, p. 13.
42. Artola, *Los afrancesados*, p. 199.
43. Azanza and O'Fárrill, *Memoria*, pp. 176–77, 279–84.
44. AHN, Estado, legajo 3003.
45. Torre, *Los campesinos navarros*, pp. 25–65.
46. The average annual product of agriculture, commerce, and industry in Navarre in the period before the war came to 71,600,000 reales. "Estado general de los productos territoriales, comerciales, é industriales del Reino de Navarra," AGN, Estadística, legajo 49, car. 18.
47. Torre, *Los campesinos navarros*, p. 29.
48. Ibid., pp. 87–91.
49. AGN, Guerra, legajo 18, car. 19. When this did not achieve the desired result, Mina directed his aide to send threatening letters to the city government demanding contributions, but they never came. After the war, Tudelans were among Mina's most implacable enemies.
50. AGN, Guerra, legajo 20. Iriberri gave 478 reales per person, two-thirds of it in money.
51. AGN, Guerra, legajo 19, car. 44.
52. AGN, Guerra, legajos 20, 21.
53. "Razón de todo lo contribuido por este valle de Echauri desde el año de 1808 hasta el de 1813," APN, Pamplona, Velaz, 1815; and "Estado que manifiesta los granos, frutos, y ganados que hubo en toda la merindad de Pamplona en el año de 1807," AGN, Estadística, legajo 33, car. 1.
54. For Arraiza, an average-sized village within the valley, an even more detailed account is available. Arraiza contributed 54,700 reales to the French, two-thirds during the difficult year of 1811. Of this total, 43 percent was in the form of money, requiring the community repeatedly to exact head taxes and violate communal sources of wealth. To the guerrillas, on the other hand, Arraiza contributed nothing in cash. In rations and goods, however, the Division took 64,800 reales. In addition, the village gave 28,800 reales to the regular Spanish and Allied troops after 1813. Per capita, Arraiza contributed 237 reales to the French, 266 reales to the Division, and 118 reales to the Allies. "Razón de lo que ha suplido este lugar de Arraiza," APN, Pamplona, Velaz, legajo 91, 1815.
55. AGN, Guerra, legajo 20, car. 5.
56. The annual farming out of public services like the supply of wine, meat, fish, and bread, together with the rents from municipal pastures and other lands, produced more than enough to cover the ordinary expenses of local governments in the Montaña. As an example, in 1800 the village of Noáin formulated a plan to repair its fountains and roads at a cost of 300 reales and noted that its treasury contained a surplus of 2,953 reales after all other expenses had been met. APN, Pamplona, Peralta, legajo 51, no. 73, 20 May 1800.
57. A more fundamental alteration occurred with respect to the system by which Echauri milled its grain. Because milling was such a sensitive and important function, a special system had been worked out in Echauri for managing it. The water mill was not

simply rented out on a contractual basis. Had this been the case, the miller would have had to make his profit by taking a portion of the grain brought to him for milling. This portion could have been increased by adulterating the flour returned to clients or by altering receipts. Echauri avoided this abuse, common and ancient in most of Europe, by placing a salaried employee in the mill. The miller, in other words, had been converted into a full-fledged public employee. This system had to be abandoned during the Napoleonic war, however, in order to raise emergency funds. The mill was leased once again. Moreover, to maximize the value of the rental, traditional price controls were dropped. The miller was allowed to sell the flour at inflated wartime prices in return for the payment of a higher annual rent than would otherwise have been possible. The community raised needed money through what amounted to a hidden tax on bread. Echauri was not able to return to the more rational system until the spring of 1817. APN, Pamplona, Velaz.

58. APN, Pamplona, Velaz, legajo 92, 1816. Echauri also sold (illegally) over three acres of its parish's land to individuals. The land was not recovered by the parish after the war, but the village agreed to pay its priest an annual sum in compensation. Ironically, this result amounted to a partial de facto fulfillment of the French and Liberal program of secularization of the church. APN, Pamplona, Velaz, legajo 96, 1829.

59. APN, Pamplona, Velaz, legajo 96, 1829. The serious nature of this debt can be appreciated when one realizes that 8,500 reales was fourteen times the annual rent Echauri collected from all of its farmed municipal services. The method of debt retirement worked out by the village in 1828 provides an insight into Echauri's egalitarian nature. Echauri divided the debt among all heads of household on a proportional basis, from Don Melchor de Mendigaña's 1,431 reales to Simona Larumbe's 4 reales. All together, individuals paid 4,898 reales. The community promised to pay the balance, although it is unclear where these new funds were supposed to originate in the difficult decades of the 1820s and 1830s. APN, Pamplona, Velaz, legajo 96, 1828.

60. APN, Pamplona, Velaz, legajos 83–96 (1798–1828). There were 6,157 acres of private farmland in the valley of Echauri.

61. Taxes and contributions were levied on the valley as a whole, and each village was assigned a percentage of the contribution based on the number of households it possessed. The villages, however, collected taxes based on individuals' ability to pay. APN, Pamplona, Velaz, legajo 89, no. 13, 11 April 1811 and legajo 92, 1815.

62. These and other figures on the sale of commons are from the APN, Pamplona, Velaz, legajos 83–91. My examination of the records from 1800 to 1808 for the valleys of Elorz, Ibargoiti, and Unciti east of Pamplona confirmed the same pattern. APN, Pamplona, Peralta, legajos 50–54.

63. APN, Pamplona, Velaz, legajos 83–96.

64. APN, Tudela, Laquidáin, Renault, Guesca y Alfaro, 1783–1818.

65. AMC, legajo 85.

66. AMC, legajo 85, no. 5.

67. Unlike the situation in many other areas of Europe where the use of commons had long been the preserve of the biggest livestock owners, and the alienation of the

commons had the potential, therefore, of damaging their interests. See, for example, Gauthier, *La voie paysanne*.

68. "Plan para la enagenación de los enfiteusis de la Ciudad de Corella," AMC, legajo 85.

69. Montoro Sagasti, *La propiedad privada*.

70. It is interesting to note, however, that the new owners of the nationalized properties, disheartened by the tenacity of the insurgents and the direction taken by the regime, began to balk at making their mortgage payments as early as August 1810. Did they already foresee the inevitable loss of these investments? AMC, legajo 85.

71. AGN, Guerra, legajos 18–21.

72. One wonders why even these fifteen were identified. In a few cases, the individuals had already been killed, and in one case there were no living relatives to punish. Most, however, had relatives that could (and probably were) taken away to prison. Perhaps the individuals listed were already known to the French and could no longer be protected. AGN, Estadística, legajo 10, cars. 38, 43–45.

73. Espoz y Mina, *Memorias*, pp. 15–16.

74. Ibid., p. 9.

75. Ibid., p. 201.

76. *Gaceta de la Mancha*, 13 April 1811.

77. Emmanuel Martin, *La gendarmerie française*, pp. 209, 219, 223–24.

78. Volunteers received one real a day in wages, plus a ration of bread, wine, and meat. Officials received more. A captain, for example, got ten reales a day, plus double rations. The commanders drew triple or quadruple rations, but no regular salary. Since the imperial armies in Spain were notorious for not paying their troops or for paying them late, it is not surprising to find desertion to the guerrillas a fairly common occurrence. "Estado de los sueldos y raciones," letter of 28 July 1818, AGN, Guerra, legajo 21, car. 20.

79. Alexander, *Rod of Iron*, p. 121.

Epilogue

1. Espoz y Mina, *Memorias*, pp. 179–80; AGN, Guerra, legajo 17, contains various complaints against Mina, the Division, and the other troops, especially on the part of the authorities in the Ribera.

2. AGN, Guerra, legajo 17, car. 30.

3. AGN, Guerra, legajo 17, car. 36.

4. "Oficio de tribunal territorial de Navarra," AGN, legajo 17, car. 41.

5. For example, the Tribunal tried to collect money from Tudela on behalf of two local merchants who had given the Division medical supplies. Letter from Tudela to the Diputación, 13 August 1814, AGN, Guerra, legajo 17, car. 42.

6. Letter from the Diputación to Mina, 18 August 1814, AGN, Guerra, legajo 17, car. 43.

7. AGN, Guerra, legajo 17, car. 45.

8. Ibid.

9. Letter of Josef Fermín La Puerta to the Diputación, 17 September 1814, AGN, legajo 17, car. 47.
10. AGN, Guerra, legajo 17, car. 46.
11. AGN, Guerra, legajo 17, car. 48.
12. "Relación dada a la Diputación del Reino por la oficialdad del primer regimiento de voluntarios de la división de Navarra," 12 October 1814, AGN, Guerra, legajo 17, car. 50.
13. The participation of at least part of the first and fourth battalions in the attempt on Pamplona may account for the absence of military accounts submitted by these corps after the war analogous to those written by the second and third battalions.
14. Using only Navarrese accounts, the number of French casualties would be much higher. Mina spoke of 40,000 killed and captured alone, not taking into account the numbers wounded. Because some of the French situation reports and correspondence are missing, it is not possible to come up with a global estimate of casualties from the French records. However, the French figures used in this work do not differ significantly except in a few cases from those of the Navarrese chronicles. Given the numbers of soldiers constantly in the hospital (over 1,000 at almost all times) and the large numbers reported evacuated to France, the number of 50,000 total casualties seems reasonable.
15. In the summer of 1811, General Blake ordered the Aragonese guerrillas Villacampa and Obispo as well as the Empecinado to join his forces in Valencia. The Empecinado wisely declined for himself, but most of his force obeyed the summons and surrendered along with the city in January 1812. The Empecinado was reduced to commanding only 400 men. By holding out, he opened himself to charges of fomenting the "damnable spirit of provincialism or so-called federalism" decried by the patriots in Cádiz. Like Blake, they thought the guerrillas should operate according to plans formulated in the army and remain "under the protection and supervision of the government." *Semanario Patriótico*, 1 August 1811. When Valencia fell, the superiority of the Empecinado's instinctive strategic decision became clear.
16. Fantin des Odoards, *Journal*, pp. 275, 288.

�֎ Bibliography

Archive and Manuscript Sources

Archives de l'Armée de Terre, Paris
C8, 351, 352, 377, 376, 378, 381, 387 (situation reports)
C8, 3–7, 252, 267–69, 206 (correspondence of French generals)
MR, 770, 774, 1349, 1777 (manuscripts of Jouffroy, Saint-Yon, Presle)
Archivo General de Navarra, Pamplona, Navarre
Sección Estadística
legajos 6–11, 16–17, 20, 25–28, 31, 33, 49 (census data, 1786–87, 1796–97)
legajos 33, 43, 49 (economic surveys)
Sección Guerra
legajos 13–14 (documents related to war with France in 1794)
legajos 15–16 (documents from 1808 in Navarre)
legajos 17–21 (documents from the War of Independence)
Archivo Histórico Nacional, Madrid
Sección Estado
legajos 13, 28 (documents of the Central Junta)
legajo 41 (papers relating to the guerrillas)
legajo 42 (papers of Spanish generals)
legajo 81 (papers of the Junta of Murcia)
legajos 3003, 3096 (intercepted French mail)
Archivo Municipal de Corella, Navarre
legajos 81–85 (correspondence, surveys for the period 1803–19)
Archivo Parroquial de Echauri, Navarre
libro de difuntos
Archivos de Protocolos Notariales, Pamplona and Tudela, Navarre
Pamplona
Manuel de Velaz, legajos 78–96, valley of Echauri, 1789–1829
Andrés Peralta, legajos 50–55, valley of Ibargoiti, 1800–1814
Javier Ros, legajos 120–21, valley of Roncal, 1800–1802

Tudela
  Miguel Guesca y Alfaro, Mariano Laquidáin, Juan Miguel Renault, Manuel Resa,
    unnumbered, Corella, 1783–1818
Biblioteca Nacional, Madrid
  manuscritos

Periodicals

El Robespierre español, amigo de las leyes ó questiones atrevidas sobre la España, 1811–12.
El Semanario Patriótico, 1808–12.
Gaceta de Madrid, 1808–12.
Gaceta de la Mancha, 1811.
La Centinela de la Patria, 1810.

Books and Articles

Abellán, José Luís. *Liberalismo y romanticismo*. Madrid, 1984.
Adjutant I. *Souvenirs de la Guerre d'Espagne par un adjutant de chausseurs*. Paris, 1893.
Alcaide Ibieca, Augustín. *Historia de los dos sitios que pusieron a Zaragoza en los años de 1808 y 1809 las tropas de Napoleón*. Madrid, 1830.
Alcázar, Cayetano. "El Madrid del Dos de Mayo." In *Itinerarios de Madrid*. Madrid, 1952.
Alexander, Don. *Rod of Iron: French Counterinsurgency Policy in Aragon during the Peninsular War*. Wilmington, Del., 1985.
Alía y Plana. "El primer lunes de Mayo de 1808 en Madrid." In *Madrid, el 2 de Mayo de 1808, viaje a un día en la historia de España*, pp. 105–38. Madrid, 1992.
Anes, Gonzalo. *El antiguo régimen: los Borbones*. Madrid, 1975.
Anna, Timothy E. *Spain and the Loss of America*. Lincoln, Neb., 1983.
Aragó, Jacques. *José Pujol (a) Boquica, jefe de bandidos*. Barcelona, 1841.
Armiño, Mauro, ed. *Lucha de guerrillas según los clásicos de marxismo-leninismo*. Madrid, 1979.
Artola, Miguel. *Los afrancesados*. Madrid, 1976.
———. *La burguesía revolucionaria*. Madrid, 1973.
———. "La guerra de guerrillas." *Revista de Occidente* 10 (January 1964): 12–43.
———. *Los orígenes de la España contemporánea*. Madrid, 1946.
Atlas de Navarra: geográfico, económico, histórico. Pamplona, 1977.
Ayerbe, D. Pedro María de Urries, Marqués de. *Memorias del Marqués de Ayerbe sobre la estancia de D. Fernando VII en Valençay y el principio de la guerra de la independencia*. Zaragoza, 1893.
Aymes, Jean-René. *La Guerre d'Independence Espagnole, 1808–1814*. Paris, 1973.
Azanza, Miguel José de, and Gonzalo O'Fárrill. *Memoria de Miguel José de Azanza y Gonzalo O'Fárrill sobre los hechos que justifican su conducta política, desde marzo de 1808 hasta abril de 1814*. Paris, 1815.
Barahona, Renato. *Vizcaya on the Eve of Carlism: Politics and Society, 1800–1833*. Reno, Nev., 1989.

Barbero, Abilio, and Marelo Vigil. *La formación del feudalismo en la península ibérica.* Barcelona, 1979.

Bayod Pallares, Roberto. *Suministros exigidos al pueblo aragonés para el ejército napoleónico-francés.* Zaragoza, 1979.

Bergeron, Louis. *France under Napoleon.* Princeton, N.J., 1981.

Bigarré, Auguste Julien. *Mémoires du général Bigarré, aide de camp du roi Joseph, 1775–1813.* Paris, 1898.

Blaze, Sébastien. *Mémoire d'un aide-major sous le Premier Empire.* Paris, 1986.

Blum, Jerome. *The End of the Old Order in Rural Europe.* Princeton, N.J., 1978.

Bonaparte, Joseph. *Mémoires et correspondance politique et militaire du Roi Joseph.* 10 vols. Paris, 1854–55.

Bonaparte, Napoleon. *The Confidential Correspondence of Napoleon Bonaparte with His Brother Joseph.* 2 vols. London, 1856.

Bourgoing, Jean François, Baron de. *Nouveau voyage en Espagne ou tableau de l'état actuel de cette monarchie.* 3 vols. Paris, 1789.

Bullón de Mendoza, Alfonso. *La primera guerra carlista.* Madrid, 1992.

Canga Argüelles, José. *Diccionario de hacienda.* 5 vols. London, 1827.

——— . *Observaciones sobre la historia de la guerra de España que escribieron los señores Clarke, Southey, Londonderry, y Napier.* 5 vols. Madrid, 1833–36.

Capmany y de Montpalau, Antonio. *Centinela contra los franceses.* Madrid, 1808.

Carles Clemente, Josep. *Las guerras carlistas.* Barcelona, 1982.

Caro Baroja, Julio. *La hora navarra del XVIII.* Pamplona, 1969.

——— . *Los pueblos de España.* Madrid, 1981.

——— . *Vecindad, familia, y técnica.* San Sebastián, 1974.

Carr, Raymond. *Spain, 1808–1975.* London, 1975.

Carrión, Pascual. *Los latifundios en España.* Madrid, 1932.

Censo de frutos y manufacturas de España é islas adyacentes. Madrid, 1803.

Censo de la población de el año de 1797, executado de orden del Rey en el de 1801. Madrid, 1801.

Censo de la riqueza territorial é industrial de España en el año de 1799. Madrid, 1803.

Censo español executado de orden del rey, comunicada por el excelentísimo señor conde de Floridablanca, primer secretario de Estado y del despacho, en el año de 1787. Madrid, 1787.

Cevallos, Pedro. *Exposición de los hechos y máquinaciones que han preparado la usurpación de la corona de España y los medios que el Emperador de los franceses ha puesto en obra para realizarla.* Cádiz, 1808.

Clopas Batlle, Isidro. *El invicto Conde del Llobregat y los hombres de Cataluña en la Guerra de la Independencia.* Barcelona, 1961.

——— . "La lucha heróica del guerrillero en la Guerra de la Independencia." In *Estudios de la Guerra de la Independencia y su época,* vol. 2. Madrid, 1966.

Conard, Pierre. *La constitución de Bayonne.* Lyon, 1909.

——— . *Napoléon et la Catalogne.* Paris, 1909.

Connelly, Owen. *Blundering to Glory: Napoleon's Military Campaigns.* Wilmington, Del., 1987.

Corona, Carlos E. "Precedentes ideológicos de la Guerra de la Independencia." In *II Congreso histórico internacional de la Guerra de la Independencia y su época*, vol. 1, pp. 5–24. Zaragoza, 1959.

Coverdale, John. *The Basque Phase of Spain's First Carlist War*. Princeton, N.J., 1984.

Desboeufs, Marc. *Souvenirs du Capitaine Desboeufs, les étapes d'un soldat de l'empire*. Paris, 1901.

Desdevises du Dezert, Georges. *L'Espagne de l'Ancien Régime*. 3 vols. Paris, 1897.

Documentos inéditos que pertenecieron al general Castaños. Madrid, 1890.

Domínguez Ortiz, Antonio. *La España de Goya*. Madrid, 1984.

Escoiquiz, Juan. *Idea sencilla de las razones que motivaron el viaje del Rey Fernando VII a Bayona en el més de abril de 1808, dada al público de España y de Europa*. Madrid, 1814.

Esdaile, Charles J. *The Duke of Wellington and the Command of the Spanish Army*. London, 1990.

———. *The Spanish Army in the Peninsular War*. Manchester, 1988.

———. "Spanish Guerrillas: Heroes or Villains?" *History Today* 38 (April 1988): 28–35.

Espoz y Mina, Francisco. *Memorias*. In *Biblioteca de autores españoles*, vols. 146–47. Madrid, 1962.

Espoz y Mina, María Juana de la Vega, Condesa de. *Memorias íntimas*. In *Biblioteca de autores españoles*, vol. 147. Madrid, 1962.

Estado general de los frutos, ganados, y primeras materias de las artes de todas las provincias de España é islas adyacentes en el año de 1799. Madrid, 1803.

Fantin des Odoards, Louis Florimand. *Journal du Général Fantin des Odoards; étapes d'un officier de la grande armée, 1800–1830*. Paris, 1895.

Fontana, Josep. *Cambio económico y actitudes políticas en la España del siglo XIX*. Barcelona, 1973.

———. "Guerra, revolución, y cambio social." In *La Guerra de la Independencia y su momento histórico*, vol. 1. Santander, 1982.

———. *La quiebra de la monarquía absoluta*. Madrid, 1971.

Forcada Torres, Gonzalo. *Tudela durante la Guerra de la Independencia*. Pamplona, 1962.

———. *Tudela durante la Guerra de la Independencia: prisión y muerte del Conde de Fuentes*. Pamplona, 1961.

Foy, Maximilien Sébastien, Comte. *Histoire de la guerre de la péninsule*. 4 vols. Paris, 1827.

Fugier, André. *Napoléon et l'Espagne, 1799–1808*. Paris, 1930.

Galería militar contemporánea. Biografías. Vol. 2. Madrid, 1846.

Galobarde, Miguel. *El dominio francés en el Ampurdán durante la Guerra de la Independencia*. Zaragoza, 1964.

Gallego y Burin, Antonio. *Granada en la Guerra de la Independencia*. Granada, 1923.

Gambra, Rafael. *Guerra realista*. Pamplona, 1972.

———. "El Valle de Roncal en la Guerra de la Independencia." *Príncipe de Viana* 20, nos. 76–77 (1959).

García Prado, Justiniano. *Historia del alzamiento, guerra, y revolución de Asturias*. Oviedo, 1953.

García Sanz, Angel. *La respuesta a los interrogatorios de población, agricultura é indústria de 1802*. Pamplona, 1983.

Gates, David. *The Spanish Ulcer: A History of the Peninsular War.* London, 1986.

Gauthier, Florence. *La voie paysanne dans la Révolution française: l'exemple de la Picardie.* Paris, 1977.

Geoffroy de Grandmaison, Charles Alexandre. *L'Espagne et Napoléon.* 3 vols. Paris, 1925–31.

———. "Le gouverneur français de Fuentes et de Huesca." In *La Guerra de la Independencia y su época*, pp. 5–23. Zaragoza, 1909.

Gleig, George Robert. *The Subaltern.* London, 1825.

Glover, Michael. *Legacy of Glory: The Bonaparte Kingdom of Spain.* New York, 1983.

Godoy, Manuel. *Memorias.* In *Biblioteca de autores españoles*, vols. 88–89. Madrid, 1965.

Gómez de Arteche y Moro, José. *La Guerra de la Independencia.* 14 vols. Madrid, 1868.

———. "Juan Martín el Empecinado." In *La España del siglo XIX*, pp. 81–132. Madrid, 1886.

Gómez Chaparro, Rafael. *La desamortización civil en Navarra.* Pamplona, 1967.

Gómez Imaz, Miguel. *Los periódicos durante la Guerra de la Independencia.* Madrid, 1910.

Gómez Marín, José Antonio. *Bandolerismo, santidad y otros temas españoles.* Madrid, 1972.

Goodspeed, D. J. *The British Campaigns in the Peninsula.* Ottawa, 1958.

Gras y de Esteva, Rafael. "Notas sobre la dominación francesa en Lérida." In *II Congreso de la Guerra de la Independencia y su época*, vol. 2. Zaragoza, 1959.

———. *Zamora en tiempo de la Guerra de la Independencia.* Madrid, 1913.

Grasset, A. *La Guerre d'Espagne.* Paris, 1914.

Herr, Richard. *The Eighteenth Century Revolution in Spain.* Princeton, N.J., 1958.

———. "Good, Evil, and Spain's Rising against Napoleon." In *Ideas in History: Essays Presented to Louis Gottschalk*, edited by Richard Herr and Harold T. Parker, pp. 157–81. Durham, N.C., 1965.

———. *Rural Change and Royal Finances in Spain at the End of the Old Regime.* Berkeley, Calif., 1989.

Hugo, Joseph Leopold Sigisbert. *Mémoires du Général Hugo.* Paris, 1934.

Huici Goñi, María. *Las Cortes de Navarra durante la edad moderna.* Pamplona, 1963.

Ibañez de Ibero, Carlos. *Episódios de la Guerra de la Independencia.* Madrid, 1963.

Instrucción para guerrillas de infantería. Isla de Leon, 1812.

Iribarren, José María. *Espoz y Mina, el guerrillero.* Madrid, 1965.

———. *Espoz y Mina, el Liberal.* Madrid, 1967.

Izquierdo Hernández, Manuel. *Antecedentes y comienzos del reinado de Fernando VII.* Madrid, 1963.

Johnston, S. H. F. "The Contribution of British Historians to the Study of the Peninsular War." In *Estudios de la Guerra de la Independencia y su época*, vol. 2, pp. 133–38. Madrid, 1966.

Jomini, Henri. *Précis de l'art de la guerre.* Paris, 1838.

Juretschke, Hans. *Los afrancesados en la Guerra de la Independencia.* Madrid, 1962.

———. *Vida, obra, y pensamiento de Alberto Lista.* Madrid, 1951.

Laborde, Alexandre Louis Joseph, Comte de. *Itinéraire descriptif de l'Espagne et tableau élémentaire des différentes branches de l'administration et de l'industrie de ce royaume.* 5 vols. Paris, 1808.

Las Cases, Emmanuel, Comte de. *Mémorial de Sainte-Hélène.* 2 vols. Paris, 1961.

Llopis, Salvador. *Un héroe inédito: páginas nuevas de los sitios de Ciudad Rodrigo y de la Guerra de la Independencia.* Salamanca, 1963.

Llorente, Juan Antonio (pseud. Juan Nellerto). *Memoria para la historia de la revolución española.* Paris, 1814.

Louis-Lande, L. *Basques et Navarrais.* Paris, 1878.

Lovett, Gabriel. *Napoleon and the Birth of Modern Spain.* 2 vols. New York, 1965.

Madoz, Pascual. *Diccionario geográfico-estadístico-histórico de España y sus posesiones de ultramar.* 16 vols. Madrid, 1845–50.

Madrid, el 2 de Mayo de 1808, viaje a un día en la historia de España. Madrid, 1992.

Martín, Andrés. *Historia de los sucesos militares de la División de Navarra, y demás acontecimientos de este Reyno durante la última guerra contra el Tírano Napoleón.* 2 vols. Pamplona, 1953.

Martin, Emmanuel. *La gendarmerie française en Espagne, campagnes de 1807 á 1814.* Paris, 1898.

Martínez Ruiz, Adolfo. *El reino de Granada en la Guerra de la Independencia.* Granada, 1977.

Martínez Salazar, Andrés. *De la Guerra de la Independencia en Galicia.* Buenos Aires, 1908.

Marx, Karl. *Revolution in Spain.* Westport, Conn., 1975.

Mercader Riba, Juan. *Barcelona durante la ocupación francesa.* Madrid, 1949.

———. *José Bonaparte, Rey de España.* Madrid, 1971.

Mesonero y Romanos, Ramón de. *Memorias de un setentón.* Madrid, 1961.

Mina Apat, María Cruz. *Fueros y revolución liberal en Navarra.* Madrid, 1981.

Miranda Rubio, José. *La Guerra de la Independencia en Navarra.* Pamplona, 1977.

Mitchell, Harvey. "Tocqueville's Mirage or Reality? Political Freedom from Old Regime to Revolution." *Journal of Modern History* 60 (March 1988): 28–54.

Montoro Sagasti, José. *La propiedad privada y la comunal en la ciudad de Olite.* Pamplona, 1929.

Mutiloa Poza, José María. *La desamortización eclesiástica en Navarra.* Pamplona, 1972.

Nadal, Jordi. *La población española.* Barcelona, 1976.

Napier, William. *History of the War in the Peninsula and in the South of France.* 5 vols. New York, 1882.

Olcina, Evarist. *El Carlismo y las autonomías regionales.* Madrid, 1973.

Olóriz, Hermilio. *Navarra en la Guerra de la Independencia.* Pamplona, 1910.

Oman, Charles. *The History of the Peninsular War.* 7 vols. London, 1903–30.

———. *Studies in Napoleonic Wars.* London, 1929.

Ontañon, Eduardo. *El Cura Merino.* Madrid, 1933.

Palafox, Jose de. *Autobiografía.* Edited by J. García Mercadal. Madrid, 1966.

Pardo de Andrade, Manuel. *Los guerrilleros gallegos de 1809.* La Coruña, 1892.

Pérez de Guzmán, Juan. *El 2 de Mayo de 1808.* Madrid, 1908.

Pérez Goyena, Antonio. *Ensayo de bibliografía navarra.* Pamplona, 1953.

Priego López, Juan. *La Guerra de la Independencia.* 4 vols. Madrid, 1972.

Proclama de Napoleón Bonaparte a los Españoles y la anti-proclama o repuesta a dicha proclama por un patriota español, natural de Lucena. Málaga, 1809.

Puig i Oliver, María. *Girona francesa, 1812–1814: L'anexió de Catalunya a Franca i el domini napoleònic a Girona.* Girona, 1976.

Puigblanch, Antoni. *Opúsculos gramático satíricos.* 2 vols. Barcelona, 1976.

Ramos Oliveira, Antonio. *Politics, Economics, and Men of Modern Spain.* New York, 1972.

Rico, Juan. *Memorias históricas sobre la revolución de Valencia.* Cádiz, 1811.

Ringrose, David R. *Transportation and Economic Stagnation in Spain, 1750–1850.* Durham, N.C., 1970.

Rocca, Albert Jean. *Memoirs of the War of the French in Spain.* London, 1815.

Rodríguez Garraiza, Rodrigo. *Tensiones de Navarra con la administración central.* Pamplona, 1974.

Rodríguez-Solís, Enrique. *Los guerrilleros de 1808, historia popular de la guerra de la independencia.* 2 vols. Madrid, 1887.

Romero de Solis, Pedro. *La población española en los siglos XVIII y XIX.* Madrid, 1973.

Roux, Georges. *Napoléon et le guêpier espagnole.* Paris, 1970.

Roy, Just Jean Etienne. *Les Français en Espagne, souvenirs des guerres de la péninsule, 1808–1814.* Tours, 1880.

Saavedra, Pegerto. *Economía, política, y sociedad en Galicia: la provincia de Mondoñedo, 1480–1830.* Madrid, 1985.

Sahlins, Peter. *Boundaries: The Making of France and Spain in the Pyrenees.* Berkeley, Calif., 1989.

Saint-Yon, Alexandre. *Les deux Mina.* 3 vols. Paris, 1835.

Sánchez-Albornoz, Claudio. *Orígenes y destino de Navarra.* Barcelona, 1984.

Sánchez Gómez, Miguel Angel. "Aproximación a la demografía montañesa durante la Guerra de la Independencia." In *La Guerra de la Independencia y su momento histórico.* Santander, 1982.

Servicio Histórico Militar. *Guerra de la Independencia.* Madrid, 1972.

Simón Segura, Francisco. *La desamortización española del siglo XIX.* Madrid, 1973.

Soult, Nicolas Jean. *Mémoires du maréchal.* Paris, 1955.

Southey, Robert. *History of the Peninsular War.* 3 vols. London, 1823.

Suárez, Federico. *El proceso de la convocatoria a cortes.* Pamplona, 1982.

Suchet, Louis Gabriel. *Memoirs of the War in Spain from 1808 to 1814.* 2 vols. London, 1829.

Thiry, Jean. *La Guerre D'Espagne.* Paris, 1965.

Tomas y Valiente, Francisco. *El marco político de la desamortización.* Barcelona, 1971.

Tomkinson, Henry. *The Diary of a Cavalry Officer in the Peninsular War and Waterloo Campaign, 1809–1815.* New York, 1895.

Toreno, José María. *Historia del levantamiento, guerra, y revolución de España.* 3 vols. Paris, 1851.

Torre, Joseba de la. *Los campesinos navarros ante la guerra napoleónica: financiación bélica y desamortización civil.* Madrid, 1991.

Townsend, Charles. *A Journey through Spain in the Years 1786 and 1787.* London, 1791.

Un Monge Benito del Monasterio de Arlanza. *Memorias sobre la Reconquista de Zaragoza.* Madrid, 1815.

Valencina, Ambrosio de. *Los capuchinos de Andalucía en la Guerra de la Independencia.* Seville, 1910.

Vicens Vives, Jaime. *An Economic History of Spain*. Princeton, N.J., 1969.

————. "La Guerra del Frances." In *Moments crucials de la historia de Catalunya*. Barcelona, 1956.

Vilar, Pierre. "Patrie et Nation dans le Vocabulaire de la Guerre d'Independence Espagnole." In *Patriotisme et Nationalisme en Europe à l'époque de la Révolution française et de Napoléon*. Paris, 1973.

————. "Quelques aspects de l'occupation et de la résistance en Espagne en 1794 et au temps de Napoléon." In *Occupants et occupés*, pp. 225–47. Brussels, 1969.

Whyte, William Foote, and Kathleen King Whyte. *Making Mondragón: The Growth and Dynamics of the Worker Cooperative Complex*. Ithaca, N.Y., 1988.